State and Society in Contemporary Korea

The papers in this volume grew out of a workshop sponsored by the Joint Committee on Korean Studies of the Social Science Research Council and the American Council of Learned Societies.

Edited by Hagen Koo

State and Society in Contemporary Korea

Cornell University Press
Ithaca and London

First published 1993 by Cornell University Press.

International Standard Book Number 0-8014-2867-X (cloth)
International Standard Book Number 0-8014-8106-6 (paper)
Library of Congress Catalog Card Number 93-25325

Printed in the United States of America

Librarians: Library of Congress cataloging information appears on the last page of the book.

∞ The paper in this book meets the minimum requirements of the American National Standard for Information Sciences—Permanence of Paper for Printed Library Materials, ANSI Z39.48-1984.

Contents

Preface vii

Contributors ix

Introduction: Beyond State-Market Relations *Hagen Koo* 1

1 Political Cleavages in South Korea *Jang Jip Choi* 13

2 The State, Politics, and Economic Development in Postwar South Korea *Stephan Haggard and Chung-in Moon* 51

3 The South Korean Bourgeoisie: A Class in Search of Hegemony *Carter J. Eckert* 95

4 The State, *Minjung*, and the Working Class in South Korea *Hagen Koo* 131

5 The Agony of Cultural Construction: Politics and Culture in Modern Korea *Uchang Kim* 163

6 The Corporate State in North Korea *Bruce Cumings* 197

7 Strong State and Contentious Society *Hagen Koo* 231

Index 251

Preface

This book was conceived with two objectives in mind. One was to contribute to the growing literature on the political economy of South Korean development by broadening its focus from state-economy relations to state-society relations and thereby bringing to light the complexity and density of social and political change associated with economic growth. The other was to meet a pressing demand in the field for some good comprehensive books on contemporary Korean society, both North and South, especially for books to be used in upper-division or graduate courses. Although the literature on Korea is growing rapidly, it is overrepresented by a genre of South Korea's economic success stories. Fine anthropological studies on particular aspects of Korean culture and society also exist, but there are few works that offer a broader picture of Korean society and of the ways in which Korea has experienced economic and social transformation in the modern period. The absence of such books has long frustrated those who teach courses on Korea and those who want to incorporate more material on Korea into general area studies.

Taking state-society relations as an analytical and interpretive scheme, this book looks into the distinct pattern of Korea's transition to a modern industrial society. While concerned with the important role of the state in shaping the dominant pattern of economic growth, the authors of the essays presented here are more interested in analyzing the societal forces that have been historically formed and have impinged upon the state. What Korea has experienced in modern times is an immensely more complex and dynamic process than is commonly represented in the economic development literature, a process filled with conflicts, contradictions, and the spirited reactions of individuals to their experiences of change. In this book the authors explore aspects of Korean modernization so far overshadowed by the search for the causes of South Korea's economic success.

In many ways, the book is a product of the Joint Committee on Korean Studies of the Social Science Research Council and the American Council of Learned Societies. While I was a member of this committee, there was constant discussion about the need for going beyond the current developmental concerns and casting Korean modernization in a broader and richer historical and cultural context. Toward this end, the JCKS funded two small workshops, in 1988 and 1989, attended by the contributors to this book and by B. C. Koh and Nancy Abelmann. I sincerely regret that Koh's and Abelmann's papers are not included in the volume. And I thank the SSRC and ACLS for their support and especially the JCKS members for their collegiality during the course of the project.

Passages from "Maybe" by Pak No Hae, from *Dawn of Labor,* Pulbbit poem series no. 5, Pulbbit Publishing Company, are reprinted by permission of the publisher.

I also thank several people who read and gave helpful suggestions on various drafts of chapters: Yunshik Chang, Brian Folk, Hong Young Lee, Timothy Lim, Ravi Palat, Ned Shultz, Alvin So, Patricia Steinhoff, Rob Wilson, and above all, two anonymous readers of the manuscript for Cornell University Press. Finally, I thank Roger Haydon, our editor at Cornell, for handling our manuscript smoothly, with a good sense of judgment, efficiency, and humor.

HAGEN KOO

Honolulu

Contributors

Jang Jip Choi is Professor of Political Science at Korea University, Seoul, Korea.

Bruce Cumings is Professor of East Asian and International History at the University of Chicago.

Carter J. Eckert is Professor of Korean History at Harvard University.

Stephan Haggard is Professor in the Graduate School of International Relations and Pacific Studies, University of California, San Diego.

Uchang Kim is Professor of English Literature at Korea University, Seoul, Korea.

Hagen Koo is Professor of Sociology at the University of Hawaii at Manoa.

Chung-in Moon is Associate Professor of Political Science at the University of Kentucky.

State and Society in Contemporary Korea

Introduction: Beyond State-Market Relations

Hagen Koo

Korea is widely known for having exceptionally strong states.[1] Whether in the capitalist South or the Communist North, the state clearly overpowers civil society with an impressive capacity to penetrate into society and mold the behavior of social groups and individuals. North Korea, of course, is a supreme case of a monolithic, totalitarian state, resembling the Orwellian state of 1984; the civil society that exists is neither heard or seen, except in its ritualistic echoes of state power. While communist states have been crumbling one by one following the resurrection of angry civil societies, North Korean rulers seem to be living in another world and in another age, enjoying absolute control over an obedient population. Whatever hidden civil resistance and political conflict exist or may exist, the ability of

1. In his informed survey of state strength in the modern world, Migdal observes that "strong states have been a rarity," noting that "only a handful of Asian, African, and Latin American states fall high on the continuum of 'stateness,' or state capabilities. Israel, Cuba, China, Japan, Vietnam, Taiwan, North Korea, and South Korea have been among the highest in state capabilities from those continents." Joel Migdal, *Strong Societies and Weak States: State-Society Relations and State Capabilities in the Third World* (Princeton: Princeton University Press, 1988), p. 269.

North Korean rulers to manage and tame society is truly impressive and must be the envy of all Communist rulers.

The state in South Korea is equally remarkable for its strength. For a capitalist society, the South Korean state possesses an unusual degree of autonomous power and maintains tight control over the economy and society. Power is highly concentrated in the executive organs of government with an enormous amount of coercive and allocative authority in the hands of state executives. Hardly anything socially consequential in South Korea is left untouched by the regulatory actions of the state, and few groups or organizations in society exist without some kind of state sanction.

The South Korean state has recently received special attention with regard to its role in economic development. Although it is true that all modern states intervene in their economies in one way or another, the South Korean state stands out in terms of the depth of such intervention, its dirigist policy implementation, and its ability to discipline the business sector while maintaining tight control over labor organizations. A growing literature on South Korean development, therefore, assigns the highest importance to the character and role of its developmental state for South Korea's economic success.

This view is apt to lead to an image of Korean society as being highly homogeneous, pliant, and well managed by a strong paternalist state. In this image, Korean people seem to have not only few opportunities but also no strong desire to organize private interests in confrontation with the state. While civil society is hampered in its autonomous development, the state nonetheless seems responsive to the people's demands and has been efficient in delivering economic goods to its citizens. This is a popular image, conjured up in such terms as "Korea, Inc.," coined after "Japan, Inc." The term indicates more than close collaboration between the government and the business community; it suggests broader state-society relationships that are by and large harmonious, reciprocal, and cohesive in relations with outsiders. As such, Korea is seen as just one representative example of the generic East Asian or post-Confucian state model.

Fairly accurate though it may be in describing the Korean state, this model tends to mischaracterize the true nature of Korean civil society, which, as we have observed historically and in more recent periods, is far from weak, submissive, and quiescent. Korea's recent history has been characterized by an enormous amount of social conflict and struggle, most of which was directed against state power. Korea's transition to the modern era was marked by massive peasant rebellions, called the Tonghak Uprisings (1894), which, had there been no foreign intervention, could have put an early end to Korea's ancient regime. The Japanese colonial regime in Korea (1910–45) faced tenacious resistance movements, the most memorable of which was the March First Movement in 1919, a spontaneous, nationwide, nonviolent protest involving millions of Koreans. Neither police repression nor the sophisticated cultural policy of the colonial government succeeded in taming the Koreans, and Korean resistance made Japanese rule in Korea much more difficult and coercive than in other parts of Japan's colonial empire.

The abrupt ending of colonial rule triggered an explosion of political activities and civil strife. As well as the usual turmoil and confusion that one would expect to accompany sudden liberation, there were also widespread political mobilizations throughout the country. Peasants organized village committees for self-government; workers took over Japanese-owned factories; and political organizations of all ideological stripes arose to compete for power. It was truly a revolutionary period; civil society suddenly exploded with pent-up grief over past injustices and with high hopes for creating a new independent state, only to be suppressed again by an external power.[2]

The more recent history of South Korea is also remarkable for its political volatility. The autocratic regime of Syngman Rhee was toppled by the April 19 Student Uprising in 1960. The first democratic government of Chang Myon, plagued by incessant street demonstrations and a faltering economy, barely survived one year. Park Chung Hee came to power in 1961 through a bloodless coup, shook up the economy, and pushed the country into a high-geared race for economic prosperity. Despite the admiration of outsiders for the Korean government's creation of the "Korean miracle," Park was never successful at buying popular support with his economic achievements. His regime was continuously plagued by dissident movements, student demonstrations, and grass-roots labor protests. The corporatist labor regime that worked so well in neighboring East Asian economies faltered in the face of tenacious workers' struggles to form independent unions.

The transition from the Park regime (1961–79) to the Chun regime (1980–87) was also marked by an immediate activation of civil society,

2. See Bruce Cumings, *The Origins of the Korean War: Liberation and the Emergence of Separate Regimes, 1945–1947* (Princeton: Princeton University Press, 1981).

accompanied by a level of labor strife and civil protests that had not been seen since the immediate postliberation period. Chun Doo Hwan came to power only after the bloody suppression of a civil uprising in Kwangju, which left a deep scar in South Korea's political history and sowed the seeds for the infamous demise of his regime. Civil society became highly splintered and politicized under Chun's harsh authoritarian rule, and 1987 witnessed another uprising. This time many middle-class citizens joined students in large-scale street demonstrations to force Chun to transfer power through a direct presidential election. In this way the Korean transition to democracy deviated from the top-down, elite-initiated process found in such neighboring countries as Taiwan, Hong Kong, and Singapore; the Korean transition from authoritarian rule has involved a far more active struggle by civil society against state power.[3]

Clearly, South Korea is by no means a docile and quiescent society happily engaged in the pursuit of economic prosperity led by a strong, mercantile state. A weak society is not a logical correlate of a strong state, nor does an "overdeveloped" state structure necessarily produce an underdeveloped civil society. Modern Korean history demonstrates complex, dialectic relationships between the state and civil society, far more dynamic and conflict-ridden than is usually assumed in the literature.

The main objective of this book is to present a comprehensive analysis of the social, political, and economic changes that Korea has undergone since the end of World War II. This analysis uses the relations between state and society as its basic interpretive framework for comprehending the dominant forms of social transformation in contemporary Korea. A central assumption shared among the authors represented in this collection is that the society-centered perspective, which has been predominant in social science until recently, is clearly insufficient for studying social and political change in Korea.[4] The magnitude of social change experienced by Korea

3. Tun-jeng Cheng, "Democratizing the Quasi-Leninist Regime in Taiwan," *World Politics* 41 (1989): 471–99; Larry Diamond, Juan Linz, and S. M. Lipset, eds., *Democracy in Developing Countries: Asia,* vol. 3 (Boulder, Col.: Lynne Rienner, 1989): 1–52; Alvin Y. So and Sai-Hsin May, "Democratization in East Asia: Comparing the Taiwan Breakthrough and the Hong Kong Frustration," paper presented at the annual meetings of the American Sociological Association, Washington, D.C., 1990.

4. The most cogent critique of the society-centered perspective is Theda Skocpol, "Bringing the State Back In: Strategies of Analysis in Current Research," in *Bringing the State Back In,* ed. Peter Evans, Dietrich Rueschemeyer, and Theda Skocpol (New York: Cambridge Univer-

in the contemporary period and its sources, mechanisms, and consequences cannot be adequately accounted for by social dynamics emanating from within society alone. Neither the liberal-pluralist theory of politics nor the modernization theory of social change is capable of identifying the most crucial mechanism of social change in Korea—which we believe to be the state. The same limitation is more or less true of Marxist theory, which views the state as a tool of class domination or as a reflection of class relations rooted in the mode of production.[5] In Korea, the state clearly enjoys more autonomy from class power than is commonly assumed in Marxist literature, and it has played an independent role in the making and unmaking of classes.

At the same time, we recognize that the state-centered perspective, which is currently in vogue, especially in studies of East Asian economic development, has its own limitations.[6] While correctly stressing the key role played by the state in economic and social development and thereby correcting the deficiencies of the society-centered approach, the state-centered approach tends to err in the opposite direction by overstressing the independent role of the state at the expense of societal forces. In efforts to highlight the significance of the state as an autonomous actor, analyses conducted in the statist perspective often ignore that the state is embedded in society and draws its essential characteristics from society itself. Both state autonomy and state strength are the products of interactions between the state

sity Press, 1985); see also John Hall, "Introduction," in *States in History,* ed. John A. Hall (Oxford: Basil Blackwell, 1986).

5. Nicos Poulantzas, *Political Power and Social Classes* (London: New Left Books, 1974); David Gold, Clarence Lo, and Erik Wright, "Recent Development in Marxist Theories of the Capitalist State: Part 2," *Monthly Review* 27 (1975): 29–43; Gosta Esping-Anderson, Roger Friedland, and Erik Wright, "Class Struggle and the Capitalist State," *Kapitalistate* 4–5 (1976): 186–98; Bob Jessop, *The Capitalist State* (New York: New York University Press, 1982), and *State Theory: Putting Capitalist States in Their Place* (University Park: Pennsylvania State University Press, 1990).

6. Some good examples of state-centered analysis of the newly industrialized economies in East Asia are Frederic Deyo, ed., *The Political Economy of the New Asian Industrialism* (Ithaca: Cornell University Press, 1987); Alice Amsden, *Asia's Next Giant: Late Industrialization in Korea* (New York: Oxford University Press, 1989); Stephan Haggard, *Pathways from the Periphery: The Politics of Growth in the Newly Industrializing Countries* (Ithaca: Cornell University Press, 1990); Robert Wade, *Governing the Market: The Role of Government in East Asian Industrialization* (Princeton: Princeton University Press, 1990); Gary Gereffi and Donald Wyman, eds., *Manufacturing Miracles: Paths of Industrialization in Latin America and East Asia* (Princeton: Princeton University Press, 1990).

and society, in which even a weak society finds diverse ways to influence state structure. State strength is neither absolute nor fixed, but rather varies according to social struggles and accommodations in multiple arenas.[7] The state must continuously compete with social groups and classes to maintain control over the people and their behavior, and the state's control may change significantly from one sector to another and from one issue to another.

The approach taken in this book, therefore, seeks to go beyond the unnecessary dichotomy of state-centered versus society-centered approaches by paying close attention to the complex, dynamic, and dialectic relationships between the state and society.[8] While stressing the important role of the state in Korea's socioeconomic transformation, the authors are primarily interested in analyzing the nature of social conflicts and contradictions generated by the relationships between the state and civil society and the nature of social change shaped by these conflicts.

In order to explain the distinctive contribution this book seeks to make, it is useful to describe how our approach differs from that of the current political economy literature on East Asian economic development. The political economy literature addresses basically one key question: What made the East Asian "economic miracle" possible? Put differently, what causal factors explain the remarkable economic performances of the East Asian capitalist economies? The focus of the debate has been on the relative importance of the state and the market for economic growth: Is the East Asian economic success attributable principally to the state or to free-market mechanisms? Recently, analytic attention has gradually shifted to the institutional underpinnings of economic performances, but the overriding concern is still confined to the state-market relations.[9]

Although this book addresses issues prominent in this literature, our main concern is not primarily with state-market relationships but more broadly with the relationships between the state and civil society. By "civil

7. Migdal, *Strong Societies and Weak States.*

8. A major thrust of theoretical development in the state literature stresses the embedded character of the state in socioeconomic and sociocultural contexts. See Karen Barkey and Sunita Parikh, "Comparative Perspectives on the State," *Annual Review of Sociology* 17 (1991): 523–49.

9. See two excellent reviews of this literature: Robert Wade, "East Asia's Economic Success: Conflicting Perspectives, Partial Insights, Shaky Evidence," *World Politics* 44 (1992): 270–320; and Ziya Önis, "The Logic of the Developmental State," *Comparative Politics* 24 (1991): 109–26.

society," I mean both market and nonmarket spheres of social relations, comprising a multitude of "market-regulated, privately controlled, or voluntarily organized" activities.[10] The term also encompasses a complex of ideological and cultural relations, spiritual and intellectual life, and the political expressions of those relations. While the European literature on civil society is much concerned with a broad spectrum of sociopolitical processes, such as class formation, social movements, and cultural representations, the East Asian literature confines its focus to the interplay of the "developmental state" and the market, more or less separate from the broader context of civil society. This narrow economistic approach results in a tendency to exaggerate the autonomy and strength of the East Asian state and to interpret economic growth in isolation from other political and social changes. An obvious danger of such an approach is a reification of the concept of the state, as often found in many stylistic accounts of the East Asian developmental states.

So, rather than trying to add another book to the already copious literature on East Asian economic success, we have aimed to fill large gaps created by the current preoccupation with the East Asian development model. In analyzing the relationship between the state and society, we have emphasized those spheres of civil society which have been underanalyzed—emerging class forces, political cleavages, crises of hegemony, social movements, cultural reactions to modernity, and the like. All these elements of civil society bear directly on, and are intimately affected by, the nature of state power and market processes. The notion of a "developmental state," on which so much scholarly attention has been focused, represents only one facet of the relationships between the state and civil society. Although this concept helps highlight a particularly important element of the East Asian capitalist model of economic development, it does not facilitate grappling with the totality of economic, political, and social transformations that the Korean people have experienced in modern times. Given its broad focus, this collection pays as much attention to the phenomena of culture and ideology as to economic and political issues, for culture and ideology constitute vital aspects of civil society, which are intimately related to the political economy itself.

Contemporary Korea, that is, the period since its independence from

10. John Keane, "Introduction," in *Civil Society and the State: New European Perspectives*, ed. Keane (London: Verso, 1988), p. 1.

Japanese colonial rule in 1945, is the main focus of all the chapters; nonetheless, they all look back to the colonial period (1910–45) or further. The colonial period is especially important for contemporary analyses, because it was during this time that much of the initial transformation occurred, causing the Korean people great pain and resentment.

We regret that only one chapter is devoted exclusively to North Korea, a reflection of the dearth of scholarship on that area. Although several excellent studies on certain features of the North Korean political system exist, scarcely any systematic study is available on the nature of society and its relationships with the state, simply because data required for such an analysis are unavailable at present. Thus in order to maintain our analytic focus, we had no choice but to give little space to North Korea.

The topics covered here deal with several crucial dimensions of social transformation in contemporary Korea. Though not comprehensive, chapters that follow offer a good picture of the nature of the Korean state and society and the ways in which the two have interacted to weave a turbulent modern history.

In Chapter 1, Jang Jip Choi presents an overall analysis of Korean political history since independence. He describes the geopolitical context in which antagonistic states emerged on the Korean peninsula and explores the sources of the continuous political conflict that has characterized state-society relations in South Korea. He concentrates on three major "cleavages" of conflict, involving issues of democracy, economic justice, and reunification, along which political dynamics in South Korea have evolved, generating cycles of mobilization and demobilization of civil society and unpredictable changes on the political terrain. These social cleavages appeared in a historical sequence, the author argues, from the issue of democracy, to that of economic justice, and finally to the question of reunification. This chapter provides a powerful, yet sensitive historical account of why these issues have emerged as principal axes of social conflict at given historical junctures, how they have shaped the relationship between the state and society, and in which direction the sociopolitical order of South Korea is heading.

In Chapter 2, Stephan Haggard and Chung-in Moon divide the recent history of South Korean economic growth into several periods in terms of development strategy and major economic policies, and examines both the domestic and international factors responsible for these economic transitions. The South Korean economy has undergone several major transitions in terms of development strategies: the shift from import-substitution industrialization to export-led industrialization in the early 1960s, industrial deepening toward heavy and chemical industries in the mid-1970s, economic liberalization and structural adjustment in the 1980s, and economic changes associated with a democratic transition since 1987. Exploring each of these economic transitions, the authors present a comprehensive political economy account of South Korea's development since the end of World War II. Setting against several major theoretical perspectives that explain successful performances of the East Asian capitalist economies, Haggard and Moon stress that institutional factors, including the autonomy and capacity of the state, its internal decision-making structure, and the broad rules of the political game itself account for the changes in South Korea's development strategies.

In Chapter 3, Carter Eckert describes the origin and development of Korean capitalism. He examines an interesting puzzle about the growth of the Korean capitalist class—the fact that "the Korean bourgeoisie remains, despite its wealth and increasing political influence, a decidedly unhegemonic class, estranged from the very society in which it continues to grow." Indeed, despite the amount of credit awarded to their role in South Korea's economic development, large conglomerate business groups *(chaebŏl)* have been the focus of intense popular resentment and opposition in South Korea. The author explains this interesting phenomenon in terms of several factors, including the historical (especially colonial) contexts in which Korean capitalism emerged, Confucian cultural legacies, and the aggressive and selfish manner in which chaebŏl owners have accumulated wealth. But the strongest emphasis in this analysis is placed on the long and special relationship between the authoritarian state and big business. The new bourgeoisie was hampered in establishing its social and moral authority in society because its economic rise was based primarily on special privilege and protection provided by the state and because it has supported authoritarian regimes to further its own interests.

In Chapter 4, I change the focus from the capitalist class to the working class. One salient consequence of South Korean industrialization is the rise of a large industrial working class and its impressive development in class consciousness and organization. In this chapter I provide a short history of the Korean labor movement since the colonial period and analyze the specific ways in which this working-class movement has been shaped by the state's strategy of capital accumulation and labor control. Unlike other newly industrialized countries in East Asia, South Korea has seen an aggressive labor movement and the rapid development of workers' collective consciousness and class solidarity. Of particular importance in this regard is the interpenetration of worker struggles in the industrial arena and the broader social and political movement called the *minjung* movement. I explain this development by examining the central role of the state in the development of both movements.

In Chapter 5, Uchang Kim turns to the realm of culture, describing the intricate relationships between Korea's political history and literature as they have evolved from the colonial period through the tumultuous years of postliberation to the present era of industrialism. His description centers on inherent clashes between external forces (morality, ideology, and politics) and the lived experiences of individuals, and clashes between societal demands and aesthetic concerns of cultural workers. So, rather than a dualistic model of state-society relations, the author posits tripartite relationships among state, society, and culture, in which culture stands on the side neither of society nor of the state. The development of Korean literature demonstrates that societal demands on culture have been even more insistent and difficult to resist than political ones, because of the particular nature of modern Korean history, which has continuously generated agony, guilt, repression, and bad memories, and because of the absence of a stable moral and political order in recent years. In the absence of a stable moral and political order, Kim argues, "cultural activities come, paradoxically, to take upon themselves the task of providing it, with the result that the task of culture is narrowed down to what is demanded by moral duties and political objectives, losing the fuller human dimension of the aesthetic." The fate of Korean culture, therefore, has been a cyclical process of "politicization, depoliticization, and repoliticization."

Chapter 6, by Bruce Cumings, brings North Korea into the overall picture. The author dismisses a previously popular understanding of the North Korean political system as little more than an imposition of the Soviet system of Stalinism. Such a view does not explain why the Democratic People's Republic of Korea (DPRK) remains strong even after the collapse of the Soviet Union and its East European satellites. The remarkable political stability of the North Korean system cannot be adequately understood in terms of such conventional categories as totalitarianism, proletarian dictatorship, or personality cult. One explanation for its stability, the author argues, is a distinct form of socialist corporatism that North Korean leaders developed by melding diverse elements drawn from the Soviet and Chinese models, traditional Korean culture, geopolitics, and past experiences of independence struggles. Salient features of North Korean corporatism include familism, nationalism, voluntarism, and heavy reliance on a maximum leader. Although it uses classic corporatist verbiage and images, North Korean corporatism diverges significantly from its counterparts in both Europe and Latin America. Both the apparent stability of the North Korean political system and its potential for instability derive from its distinctive form of socialist corporatism.

Two important themes run through the analyses in this collection. One is the strength and pervasiveness of the Korean states, which in both Koreas display an unusual degree of independence from social forces. Both states are capable of setting the direction of social and economic change and molding the behavior of individuals and groups in society. The state is therefore the most critical variable explaining virtually all major aspects of historical change in Korea. The other theme is that despite the state's dominance, Korean society is far from weak and submissive, and accordingly state-society relationships cannot be characterized as peaceful and harmonious. Modern Korean history, as described in these chapters, eminently demonstrates the unruly, volatile character of civil society in Korea, which has often erupted to confront mighty state power whenever the state's grip on society loosened even slightly. State control of society has thus never been fully assured; an extra dose of repression and ideological mobilization has frequently been used.

What, then, accounts for this particular pattern of state-society relations in Korea? Specifically, what are the historical origins of strong states on the Korean peninsula, and what is responsible for such highly contentious, conflict-prone relations between the state and society in South Korea? In the concluding chapter, I address this question and try to formulate an explanation based on the analyses presented in this book as well as from my own study.

1
Political Cleavages in South Korea

Jang Jip Choi

Political conflict in South Korea takes place around political cleavages created after liberation in 1945. These cleavages were produced by the circumstances in which the state and civil society emerged. Simply put, the South Korean state, from its inception, was authoritarian, while civil society was forcibly depoliticized. In this chapter I examine the history of South Korea's authoritarian state and the popular masses' recurring demand for democratization and political participation from the end of the colonial period to the present, against the backdrop of rapid capitalist industrialization and diversification of economic interests.

In this analysis, "state versus civil society" is the central motif. Civil society is conceptualized as a network of organizations or a structure of classes, which emerge at certain historical junctures as articulate political and social groups to advocate common interests. The state, however, is society's ruling body and its central controlling structure. If we examine South Korea's political history with this interpretive framework, we see a long-standing alienation between the state and society in Korea from the First Republic to the present, punctuated by periods of intense conflict. In thus outlining the history of postwar politics in South Korea, two assumptions are made: that the development of civil society is critical to the formation of a political system based on widespread consensus, rather than force; and that the institutionalization of democratic structures, at the levels of politics and of culture, requires a counterhegemonic movement to dismantle the present structures of domination and oppression.

By the time of liberation from Japanese colonialism in 1945, a revitalized civil society had emerged, one that contained the seeds of a new, more just political order. That the postliberation period actually laid the foundation for fratricidal war had less to do with sociopolitical conditions inside Korea than with developments in international politics. Weighing the relative importance of internal versus external factors in contemporary politics is in itself not important here. The purpose is, rather, to examine how the two interacted, how that relationship was structured, and what impact the relationship had on the course of modern Korean history.

In analyzing the fractious history of state-society relations since liberation, in this chapter I focus on three distinct but interlinked cleavages along which political confrontations have taken place: (1) democracy versus authoritarianism; (2) economic justice versus development; and (3) populist versus conservative reunification. The salience of any particular cleavage during a given historical period was determined by the changing international context and the shifting power relationship between the state and civil society within South Korea.

Immediately after liberation, conflict between contending political forces raged along all three cleavages. However, after the founding of the First Republic in 1948 and the elimination of leftist forces in the South, the second and third cleavages were deferred through both force and ideological measures. Thereafter, at specific historical junctures these three cleavages have appeared on the political terrain in a definite historical sequence: first, the issues of democracy, then those of economic justice, and finally the question of reunification.

Liberation and the Burgeoning of Civil Society

Liberation from Japanese colonial rule brought but a fleeting moment of jubilation. With the collapse of Japanese colonialism the political atmosphere decidedly favored revolutionary nationalism. Within days after liberation, numerous political organizations were established spontaneously in cities and throughout the countryside,[1] attracting masses of workers and peasants. Of these organizations, the "people's committees" were the most consequential. These committees, along with many labor and peasant organizations, became the organizational base for "Kŏnjun" (Chosŏn kŏnguk chunbi wiwonhoe; Committee for the Preparation of Korean Independence) (CPKI) and "Ingong" (Chosŏn inmin konghwaguk; Korean People's Republic), with political structures that began to evince all the characteristics of an independent, functioning state.[2]

The division and occupation of Korea by Soviet and U.S. troops, however, completely undermined the Korean people's efforts to establish an independent political system. The division of Korea along the thirty-eighth parallel was unilaterally declared by the United States as a part of its postwar global strategy. In this way, without having given their consent, the Korean people became victims of U.S. and Soviet strategic interests. With the announcement that the United States would occupy the southern half of Korea, former Japanese collaborators and conservative forces in Korean society also began to organize. Thus, after the U.S. forces arrived, they encountered an array of revolutionary and counterrevolutionary political and social groups.[3]

1. These political and social organizations appeared before the arrival of the U.S. forces on September 8, 1945. By the end of August 1945, 145 local branches of the Committee for the Preparation of Korean Independence (CPKI) had been organized. Minjujuŭi minjok chonsŏn, *Chosŏn haebangillyŏnsa* [The Korean history of the first year of liberation] (Seoul: Munuinsokwan, 1946), p. 81.

Also, by the end of October 1945, people's committees had been organized in 7 provinces, 12 cities, and 131 *kun* (counties). Kim Nam-sik, *Namnodang yŏngu* [A study of the South Korean Labor Party] (Seoul: Tolpekae, 1984), p. 117. The actual number of social and political organizations, including labor, peasant, women's, student, and various youth groups, was far higher. See Bruce Cumings, *The Origins of the Korean War,* vol. 1 (Princeton: Princeton University Press, 1981), pp. 68–100, 265–350.

2. The Korean People's Republic (KPR) was formed just before the U.S. occupation forces landed. The impetus for the formation of the KPR originated from the CPKI. The political framework of the KPR encompassed both the Left and the Right, but compared with the CPKI, the leadership of the KPR was dominated by the Left. On October 10, 1945, the U.S. military government refused to recognize the KPR's authority. On the relationship between the KPR and the U.S. military government in South Korea, see Kim Nam-sik, *Namnodang yŏngu,* pp. 117–57.

3. The sudden appearance of new political organizations, after the U.S. occupation forces arrived, is distinguishable from the phenomenon of spontaneous organizing which took place before their arrival. With the establishment of the U.S. military government, the rightists and the former Japanese collaborators hurriedly organized a variety of counterrevolutionary

Here, we must take into consideration the intensity of politically suppressive measures carried out by the Japanese during the colonial period.[4] Except for the state-sponsored and collaborating groups, the immense security system of the Japanese police had derailed all attempts to organize sociopolitical demands from below. In that sense, leadership of the Korean independence movements, whether Communist or conservative nationalist, had maintained a subterranean existence within Korea, while in the peripheries of the Japanese empire the movements were scattered geographically, with multiple centers of leadership.

With the sudden collapse of the Japanese empire, and with the nation divided and occupied by two ideologically opposing forces, a whole spectrum of political leaders appeared, and several youth, student, women's, religious, and cultural groups were organized with various political and social objectives. Postliberation Korean politics, then, has to be understood in historical terms: the harsh nature of colonial rule, the way in which the Pacific war ended, the temporary immobilization of the Japanese coercive apparatuses, tremendous population movement, and the sheer politicizing force of historical events.

To this we must add additional—and what proved to be decisive—structural factors: the unnatural division of Korea, occupation by foreign troops, and the insertion of U.S. and Soviet interests into Korean politics. It is in this context that the historical significance of political entities like Kŏnjun and Ingong should be evaluated. The Committee for the Preparation of Korean Independence and the Korean People's Republic embodied all the characteristics of what Gramsci would call a "national-popular collective

---

groups in response to the organized forces of revolutionary nationalism. Central among these was the Emergency Political Council (later referred to as the Emergency National Council), a right-wing united front. By February 1946, under the direct supervision of the U.S. military government, the Representative Democratic Council was formed, with Syngman Rhee as chairman and Kim Ku as vice chairman. This council was to have laid the basis for the formation of a separate regime in the South. And the organizations created by the right-wing conservatives during this period included shadow organizations, with faked membership lists and little mass support. These right-wing organizations were organized to increase the Right's representation on the U.S.-Soviet Joint Commission established in early 1946.

4. On this, see Bruce Cumings, "The Legacy of Japanese Colonialism in Korea," in *The Japanese Colonial Empire, 1895–1945,* ed. Ramon H. Myers and Mark R. Peattie (Princeton: Princeton University Press, 1984), pp. 478–96.

will" based on an emerging progressive "historical bloc."[5] It was here that a principal postcolonial issue was projected, welding together a wide configuration of social forces, capable, it seemed, of mastering the moment of revolutionary change to usher in a new nation and a new history.

In their various claims to political legitimacy and in their attempts to build a political base, nationalist leaders, whether conservative or Communist, all aimed to establish an independent nation-state and rid Korea of all vestiges of colonial rule. Thus, in the immediate postliberation period, there emerged a common vocabulary and a political scene not yet split along rigid ideological lines.

The intervention and ensuing rivalry between the United States and the USSR, however, rather than facilitating the emergence of a national consensus, polarized the political terrain and made it impossible for various Korean groups to consolidate around a common axis of nationalism. Refusing to deal with the Korean People's Republic organized and led by revolutionary nationalists, the United States committed itself to Syngman Rhee, to the wealthy elites organized around Hanmindang (the Korean Democratic Party), and to that large pool of Koreans who had served the Japanese as administrators and functionaries. Police, military personnel, and bureaucrats who had served the Japanese empire now found new employment serving the interests of the United States. For the Korean *minjung*,[6] however, the restoration of former Japanese collaborators to positions of power

5. On this notion, see Antonio Gramsci, *Selections from the Prison Notebooks,* trans. Quintin Hoare and Geoffrey Nowell Smith (New York: International Publishers, 1971), pp. 130–33, 421 and fn. 65.

6. *Minjung,* as used in this chapter, is defined in terms of several overlapping meanings. First, in the context of capitalist production relations, i.e., in the contradiction between capital and labor, the *minjung* is made up of workers, peasants, the lower middle class, and the urban poor. Second, at the political level, the *minjung* consists of those who are made peripheral to, or alienated from, the political process because of direct and indirect restrictions placed on political participation by the authoritarian regime. Third, the *minjung* is made up of those sectors in society adversely affected by the division of Korean peninsula and South Korea's dependent and subordinated relationship to the United States. Last, while the *minjung* exists objectively, as outlined above, the actual social composition of the *minjung,* at the level of praxis, is constituted by a collective historical consciousness that is alienated from existing relationships of domination. This collective consciousness can be traced back to the experiences of the *minjung* during the great Tonghak Revolution at the end of the nineteenth century. Thus, the *minjung* is not a fixed or limited sociopolitical entity, but embodies a dynamic, liberating subjectivity that arises from a history of oppression.

negated the very meaning of liberation. The U.S. occupation meant salvation for the Japanese collaborators, while for the Korean people, it meant the restoration and strengthening of the colonial structures of domination and control. The U.S. military government, in its bid to will the future of Korea, imposed its own agenda on Korean politics. Liberation, then, brought but a temporary reprieve from the intimidation and violence of the coercive state apparatuses, causing civil society to become rapidly alienated from the U.S. military government and its Korean allies.

Formation of the Overdeveloped State and the First Cleavage

With the early development of the cold war in Korea, the U.S. military government quickly settled for a strategy of creating an anti-communist bulwark in the South. Measures were taken to debilitate the nationalist forces on the Left and even on the Right,[7] to depoliticize civil society, and to destroy the social foundations on which a unified nation-state could be established. These measures, carried out in the name of anti-communism, followed the dictates of U.S. strategic interests in opposition to the balance of social and political forces in Korea favoring revolutionary nationalism over anti-communism.

In this process, the colonial state structure inherited by the United States was greatly expanded, while civil society was restrained and bound by a combination of oppressive laws and brute force. This process is clearly evident in the U.S. military government's policies toward labor in southern Korea. By November 1945, "Chŏnp'yŏng" (Chosŏn nodong chohap chŏnguk p'yŏnguihoe; National Council of Korean Trade Unions) had rallied 1,194 trade unions under its umbrella, representing two hundred thousand union members.[8] By the end of 1945 this number had grown to over half a million—virtually the entire nonagricultural workforce. By September 1947, however, the number of union members under Chŏnp'yŏng had shrunk to almost zero, while the rightist trade union "Noch'ong" (Hanguk nodong chohap ch'ong yŏnmaeng; Federation of Korean Trade Unions)

7. For example, nationalists like Kim Ku and other leaders of the Korean Provisional Government were excluded from access to political power because of their opposition to the policies of the U.S. military government.

8. On this, see the Federation of Korean Trade Unions, *Hanguk nodong chohap undongsa* [The history of the Korean labor union movement] (Seoul: Koryŏ Sŏjok, 1979), pp. 265–66.

counted forty thousand members. Here we notice an interesting contrast with the Japanese occupation experience; in Japan it wasn't until 1949 that the United States expelled leftist leaders from the trade union movement and took limited measures to depoliticize labor.[9] In Korea, the "red purge" began almost immediately. The goal of U.S. policy was not limited to erasing the leftist slant of the trade unions. It was a policy that sanctioned extreme measures to root out leftist unions altogether, to replace them with anti-communist ones, and to otherwise thoroughly depoliticize labor.

The nationwide people's uprising in October and November 1946 demonstrated that civil society overwhelmingly opposed both the creation of a separate regime in the South and the class structure inherited from the colonial period. This event, and many others, challenged the very foundation of the U.S. military government's policies and put civil society on a collision course with the U.S. occupation authorities. The political alliance struck between the U.S. military government and Korean elites encountered great difficulty in eliciting consent, not to mention support, from the Korean masses. The policy of depoliticizing civil society, then, was the necessary counterpart, and prerequisite, to efforts at organizing political and social forces that would support the American position.

For its part, the military government authorities tried to build a political coalition based on three ideological goals: the creation of an anti-communist state, the establishment of a capitalist economy, and the institutionalization of democracy based on a parliamentary system of political representation. Unfortunately, in post-1945 Korea, capitalism, anti-communism, and parliamentary democracy did not occupy privileged positions in the political discourse—nor were these three goals necessarily complementary. The vast majority of Koreans, except those allied with the U.S. military government, would not accept capitalism and anti-communism if instituting them meant preserving the colonial structure of land ownership and division of the country.[10]

9. For the information of the labor union movement in the immediate postwar years, see Okochi Kazuo, *Sengo Nihon no rodoundo* [The labor movement in postwar Japan] (Tokyo: Iwanami shoten, 1956).

10. Land reform was one of most important political issues of the postliberation period, and class conflict was very intense on this issue. The revolutionary nationalists, together with the *minjung*, called for fundamental land reform, i.e., redistribution of land to tenant farmers without compensating the landlords. However, the U.S. military government, and the Korean rightists, either insisted on a very moderate land reform program or opposed land reform altogether. It was not until just before the outbreak of the Korean War that the law on land

By creating a separate regime in the South (the First Republic), the U.S. military government privileged the establishment of a capitalist market economy and an anti-Communist state over the establishment of a democratic political order. Thus while publicly championing the ideals of democracy, the occupation forces crushed popular democratic demands and helped Syngman Rhee establish autocratic power over a forcibly depoliticized society. Herein lies the origin of the first political cleavage: the contradiction between the democratic ideals proclaimed by the state, on the one hand, and its authoritarian practice, on the other. Thus was set a pattern that was to be repeated in subsequent chapters of Korean history: confrontation over the legitimacy of the ruling regime on the basis of democratic norms versus authoritarian practice.

From the beginning of the First Republic, institutions that were meant to give the regime a democratic facade faced severe challenges on two levels. First, a series of revolts followed the establishment of the First Republic, ranging from a full-scale guerrilla war on Cheju Island to subsequent uprisings in Yŏsu and Sunch'ŏn. These massive protests against the establishment of a separate government in the South were answered by a further expansion of the police force and the enactment of laws, most notably the National Security Law (enacted in December 1948), which gave the state complete freedom in the use of coercive powers. There is therefore a continuity in the deployment and use of coercive power from the Japanese colonial period and the U.S. occupation to the creation of the First Republic in South Korea.

The use of this power became institutionalized under the Rhee regime in its campaign to exterminate leftists—and to silence his conservative critics. The exclusion from politics of even the conservative opposition created another source of political challenge to the legitimacy and viability of the parliamentary system under Rhee. There was an economic aspect to this as well. Specifically, Hanmindang, which had emerged as the party of the

---

reform was enacted, but land reform was actually carried out only after the war. The radical land reform program in North Korea began in 1946, and the redistribution of land that took place under the auspices of the North Korean military when they swept southward at the start of the Korean War greatly influenced the politics of land reform in South Korea. There are numerous studies on the topic of South Korean land reform; for an overall analysis, see Yu In-ho, "Haebanghu nongji kaehyukui sŏnggyuk" [The character of land reform after liberation], in *Haebang chŏnhusaui insik* [Interpreting Korean history before and after liberation], vol. 1, ed. Song Kon-ho et al. (Seoul: Hankilsa, 1979), pp. 371–448.

landed class in opposition to Rhee, lost its economic base through the land reform program. The land reform program in the South, in contrast to the North, required that the landlord be compensated for the land turned over to the tenant. Even this moderate program, however, was opposed by the landlords and conservative elements, as represented by Hanmindang.

Thus, soon after the war ended, the landed class was transformed into an urban class, and the power relationship between Rhee, who had command over the powerful state apparatus, and Hanmindang, whose economic base had been expropriated, became lopsided. An acute conflict existed, however, between the Rhee regime and civil society. The strong state–weak society relationship imposed by the U.S. military government was carried over into the First Republic established in 1948. The state was strong because even though it lacked hegemony, it was equipped with coercive apparatuses able to suppress powerful emerging social forces that were principally responsible for activating civil society. But society was weak as a result of the exercise of repressive state power. If we compare 1948 with the period immediately after liberation, when a revolutionary atmosphere swept the country, the difference is striking indeed.

This precipitous decline of civil society had little to do with the internal dynamics of South Korean society; rather, this decline must be attributed to U.S. military government policy and the vast resources mobilized to achieve its objectives. The legitimacy of the First Republic was fragile and vulnerable because the power of the South Korean state was perceived as deriving from its American benefactor. If the United States had reduced or withdrawn its support from the ruling regime, political conflicts or upheavals could have (and indeed probably would have) occurred within society to restore the previous relationships of power. The Korean War, then, should not be interpreted as a confrontation between liberal democracy and communism, but, on one level, as a violent attempt to restore relationships of power established soon after 1945—relationships that had been established before the distorting influence exerted by division and the occupation by U.S. and Soviet troops.

The Korean War and Its Political Consequences

The Korean War was the most decisive turning point in modern Korean history, the denouement of everything that preceded it: the colonial experience, liberation, division, and occupation. At the same time, it became the point of departure for all post–Korean War politics. For the state–civil society relationship as well, the Korean War was critical in shaping the parameters of conflicts to come. Whereas before the war, the South Korean state had a weak local base of support, the war gave the state an ideological basis for building its legitimacy. Anti-communism, articulated and experienced in everyday life, became the premier motif for ideological legitimization of the South Korean state. For this reason, no other event comes close to the Korean War in terms of its determining force on the establishment of that relationship.

The Korean War transformed the South Korean state from an extremely unstable and fragile anti-communist state into a powerful bureaucratic one ruled by an authoritarian regime. This regime, in turn, was supported by a military force that was huge relative to the population and the size of the economy. The size of the Republic of Korea (ROK) Army grew from a mere 150,000 before the war, to over 600,000 at the time of the cease-fire.[11] The police force also expanded greatly after the war. Obviously, it was the Korean War and not the productive growth of society that prompted such state growth, and it was mainly through massive aid provided by the United States that such a powerful state was maintained. It is in this sense that South Korea's postwar state may be called an "overdeveloped state."[12]

After the Korean War, the South Korean economy became fully incorporated into the world capitalist system. With the economy devastated by war, the state came to dominate the economic and financial sectors through receiving and allocating foreign aid. Through this process, economic elites who emerged after the Korean War came to owe their socioeconomic status to the good graces of the regime in power. In the late 1950s, when the wartorn economy was being reconstructed, about 70 percent of the government's total revenue came from foreign aid.[13] Since the government con-

11. Park Myung-lim, "Haebang, pundan, Han'guk jŏnjaengŭi chonch'ejŏk insik" [The holistic understanding of Liberation, division, and the Korean War], in *Haebang chŏnhusaŭi insik* [The understanding of the history before and after liberation], vol. 6, ed. Park Myung-lim et al. (Seoul: Hankilsa, 1989), p. 48.

12. The concept of an "overdeveloped state" comes from Hamza Alavi's analysis of Pakistan and Bangladesh after independence. The formation of the South Korean state after liberation does not necessarily follow the experiences described by Alavi. See Hamza Alavi, "The State in Post-Colonial Societies: Pakistan and Bangladesh," *New Left Review*, no. 74 (July–August 1972).

13. This figure is estimated from Economic Planning Board, *Korea Statistical Yearbook* (Seoul: EPB), pp. 302–30. See also Chung Il-yong, "Wŏnjo gyŏngjeŭi chŏngae" [The evolution

trolled capital and financing, and since much of the capital for government investment and financing came from U.S. aid, the economic structure that was built after the war came to be heavily dependent on foreign capital.

As for civil society, the Korean War caused tremendous suffering and psychological shock. The ferocity of war was felt immediately by every individual. Land and flesh were torn apart; no one was left untouched. But the cease-fire brought neither reconciliation nor peace. With the division reimposed along the cease-fire line (thus perpetuating the prewar division of the country), fear became an integral part of the political culture—fear of communism and of being labeled a communist. The immediate experience of war was thus appropriated by the South Korean state so that it could determine how the war would be remembered.

The wartime experience and the suffering left in its wake were articulated and rearticulated through the ideological apparatuses of the state to control the language, to set the parameters of common discourse, and to produce and reproduce an anti-communist world view that was immediate and real. The political terrain was rearranged by the terror of war, and anti-communism achieved a hegemonic hold over civil society.

Thereafter, the state could invoke anti-communism, or national security, to shore up its legitimacy. Nationalism, in this context, became transformed into a statism that privileged anti-communism over unification. The Korean War therefore gave the Rhee regime two immediate windfalls: first, political order was restored with the elimination of all leftist and progressive forces, including guerrillas who had been active in the mountains and those who had advocated peaceful unification; second, anti-communism, vindicated by the war, provided the ideological basis on which the First Republic could be consolidated. So even as the physical scars of the Korean War were disappearing, civil society was gradually withering in direct proportion to the overdevelopment of the state.

In the West, the growth of the state in the postfeudal period was historically preceded by, or occurred simultaneously with, the growth of civil society under the leadership of the emerging bourgeoisie. In this process, which spanned a century or more, the state, as it came to be differentiated from civil society, came to embody the traits and characteristics corresponding to the formation and growth of different social classes. In South

---

of the economy based on aid] in *Hanguk jabonjuŭiron* [The discussion on Korean capitalism], ed. Lee Tae-gun and Chung Un-yung (Seoul: Kkach'i, 1984), p. 148.

Korea, however, the state was established within an extremely short period of time, in the context of violent political upheaval, and historically prior to the formation of the proletariat and bourgeois classes. Before the Korean War, the state structure in South Korea, whether under the U.S. military government or under the First Republic, could not exercise hegemony over all forces in civil society. The South Korean state, to use Gramsci's phrase, had to be "protected by the armor of coercion."[14] After the war, the capitalist system of production was linked up with the world market economy led by the United States; the military establishment was newly incorporated into the state structure; and the entire governing structure of the state achieved a good deal of legitimacy, largely obscuring its fundamentally illegitimate historical origins.

By the conclusion of the Korean War, the South Korean state had become a state that could sustain itself. So long as the North Korean regime existed, the state had its historical raison d'être. The experience of war and the anti-communism as promulgated by the state became the most important and useful tools for penetrating civil society and consolidating the state's legitimacy among the people. That anti-communism could limit the parameters of subsequent political conflict testifies to the harshness of the wartime experience and the effectiveness of South Korea's ideological state apparatuses. It was under these circumstances that the class structure and characteristics of civil society came to be "overdetermined" (in Althusser's terms) by the state itself.[15]

From an Overdeveloped State to Authoritarian Developmentalism

As seen above, the period from 1945 to 1953 was filled with political upheaval, ideological polarization, death, and suffering. The overall framework for all subsequent political conflicts in South Korea was established during this period of turmoil. Immediately after the Korean War, these political upheavals and confrontations ended. However, the fundamental cleavages that had structured the politics of the pre–Korean War period made their appearance again in the post–Korean War period. When and

14. Gramsci, *Selections from the Prison Notebooks,* p. 263.

15. For this notion, see Louis Althusser, *For Marx* (New York: Vintage Books, 1970), chap. 3, "Contradiction and Overdetermination," pp. 87–128.

under what conditions these cleavages appeared over South Korea's political terrain is examined below.

At the outbreak of the Korean War, a mere 18 percent of the South Korean population was living in Seoul and other urban centers.[16] In terms of occupation, a little less than 80 percent of the population were farmers, with a minuscule 3 percent in manufacturing and mining, and the rest in the tertiary service sector.[17] These simple statistics show that in 1950 South Korean society was still in a preindustrial stage, with an unspecialized agricultural economy, and a low degree of urbanization. The devastation and economic havoc caused by the war displaced a large number of people to Seoul and other administrative centers. The service sector became bloated relative to other sectors of the economy, but by the time of the April 19 Student Uprising in 1960, the overall social structure was not much different from that of ten years earlier. The uprising began with protests against Rhee's scheme to prolong his rule through rigged elections. These protests were also aimed at government corruption and ineffectiveness, and denoted a political confrontation pitting the small urban middle class, represented by the university and the press, against the entrenched administrative and political elites. The April 19 Student Uprising, then, erupted not out of social pressure caused by capitalist development but out of political pressure. Initially, the uprising emerged from what we have called the first political cleavage, that is, the cleavage, in existence before the Korean War, between the facade of democracy on the one hand and authoritarian practice on the other. This uprising was the first direct challenge launched by civil society against the state since the Korean War, and it represented civil society's first victory over the state. But, because the uprising failed to dismantle the repressive state apparatuses—the military, police, and bureaucrats—it represented only a limited victory.

The political cleavage manifested during the April 19 uprising was accompanied by a tremendous bulwark left as a lasting legacy of the Korean War: anti-communism. Within this limited political space, the struggle was perceived and defined in terms of democracy versus dictatorship, and the legitimacy of the Rhee regime was challenged on the basis of the norms of

16. David C. Cole, "Population, Urbanization, and Health," in *The Economic and Social Modernization of the Republic of Korea,* ed. Edward S. Mason, Mahn Je Kim et al. (Cambridge: Council on East Asian Studies, Harvard University Press, 1980), p. 392.

17. The Bank of Korea, *Kyŏngje t'onggye nyŏnbo* [Economic statistical yearbook] (Seoul: Bank of Korea, 1966).

parliamentary democracy and due process. By "consensus," then, the forces that lined up against the Rhee regime did not speak for the class interests of the lower strata of society, nor did they try to organize mass political organizations. However, as the coercive power of the state became immobilized, the political fissure, contained at first at the top of the social structure, spread to the lower strata of society. With this, the boundaries of political conflict began to spread beyond that of the first cleavage, and the discourse strayed beyond the established parameters.

After the Rhee regime was toppled, a radical faction of students tried to shift the direction of the struggle to include the issue of unifying the Korean peninsula. In speaking about reunification, the language employed by these students was idealistic, advocating an extremely open (many would say naive) stand on how unification was to be achieved. These students, for example, called on the students in North Korea to join them at Panmunjŏm so that they might touch off a widespread movement that would lead to reunification. The anti-communist response came in the form of the May 16 military coup led by Park Chung Hee.

The course of events beginning with the April 19 uprising in 1960 and leading to the May 16 military coup in 1961 thus reveals another sequence of rapid expansion of civil society and subsequent reaction, and expansion, of the state—a pattern resembling that of the immediate postwar years. These events must be explained in political terms: the overdevelopment of the bureaucratic-military system both before and after the Korean War, versus a forcefully depoliticized civil society. The military coup of 1961 revealed shifting power dynamics within the power bloc, especially within the military: discontent over the political situation, corruption among the military's top echelons, rank promotions, and so on. The structure of the government established by the 1961 coup, and the "Yushin" (Revitalization) regime put in place in 1972 display the following features of state-led, authoritarian developmentalism: consolidation of a stable political base through coercive force; accelerated industrialization through tightly staged authoritarian planning, with a heavy reliance on foreign capital; and the creation of a political alliance of civilian bureaucrats, technocrats, and industrialists centered on military elites.

This regime formulated policies that favored the upper strata of the bourgeoisie, in close connection with international capital through the medium of the state. With this came the downgrading of the National Assembly's role in national affairs, the suppression of opposition parties, denial of civil rights, and the shriveling of civil society. Here, the wider public was excluded from policy formulation and political processes, while sociopolitical issues were depoliticized by privileging the "technical rationality" of the administration. Thus, a strong authoritarian developmentalist state was established and consolidated before industrialization.

Political considerations outweighed the economic in establishing the Yushin regime.[18] The Yushin constitution marks a self-made change of course on the part of the Park Chung Hee regime, a change that further narrowed the political space. The reasons for this change lie less in the exacerbation of contradictions caused by the industrialization of the 1960s than in Park's efforts to extend his term in office for life. The rewriting of the constitution sought to transform the political system into a vehicle for personalized, Caesaristic rule, so that Park, at the pinnacle of the state structure, could manipulate both the state and civil society. A pattern therefore emerges, beginning with the establishment of the Rhee regime under the auspices of the U.S. military government and continuing under the Park administration.

First, in a situation where the state has a monopoly over compulsory economic, symbolic, and ideological apparatuses, a power elite develops in possession of those apparatuses. In the process of forming a new regime, no channel for dialogue or participation is open to social or political groups representing the interests of other classes in society. The new regime, after consolidating its hold over the state structure, then defines the national interest—autonomous of popular pressures and demands, whether from the newly emerging bourgeoisie or the working classes. In determining what the "national interest" is, and how it is to be served, the regime seeks to lay the basis for its legitimacy and to institutionalize its rule. When a new regime comes to power, overturning the old by violent means, political institutions, political parties, and interest groups must be either reconstituted or their leadership reshuffled. In this sense, an overdeveloped state

18. There are a number of studies on the causes of the installation and character of the Yushin system that are, more or less, different from my point of view. Many of them apply Guillermo O'Donnell's notion of "bureaucratic authoritarianism" and assume economic factors to be the principal cause. See Kang Min, "Kwanryojŏk kwŏnwijuŭiŭi Han'gukjok saengsŏng" [The emergence of Korean bureaucratic authoritarianism], *Korean Political Science Review* 17 (1983), and Han Sang-jin, "Bureaucratic Authoritarianism and Economic Development in Korea during the Yushin Period," *Dependency Issues in Korean Development*, ed. Kim Kyong-dong (Seoul: Seoul National University, 1987), pp. 362–74.

implies a weak civil society: in spite of the social differentiation and diversification of economic interests brought about by industrialization, the network between political and social groupings that reflect divergent interests is kept fragile, tenuous, and incapable of setting the political agenda.

In such a situation, it is unlikely that the state elites will feel pressured to include political and social groups in the ruling bloc; this in turn decreases the possibility for political compromise through institutional means. Important policies or decisions are thus made within a small closed circuit, that is, by the head of state assisted by an entourage of bureaucrats and technocrats. This is how Park and his Democratic Republican Party dictated in the early 1960s what the supreme national goal was to be: national security and economic prosperity through export-oriented industrialization.

State-Led Industrialization and the Shaping of a Second Cleavage

Having come to power in 1961 through a military coup, the Park regime tried to compensate for its lack of legitimacy by pursuing a program of accelerated economic growth. Beginning in the mid-1960s, the South Korean economy grew rapidly, with light industry leading the way. During this period a large industrial workforce was created, and tremendous socioeconomic changes occurred, leading to intensified conflict between social strata. Clashes over production relations and over the distribution of benefits of economic growth then resulted in the formation of the second cleavage.

The socioeconomic condition of South Korea, which until the early 1960s exhibited only incremental change, underwent drastic and fundamental changes during the 1960s and 1970s. Within a short span of time, by the mid-1970s, the bulk of the population had migrated to the cities and the farming population had declined by nearly half. While the agricultural sector became subordinated to the export-industrial sector, the movement of farmers from the countryside to the cities exceeded the speed of industrialization. This population shift, involving nearly 20 percent of the population within a ten-year period, is quite unprecedented—even greater than that which took place during the course of the Korean War.[19] This movement

19. Between 1967 and 1976, about 6.7 million people migrated from rural areas to cities and between 1949 and 1955 the population movement is estimated about 1.8 million. See

to the cities to seek employment accelerated the process of occupational differentiation and diversification of economic interests and engendered aspirations that were pluralistic and multitiered. Although these newly created interests were prevented from being expressed politically, they nevertheless provided the social basis for the expansion of civil society.

Out of this process, the structure of society was reconstituted in pyramidal form. At the top rested the upper bourgeoisie favored by the political regime, high technocrats and bureaucrats in the public sector, and senior executives from the major firms, along with a collection of small-business owners. Below this elite lay the middle echelon managers, the petite bourgeoisie, and white-collar workers. And forming the huge base for this structure were the industrial and service sector workers, peasants, miners, fishermen, peddlers, the underemployed, and the jobless.[20]

Although income levels for the population as a whole significantly increased, the social and economic gap between classes widened even more. For the lower classes, despite the increase in the absolute income, what amounted to a revolution in expectations brought about a keen sense of deprivation and alienation from the sociopolitical system. The extent of this alienation among the fundamental classes, especially among industrial workers, was manifested eloquently in protests throughout the Yushin years.

The political power structure remained paralyzed between Park's assassination by his own intelligence chief in October 1979 and the proclamation of martial law in May 1980. Workers nationwide launched a series of strikes and other collective actions, for example, at the Sabuk coal mine in Kangwon province, the Tongguk Steel Mill in Pusan and Inchon, and at the Hyundai Group's Inchon Steel Mill. Scenes such as these, and the possibility that the strikes could spread even further, caused the political elite and the bourgeoisie to feel a sense of crisis. It is worthwhile to compare this period with the situation immediately following the April 19 Student Uprising in 1960. In 1960, as in early 1980, the coercive apparatuses were temporarily immobilized. In 1960, labor disputes increased more than twofold, over the year before, while in 1980, in the four-month period preced-

---

Song Byung-nak and E. S. Mills, *Sŏngjanggwa tosihwa munje* [Economic growth and urbanization] (Seoul: Korean Development Institute, 1980), p. 78.

20. For a discussion about the changing trend in class structure during 1970s, see Kim Chin-kyun, "Hanguk sahoeŭi kegŭp kujo" [The class structure in Korean society], in *Hanguk sahoe pyŭndong yŏngu* [The studies of social change in Korean society] (1), ed. Chung Yun-hyung, Kim Chin-kyun et al. (Seoul: Minjungsa, 1984).

ing the proclamation of martial law, the number of labor disputes increased by more than fourfold compared with all of 1979.[21]

From this we can infer the following: In 1960, as in 1980, crises within the ruling regime and the concomitant paralysis of the coercive apparatuses allowed workers to demonstrate their class aspirations through collective action; however, in both relative and absolute terms, the strikes and other actions in 1980 were much more massive and intense, reflecting the tremendous expansion of the industrial workforce in the twenty-year period, as well as the depth of its accumulated discontent.

The income of the industrial workers at large plants, compared to that of the urban poor, is relatively high. However, the wages of these workers still amount to less than a fifth of middle-level managers and white-collar workers. To this source of dissatisfaction can be added other factors: a system of health insurance tailored for the middle class, paucity of social services, and a "development first" logic that had little regard for the plight of the workers. Here, then, was the structural basis for the political alienation of a large segment of the economically active population.

This alienation was articulated politically as rejection of the authoritarian political system and of the highly exploitative and oppressive system of production. Opposed to this, the collective vision that emerged from the workers' struggles was radically egalitarian and communitarian.[22] The militancy of the workers, then, and the countervision that they projected, had as its structural basis the absence of institutional mechanisms through which workers could articulate and assert their views and interests. The existing mechanisms of industrial relations, because their essential function was to limit and control the workers' demands, became impotent in times of intense labor strife. Mobilized through rapid industrialization, yet excluded from the sociopolitical system, and with only a top-down chain of command linking the workers to the state elites, the workers responded by organizing democratic unions through which they solidified their ranks and

21. There were 848 disputes during the four-month period from January to April 1980. See Economic Planning Board, "Nodong kwankye charyo" [The material concerning labor] (Seoul: EPB, 1980), p. 108.

22. This description of the labor movement is based on my empirical study of the labor union movement during the 1960s and 1970s. See my *Labor and the Authoritarian State: Labor Unions in South Korean Manufacturing Industries, 1961–1980* (Seoul: Korea University Press, 1989).

pressed their demands. With the declaration of martial law in May 1980, however, the political terrain was restored by brute force to its former state.

The similarities to the past are readily apparent: In a situation where the central power structure was not yet consolidated, the waves of demonstrators led by students failed to dismantle the authoritarian political system. This failure, so similar in its outcome to the immediate postliberation period, when the masses demanded the liquidation of the colonial structure, and similar also to 1960, when the people tried to overthrow Rhee's authoritarian regime, nevertheless disclosed a crucial difference with its historical predecessors.

In opposition to the workers, the industrial bourgeoisie and the upper segments of the petty bourgeoisie, together with the greatly expanded middle class, formed a political alliance—albeit not in the form of a political party. This political alliance, through its silence and political passivity, actually helped maintain the existing political power structure. The emergence of this type of alliance marks a sharp break from the character of previous political struggles. Specifically, military intervention had been the decisive factor in the demise of the progressive-nationalist forces in the immediate postliberation years, and in the failure of the April 19 uprising in 1960. In 1980 another military coup, led by Chun Doo Hwan, again determined the outcome of political confrontation; but here, for the first time a new political force composed of the upper and middle classes emerged, which, through its quiescence, allowed the new regime to consolidate its power. Thus it is not accurate to say that history was simply repeating itself in 1980. Rather, the historical significance of that year lies in the fact that at a critical historical juncture the progressive forces could not draw support from the middle class that now constituted the central social strata in Seoul.

Here, Seoul must be given special consideration because of its critical place in national life—its centrality in terms of politics, economics, society, and culture. Seoul had more than its share of poor, marginalized, and potentially explosive sectors. Throughout the period of accelerated industrialization, Seoul had served as an economic magnet that drew the bulk of the demographic exodus from the countryside. Compared with other cities in Korea, moreover, Seoul had developed an extensive international network, had received most of the benefits of export-led growth, and had adopted a cosmopolitan-bourgeois culture. The dominance of Seoul's middle class extended into the cultural and intellectual life of the entire city, and the lower strata of society, however marginalized they may have been politically and economically, nevertheless followed the example of the middle class at the key historical moment. This, then, explains why the lower classes of Seoul remained passive in 1980, while in Kwangju, Pusan, and other urban and industrial centers, the lower classes aligned with the dissident forces to launch massive protests against the regime.

In cities and industrial centers outside Seoul the political and economic position of the middle class, compared with the middle class in Seoul, had been peripheral, and at the moment of insurrection, a portion of the middle class had aligned with the dissident forces. In the end, however, the political confrontation in Seoul, or lack thereof, proved decisive. Thus after the debacle of 1980, no one could deny that the new middle class in Seoul had established a strategic position in contemporary South Korean society.

The Second Cleavage: Just Distribution versus Developmentalism

On one level, the inability of the dissident forces to win the support of the middle class in Seoul in 1980 has to be explained historically. The installation of the Yushin system in 1972, which obliterated all semblance of democracy from the political scene, marked a critical point in the political development of the middle class and produced diverging political outlooks between the middle class and the dissident forces. With the proclamation of the Yushin constitution, Park and his Democratic Republican Party had scrapped democratic pretensions, and as an alternative basis for its political legitimacy, the Yushin system offered to guarantee stability, security, order, and efficiency, while pursuing high growth and prosperity.

The Yushin system tried to replace the ideals of freedom and democracy with the logic of national security and bureaucratic economic development. With this came a shift in the structure of the existing political fissure, from one located around the democracy-dictatorship axis to one revolving around the just distribution–developmentalism axis. If this displacement could be made permanent, the legitimacy of the political regime could no longer be challenged on the basis of democratic norms alone. A new question would have to be asked: Could a different political system maintain or improve the nation's gross national product?

This ideological move, accompanied by high-handed exercise of the state's coercive power, led to the political fragmentation of the middle class. The urban middle class, which had so strongly supported the April 19 student uprising and student protests against the 1965 treaty normalizing relations with Japan, slowly withdrew its support from the dissidents after 1972. This evolution of middle-class politics was in a sense forced; the middle class had to choose between economic growth and democracy. It did not have the luxury of choosing both. This evolution, then, produced its anticlimax in the spring of 1980.

It should be emphasized here that the sense of crisis felt by the middle class in 1980 cannot be traced to economic interest alone. The threat of invasion from North Korea served (and continues to serve) as a tremendous resource for the state; the stability of the existing political order was linked with the threat of invasion from the North. Thus in a time of acute crisis for the political order, as in the spring of 1980, a portion of Seoul's middle class remained on the sidelines, while the majority defended the status quo.

The dissident forces in 1980 consisted of students and middle-class intellectuals, industrial workers, and the radical wing of the church. The history of the dissident movement after the establishment of the First Republic shows that students had always played a central role in the opposition movement, providing intellectual leadership as well as an ability to organize and mobilize. The genealogy of the present student movement should be traced to its emergence under the regime of Syngman Rhee and his Liberal Party. In the late 1950s, the Rhee regime's popularity and credibility had declined even further because it was corrupt and used increasingly repressive measures to remain in power. Thereafter, students emerged as the leading force in the formation of antiregime groups; they projected a democratic outlook, were autonomous from the ruling bloc, and eventually led the opposition against the Rhee regime in the April 1960 uprising.

The student movement had not been allowed to create formal organizations outside campus through which the students could freely and independently interact with the political system. No mechanisms were available for students to incorporate their demands into public policy, and no meaningful exchange could take place between the students and the permissibly "loyal" opposition party, to say nothing of the ruling party. This alienation of the student movement from party politics continued even under the post-Rhee regime that briefly came to power after the April uprising. Throughout the 1960s the student movement remained within the confines of urban intellectual life, with no affiliation to political parties or any other social groups. It is within this context that the Chun Tae Il incident of November 1970 marks a turning point in the direction and character of the student movement. Chun Tae Il had worked as a tailor in a garment district of Seoul. After repeatedly failing in efforts to better the working conditions of the young employees in his charge, he committed suicide in public, calling on employers to adhere to standards set by labor laws. (For more discussion of this incident see Chapter 4 by Hagen Koo in this volume.)

The death of Chun Tae Il set the framework for intense self-reflection. This incident, and the tremendous moral and emotional energies generated by it, catalyzed attempts to organize democratic labor unions and transformed the labor question into a general social concern. Clubs, circles, and "underground unions" were formed inside and outside the factories. Though few in number, students and church activists became involved in these organizations—thus forming the beginnings of a link between the urban intellectual groups and the working class. These encounters between the workers and the urban intellectual groups, reacting against the repressive policies of the Park Chung Hee regime, radicalized both the student and labor movements.

A segment of the church was also radicalized. Traditionally, the Korean church has been very conservative in its political orientation. The appearance of a radical wing within Korean churches, however, mirrored the development of radical Christian movements in other parts of the Third World. The church in Korea, with its extensive international network, was an active participant in the theological transformations that took place in the 1960s. Parallel to Vatican II and the emergence of Liberation Theology in Latin America, the radical wing of the Korean church put forth a People's Theology, and created as its organizational expressions the Urban Industrial Missions, the Catholic and Protestant Farmers Federations, and human rights organizations.[23]

What we see emerging in the 1970s, then, is a close network of dissident groups composed of students and critical intellectuals, urban industrial workers, and the radical wing of the Korean church. These dissident groups, in the course of opposing the authoritarianism of the Yushin regime, merged into a loose but powerful political alliance. Toward the end of the 1970s, the opposition party, at this time called the New Democratic Party, joined this alliance. The leadership of the New Democratic Party was

23. On this subject, see Hak-kyu Sohn, "Political Opposition and the Yushin Regime: Radicalization in South Korea, 1972–79," Ph.D. thesis, Wolfson College, Oxford University, 1988.

shared by Kim Dae Jung and Kim Young Sam. This alliance between the New Democratic Party and the dissidents outlined as a common goal the return to a democratic system.

It should be noted, however, that on the issue of economic justice (i.e., just distribution of income) the New Democratic Party was much more conservative than the mainstream of the dissident movement; it did not play an important role in confronting the regime over the second cleavage. In its challenge to the ruling bloc, the dissident alliance argued that democratic principles are not contradictory to stability, security, and prosperity; rather, they contended, these goals can be more effectively realized within a democratic system. Opposed to the dissidents, the bourgeoisie and the conservative middle class raised the specter of political chaos and the possibility that continued political instability would undermine all previous economic accomplishments. This social configuration still perpetuates political conflict along the second cleavage.

Drastic Changes on the Political Terrain

The composition of the military authoritarian regime under Park Chung Hee had been bolstered by military elites, upper bourgeoisie, state managers, technocrats of the state and private sectors, and the omnipresence of U.S. strategic and economic interests. Compared with this ruling bloc, civil society was weak, and thus enabled the longevity of the Park regime. Despite this power imbalance between the state and civil society, the opposition was able to mobilize the masses at favorable historical moments, forcing the regime into crisis and breakdown, as in 1960 and in the spring of 1980. The political liberalizations that followed, however, were in both cases cut short by military coups.

This pattern changed entirely when the population of Kwangju rose up, en masse, to reject the imposition of military rule. The subsequent mass killings carried out by the military in that city created a new dialectic, which was to alter the political terrain. Not since the Korean War had the civilian population been so brutally victimized by the military.[24] The massa-

24. Kwangju, a city with a population of one million, is the center of Chŏlla province, located in the southwestern portion of South Korea. Chŏlla province was largely excluded from the industrialization process that took place in the 1960s and 1970s under the Park regime. Park Chung Hee came from Kyŏngsang province; in the process of consolidating his power, he filled the top political posts with men from his own province. At the same time,

cre in Kwangju proved to be a tremendous liability for the Chun regime; whereas during the Yushin years the Park regime had ruled through the issuance of emergency decrees, the Chun regime had to resort to direct military rule.

The Chun government developed out of the breakdown of the Yushin regime, yet Chun did not set out to reform the governing structure, nor did he change the government's major policies. In fact, his economic policies favored the big conglomerates even more, at the expense of other sectors of the economy; his highly repressive tax system, which taxed salary and wage incomes at much higher rates than income from capital and land, placed the burden of supporting the expanded state on the shoulders of the lower and middle classes.[25] At the same time, Chun copied Park's privatized authoritarian style and placed himself at the apex of a vast network of corruption and extortion. As later revealed during the National Assembly Hearings into Corruption during the Fifth Republic, this concentration and misuse of power generated visibly negative effects on the economy. In the process, the upper classes came to have ambivalent attitudes toward the Chun regime, recognizing on the one hand that Chun was a reliable guarantor of their monopoly interests, but disgruntled on the other by the extortion of political contributions and the state's meddling in business.

Among the masses, which make up about three-fourths of the economically active population,[26] dissident organizations made significant gains in

---

and with the help of Park's regime, the socioeconomic hierarchy also came to be dominated by men from Kyŏngsang province. This phenomenon both overlapped and reinforced the deeply rooted antagonism between Chŏlla and all the other provinces in South Korea. The Park regime's discrimination against Chŏlla province was one of the critical factors behind the Kwangju uprising of 1980. The hard-line military clique that grabbed power in 1980 was also led by men from Kyŏngsang province, and the military force these men unleashed against Kwangju in 1980 was particularly savage and brutal. When the democratic movement began to challenge the Chun regime a few years later, the issue of regional discrimination (i.e., discrimination against Chŏlla province), in particular the massacre in Kwangju, became a central political issue.

For a comprehensive documentation about the Kwangju massacre, see Han'guk Hyŏndaesa Saryo yŏnguso, *Kwangju owŏl hangjaeng saryojip* [Complete collection of the historical materials on the May people's uprising in Kwangju] (Seoul: P'ulbbit Publications, 1990).

25. For some critical evaluations of the economic policy under the Chun regime, see Shindong-a, ed., *Kajinjawa mot kajinja* [The haves and the have-nots] (Seoul: Dong-a Ilbosa, 1988).

26. This estimation of the size of the popular sectors during the early 1980s, including the working class, peasants, and lower middle class, is based on Suh Kwan-mo, "Han'guk sahoeŭi kyegŭp kujo" [The class structure in Korean society], in *Han'guk sahoeron* [Studies on Korean society], ed. Kim Chin-kyun, Kim Hyung-ki et al. (Seoul: Hanul Publications, 1990), p. 122.

organizing the workers, farmers, and urban poor. The Kwangju incident made the student movement even more militant in its tactics. From this point onward, student activists began to move in large numbers beyond the university campuses into the factories to establish links with the labor movement. Also, as Koo describes in Chapter 4, in the 1980s the center of the workers' movement shifted from labor-intensive, light industry (textiles, electronics, etc.), where women formed the bulk of the workforce, to heavy industry (automotive industry, shipping, etc.), made up predominantly of male workers. In all the sectors, moreover, the leaders of the official labor unions, which had heretofore adhered to the state's repressive labor policies, was challenged by the rank and file. The "no-hak yŏndae" (the worker-student alliance) became a powerful force, capable of challenging the coercive regime.[27]

Meanwhile, the middle strata, comprised of mid-echelon functionaries in the state and private sectors, urban professionals, intellectuals, and the self-employed, also turned against the regime. This middle class provided the impetus for a mass campaign in 1987 to revise the constitution of the Fifth Republic, and after a series of events, including the death of a student after police torture and Chun's public declaration of opposition to the constitutional amendment, the popular mood turned decisively against the regime. Throughout June 1987 the streets became a battle zone between the riot police and masses of demonstrators.[28] Chun's decision to defend his constitution sharply divided the ruling military elites into "hardliners" committed to ending the demonstrations through force, and "softliners" who were ready to come to terms with the opposition.[29] The June 29 declaration by Roh Tae Woo, then, represented the ascendancy of that faction in the military that was unwilling to repeat the bloody events of 1980—just when a stalemate existed between the severely weakened, divided power bloc and the vastly expanded populist democratic alliance. The

27. On the no-hak yŏndae, see Lee Chong-o, "P'alsip nyŏndae nodong undongron chŏngae kwachŏngŭi ihaerŭl wihayŏ" [Toward an understanding of a theory of labor movement for the 1980s], in *Han'guk nodong undongŭi inyŏm* [Theories in the Korean labor movement] ed. Han'gŭk Kitokyo Sanŏp kaebalwŏn (Seoul: Chongamsa, 1988), pp. 212–306.

28. For detailed information on the June 1987 Uprising for Democracy, see Hăn'guk kidokyo Sahoemunje Yŏnguwŏn, *6 wol minjuhwa taet'ujaeng* [The great June struggle for democracy], Kisayŏn Report no. 2 (Seoul: Minjungsa, July 1987).

29. On this concept, see Guillermo O'Donnell and Philippe C. Schmitter, *Transitions from Authoritarian Rule: Tentative Conclusions about Uncertain Democracies* (Baltimore: Johns Hopkins University Press, 1986), pp. 15–17, 63.

declaration, however, succeeded in separating and annexing an important section of the populist democratic alliance, namely, the urban middle class.

With the urban middle class demobilized, the populist democratic forces were not strong enough to dismantle the power bloc. The mainstream populist democratic forces were therefore compelled to compromise with Roh by giving up their maximalist goal and consented to containing the conflict to the first political cleavage, that is, around the issue of democracy versus dictatorship. If the movement had gone further, pushing the struggle to include both the first and second cleavages (democracy/just distribution versus dictatorship/developmentalism), the ruling bloc would have unleashed the full power of the repressive state apparatuses in a final showdown, and the populist democratic forces would have suffered tremendous bloodshed and crushing defeat.

Roh's declaration stabilized the immediate crisis by giving in to popular demands for direct presidential election. This modus vivendi enabled the state to emerge from this crisis unscathed, while the urban middle class congratulated itself for having forced the regime to carry out democratizing measures. Such a carrot thrown to the middle class, however, had done little to change the socioeconomic condition of the workers, and they now came to the forefront of the struggle. Not surprisingly, the middle strata did not join the workers' struggle. What was unexpected, however, was the scope and intensity of labor unrest and the speed with which the middle class abandoned the populist democratic movement. The declaration, then, decoupled the first cleavage from the second and isolated the workers along the second cleavage.

A wave of labor unrest after Roh's declaration started in Ulsan, a newly built industrial city with a heavy concentration of large, heavy, and chemical industries, and spread rapidly to Pusan, Kwangju, and the Masan-Changwon areas, and then turned northward to Taegu, Koomi, and finally arrived in the Seoul-Inchon area.[30] These strikes were initiated by young male workers who were skilled and had higher salaries than workers in the light industries located around the Seoul-Inchon area. (The size and the pattern of these labor strikes are described in Chapter 4.)

Compared with the spring of 1980, the difference is clear. The social

30. For the detailed information, see Han'guk kidokyo Sahoemunje Yŏnguwŏn, *7–8 wŏl nodongja taejung t'ujaeng* [The Great July–August workers' struggles], Kisayŏn Report no. 3 (Seoul: Minjungsa, September 1987).

forces unleashed in 1980 were an outcome of the temporary immobilization of the repressive apparatuses of the state, combined with the decrease in the real income brought about by the recession. At that time, the strikes were largely limited to small and medium-size industries and the issues were mainly economic (i.e., concerned with wages and working conditions), while the methods of protest were comparatively mild.[31]

The workers' movement of 1987, however, took place during a period of economic expansion. The workers' stance going into the strikes was very militant; their unity and organization were strong, and their methods went far beyond the legal boundaries. Many of the workers' demands were political, focused on changing repressive labor laws and obtaining the right to organize independent unions free from state and company control. Through these strikes, both the workers and the state/upper bourgeoisie became acutely aware of the strategic importance and power of the workers in the monopoly enterprises. Because of the vertical integration of the production system created by the monopoly enterprises, with its system of contractors and subcontractors, a protracted strike at any level of the production system could arrest the entire production process and create a political and economic crisis.

In response to the striking workers, the state and the upper bourgeoisie renewed their historical unity, while the state-controlled media portrayed the workers as destructive and influenced by pro-communist infiltrators. By thus utilizing all its repressive and ideological resources, Roh's ruling bloc succeeded in separating the middle class from the populist democratic forces. In confronting the workers along the second political cleavage, the ruling bloc defined the clash in terms of "bo-hyuk" (conservative-radical), that is, as conflicts between conservatives who uphold capitalist order and liberal democracy, on the one hand, and leftist revolutionaries who strive to overthrow the existing order through violent means, on the other. Through the media, memories were evoked of the left-right struggles during the turbulent postliberation years. That the middle class was vulnerable to this ideological interpellation is not surprising.

For both the middle class and the workers the central concept embodied in their political struggles of 1987 was, and continues to be, democracy.

31. Shin Kum-ho, "Nodong undongŭi taejungjŏk chŏngaewa chojikhwaŭi kwaje" [The evolution of the labor movement and the task for its organization], in *Chŏnhwan* [Transition] (Seoul: Sagyejŏl Publications, 1987), pp. 190–208.

But democracy as articulated by the middle class was limited to the discourse whose parameters were demarcated by the first political cleavage, a discourse that revolved around procedural norms of liberal democracy. But democracy as articulated by students and workers invoked a different discourse, one that gave centrality to the concepts of equality, social justice, and community, in addition to its minimum definition circumscribing deauthoritarianization with the opening of political space. It is here, then, between the terrain marked out by the first and second political cleavages, that the middle class and the dissident movement begin to speak different languages.

Evolution of the Third Cleavage: The Issue of Reunification

Analyzing why, when, and under what circumstances the issue of reunification came to the fore of South Korean politics is extremely important for understanding the entire structure of conflict established since liberation. All other political and social issues, including those of democracy and distribution, are at some level linked to the division of the Korean peninsula. It is the iniquity of history that this most fundamental issue necessarily appeared last in the sequence of unfolding political struggles. The state and civil society in South Korea will probably clash again in full force over the issue of reunification.

Reunification, which came to the forefront of political discourse during the middle of 1988, has become the most heatedly debated issue in South Korean politics. The reasons for this include the activation of the reunification movement within the opposition forces; recognition of the need for lessening of tensions by both the South and the North; and the changing international circumstances, that is, the end of the Cold War, the impact of German reunification, and the overall reconstitution of the world system.

With the reemergence of the reunification issue in South Korea, the conflict and confrontation of the immediate postliberation period have reappeared. All three cleavages now appear linked over the political terrain. How these cleavages are resolved will greatly influence subsequent developments in the relationship between the state and civil society in the South, and how and under what circumstances reunification will take place. Reunification has been the most severely suppressed issue in South Korea because of the historical/structural circumstances under which the political system in South Korea was formed. The very existence of an anti-communist state in the South, established under U.S. auspices after liberation, was predicated on the fact of national division. A separate regime in the South formed part of a Great Crescent, a system of state established by the United States to encircle the communist bloc countries, linking South Korea to a global system led by the United States.[32] The Korean War was the critical event consolidating this system, and it was in Korea that the power of this global system was especially concentrated. It is under these circumstances that the subject of reunification was kept outside the boundaries of allowable political discourse.

The appearance of reunification as a central political issue, then, took an entire generation. The circumstances making this possible were outlined above. The specific historical events that led up to this moment were the Kwangju uprising in 1980 and the June 1987 uprising, followed by massive workers' struggles. Through their activism, the workers developed a political consciousness, as they began to rethink, to rearticulate, and to challenge the mainstream perspectives on North Korea, as well as the role of the United States in Korean history and contemporary politics.

The reunification movement sought to portray North Korea in a nonhostile, positive way and to draw attention to U.S. responsibility for the division of Korea after Japan's surrender in 1945 and for the Kwangju massacre of 1980.[33] A variety of groups and associations tried to meet their counterparts in the North and set off a wave of discussions and public forums centering on postliberation history and reunification. The reunification movement thus brought to the center of the political stage the issue that most fundamentally challenged the existing political system in South Korea.

Roh responded by issuing a declaration on July 7 (1988), setting new guidelines for the state's reunification policy. Roh's Nordpolitik defined North Korea as part of one "national community" and introduced overtures for almost unlimited economic and cultural exchanges. This major policy redirection required the state to alter radically its conception of North Korea and other communist bloc countries, and to tone down, rhe-

32. Interpretive works that seriously address the concept of the Great Crescent include Michael Schaller, *The American Occupation of Japan* (New York: Oxford University Press, 1985).

33. On this, see Lee Sam-sung, "Kwangju bonggiwa migukui yŏkhwal" [Kwangju uprising and the U.S. role in it], *Sahoewa Sasang*, February 1989 (Seoul: Hankilsa).

torically at least, its anti-communist stance. The declaration thus signaled a drastically different approach toward maintaining control over the issue of reunification.

Looking back at post–Korean War history, we can locate important times when civil society broached the issue of reunification: Cho Bong Am, the presidential candidate of the Progressive Party in 1956, campaigned on a platform advocating peaceful reunification; and the April 19 student activists had called for a North-South meeting between students. That Cho Bong Am was executed by the Rhee regime and that a military coup ended the students' initiative reflect the degree to which reunification had been forcefully displaced from the arena of legitimate, everyday discourse.

In 1988, however, rather than simply repressing the reunification movement, the Roh regime in effect tried to repeat the accomplishments of the June 29 declaration, that is, to fragment the reunification movement by adopting a portion of its demands while imposing additional constraints. That the Roh regime tried to compromise with the movement forces and to pull the reunification issue into the confines of the "chedokwŏn" (institutionalized political arena) indicate the degree to which the strength of the forces had grown. The reunification issue had opened up a whole new political space in which the dissident movement could organize a broad coalition: farmers hurt by imports of U.S. agricultural products, thousands of separated families, teachers struggling to reform the curriculum and the educational system as a whole, and so on. In this way, the issue of reunification brought together a variety of groups and a whole range of issues that emanated from the fact of national division.

The July declaration, however, also unified the power bloc on the basis of confining the reunification issue to official channels, and provided conservatives with an opportunity to rearticulate their Cold War stance in a new language. Nordpolitik came to mean economic penetration into the socialist bloc countries; annexation of the conservative opposition parties from the populist nationalist movement; maintenance of the highly oppressive National Security Law; and the achievement of Southern predominance over the North in line with a drastically changing international environment. Taking advantage of the changing international scene, a grand conservative alliance was forged around the state's formulation of the issue of reunification.

The formation of such a coalition can be attributed to the internalization of the division within South Korean society. The problem of reunification is embedded in the overlap between international structures and class stratification within South Korea. Simply put, a wide configuration of groups and sectors in South Korea had benefited from the division. The technocrats, the military establishment, and the upper bourgeoisie, which previously constituted the core bloc advocating a nonconciliatory reunification policy, have now rallied around Nordpolitik based on the model of West Germany's absorption of East Germany. Nordpolitik represents the conservative bloc's aggressive reaction to both the collapse of communism in the Soviet bloc and the emergence of a populist reunification movement in South Korea. Thus it is against this backdrop that the formerly antireunification conservative bloc, which had developed in the processes of separate state formation and state-led industrialization, is now turning out to be a force for reunification.

Democratization is fundamentally linked to reunification. This becomes readily apparent when we recognize that North Korean society was similarly affected by division, leading to the emergence of a particular power structure within North Korea. This perspective, which has not been adequately addressed within the reunification movement in South Korea, tends to see North Korea only in abstract or idealized terms. But North Korea has its own internal logic, distinct from that of the South. To put it differently, reunification implies the existence of a concrete other. Thus reunification should not mean the absorption of one by the other, nor should it mean the simultaneous dismantling of both. What is needed is a reunification that comes about as a result of the prolonged preservation of two states within one unified Korea, linking the issues of national self-determination and democratization. In this sense, the task of reunification transcends the state–civil society conflict within South Korea.

The Political Opening and Its Consequences

From the vantage point of the early 1990s, after a few years of political opening, there has evidently been a high degree of continuity in the conservative ruling power structure between the ancien régime and the new Roh regime. This does not necessarily mean, however, that there have been no substantial changes in the composition of the ruling power bloc, the internal structure of the state, and the state–civil society relationship. The transition from authoritarian rule since 1987 has unmistakenly had a great impact on every important aspect of both the state and society. The upsurge of popular democratic forces led by the *minjung* unleashed the forces of civil society and enormously expanded the scope of conflicts along all three cleavages (democratization, economic justice, and reunification) to the forefront of the political agenda.

The ruling bloc's response to this political crisis was quite familiar; it defined the political situation as a public security crisis *(kongan chungguk)* in April 1989, representing a backlash to the democratization process led by the hardliners in the new regime. Its aim was to put the brakes on the mounting two-front opposition movement, the labor-led movement demanding substantive benefits for workers and the populist reunification movement led by the students and progressive church groups. But this time, unlike the coups of 1961 and 1980, the state elite's attempt to impose authoritarian rule was modest: its methods were moderate and its target was limited mainly to the radical sections of the movements. This reflected a political atmosphere in which the new regime's elites were not strong enough to recoup their losses since 1987, but at the same time the democratic forces in civil society were not powerful enough to remove them. Nevertheless, the conservative ruling elites were able to remain in power and keep the political system authoritarian to a considerable extent.

The partial success of the ruling elites is related to the weaknesses of the democratic forces. For the latter, two factors are crucial. One is the horizontal fissure that exists between social classes, particularly between the middle class and the working class. The middle class has proved how deeply it has accepted the dominant ideology and how easily it could become conservative and hostile to the working-class movement, which was becoming increasingly radicalized and vociferous as the political conflicts developed not only on the terrain of the first cleavage but also on that of the second and third ones. But middle-class complacency did not derive merely from ideology. The middle class has clearly benefited from the current economic system, so it had no reason to align itself with the working class for substantive reforms. The general prosperity of society made the labor movement a minority among the democratic movements.

The other important factor is the vertical division of society along regional lines, that is, the rise of regional discrimination against Chŏlla province.[34] In a way this regional discrimination is so powerful that it may

34. For a comprehensive collection of the studies concerning the regionalism, see Kim Hakmin and Lee Tu-yop, eds., *Chiyŏk kamjŏng yŏngu* [Studies on regional sentiments] (Seoul: Hakminsa, 1991).

constitute the fourth cleavage in South Korean politics. But it should not be understood as another cleavage, not only because it is not a kind of conflict that can be reduced to a certain fundamental and structural variant, but also because it is a cumulative result of other conflictual factors like political and economic democratization whose failure has strengthened discrimination against a particular region.

Yet no matter how spontaneous or manipulated, people from outside Chŏlla province, particularly the political and social ruling strata from Kyŏngsang province, fear the possibility of radical reforms should the Party for Peace and Democracy (PPD) and its leader, Kim Dae Jung, win in elections. So for most of Korean society, a transfer of power to the opposition party would have been identified not as a transition to democracy but as a power shift from people from Kyŏngsang to those from Chŏlla. The majority of people outside Chŏlla province have also come to hold this view. Voting patterns since the opening of the electoral arena, from the presidential election of 1987, to the March general election of 1992, and to the December presidential election of 1992, reveal the predominance of this regional consideration, which is likely to continue.[35]

In South Korea, this regionalism has had a particularly regressive impact on politics. Ultimately, regionalism represents the displaced concentration of the cleavages discussed above, not irrational, collective sentiment or ideology. Thus it led not only to the installation of the security-defined political calculations (whose initiators came from the so-called TK region (Taegu-Kyŏngsang Pukdo) but also to the formation in early 1990 of a grand ruling party named the Democratic Liberal Party (DLP) through co-opting the formerly South Kyŏngsang province-based opposition, Kim Young Sam's party, to complete the Kyŏngsang province-based conservative coalition.

Regionalism has not been confined merely to electoral politics. It has had an even more profound effect on the opposition movement, including the

35. Here I refer to the three elections since 1987: the presidential election of December 1987, the general election of April 1988, and the general election of March 1992. For the analysis of the first case, see Kim Hyung-guk, "Taet'ongryŭng sŏngŏui T'up'yo haengt'aee taehan chijŏnghakjŏk yŏnku" [The geographical approach to the voting patterns in the thirteenth presidential election], in *Han'gukŭi sŏngŏ chŏngch'ihak* [Political science on elections in Korea], ed. Kim Kwang-ung (Seoul: Nanam Publications, 1990); for the second, Park Ch'an-uk, "Sŏngŏ kwajŏngkwa taeui chŏngch'i" [Electoral process and representative politics], in ibid.; and for the third, Park Ch'an-uk, "14-dae Kukhoeuiwon ch'ong sŏngŏesŏŭi chŏngdang chiji punsŏk" [Analysis on support for the party in the fourteenth general election], unpublished manuscript, July 2, 1992.

labor movement, by vertically dividing and fragmenting it and thereby preventing it from becoming a strong political force. While the Roh regime has allowed a considerable degree of political democratization in the middle and upper classes, it has not changed its repressive policy toward the popular sector-based movements, notably the labor movement.[36] Therefore, the transition to democracy under the new regime may be characterized as highly class-specific. Under such harsh circumstances the student-led social movements and working-class movements have been subjected to their own dynamics of disintegration, which gained momentum toward the end of the 1980s: the acceleration of radicalism and fragmentation along ideological lines, which caused the loss of a sense of realism and of moral support, not only from other social sectors but also from their own ranks. No doubt, the weakening of radical social forces was prompted by the combined effects of the regime's antipopulist campaigns, both political and ideological, and the collapse of state socialism. And perhaps most important, the bulk of the working class has benefited so materially from the sustained economic growth that workers have become increasingly reluctant to support their radical leadership.[37] The rapid disappearance of the *minjung* forces from the political scene in the late 1980s is as remarkable as their potent advancement during the early 1980s.

Yet the weakening of the popular democratic forces need not immediately lead to the decline of social forces as a whole, or that of civil society. This phenomenon determines not whether civil society expands or not, but how civil society is shaped in its progressive advancement. In other words, the deauthoritarianization process in the political sphere irreversibly unleashed the forces of civil society. But civil society, in turn, has not necessarily evolved toward a progressive democracy, but in a conservative liberal direction. Under such circumstances the fragile presence, if not absence, of progressive democratic forces would, to some extent, give way to the rise of

36. From March 1988 to July 1991, 1,736 workers were imprisoned as a result of their labor movement activities—more than under the Chun regime. See Chŏnguk Nodong Johap Hyŭpuihoe (National Council of Labor Unions), "Che 6 Konghwaguk Ch'ulbŏm ihu Kusok nodongja Hyŏnhwang chosa" [Survey of the present situation concerning the workers under imprisonment since the inauguration of the Sixth Republic], *Chosa t'onggye,* no. 91–93 (July 31, 1991).

37. An indicator of this is the remarkably rapid increase in real wages: the rise in real wages during the period from 1987 to 1991 was 11% on average. For this, see the EPB, *Kyŏngje tonghyang* [Economic trends] (February 1992), p. 135; and Han'guk Nodong yŏnguwon, *Quarterly Labor Review* 4, no. 4 (April 30, 1992), p. 26.

the bourgeoisie, and pave the way for its ascendance vis-à-vis the state elites and eventually its colonization of the state. The traditional relationship between the state elites and entrepreneurs, which can be characterized as cohesive and undifferentiated, albeit dominating and subordinating, has been rapidly changing to one that is more differentiated, autonomous, and mutually dependent. Under the Roh regime the upper bourgeoisie consciously strive to convert its economic power to political power as it became increasingly distrustful of the regime's economic policies, which were inconsistent, unreliable, and often hostile to its interests.

Its manifestation was the Hyundai Group chairman Chung Ju Yung's bold challenge to the ruling political elites and his subsequent creation of a political party named the Unification National Party (UNP). This signifies that the state is no longer omnipotent. However, the UNP is not a full-fledged liberal party similar to those in Western countries. Under the new regime big business is coming to play a significant role as the role of the military has declined considerably.[38] This helps to explain how the regime could maintain itself in the face of the populist initiative surrounding reunification. As the capitalist class attempted to replace the military elites in maintaining conservative social order, capitalism cum efficiency and developmentalism may effectively supplant the previously hegemonic ideology of anti-communism. Therefore, the regime could handle the reunification issue with ever greater confidence vis-à-vis both domestic oppositions and North Korea.

The grip of the state elites and civilian politicians on the private economic sector has substantially weakened. Market forces supported by their own economic rationality and neoliberalism on a global scale have gained predominance over the state-regulated economy. The opening of the electoral arena has made political elites more dependent on entrepreneurs for campaign funds. The loci of political decision-making have widened, dispersing contact points between decisionmakers and private interests. But most important, as the nation's economy continues growing, whether quickly or slowly, private economic power itself, which is almost identical to the chaebŏls' influence, has risen correspondingly. Under such circumstances, it is

38. One indication of the political significance of the capitalist class is the UNP's success in the March 1992 general election. The December 1992 presidential election, however, demonstrated that it still lacked organizational strength and popular base to pose a serious threat to the state.

inevitable that entrepreneurs are coming to play a much greater role in politics. That is, the chaebŏls' political advance is a direct result of economic "success."

However, continuous pressures for political and economic reforms from below have placed the Roh government in a very vulnerable and contradictory position, forcing it to pursue inconsistent and schizophrenic policies that alternate between the time-honored, growth-oriented economic policy and a mildly reformist policy aimed at more balanced growth and stabilization. No matter how ineffective, the Roh regime was the first one that seriously attempted to pursue reform-minded policies, to reduce the economic monopoly of the chaebŏls and to improve welfare.[39] Though timid and inconsistent, the reformist policy was threatening enough for entrepreneurs and stimulated their attempts to undo it, by supporting, behind the scenes, the establishment of the DLP, or by creating their own party outright in the case of the UNP. To some extent, therefore, the democratization process had effect of widening the schism between the state elites and chaebŏls.

Conclusion

Through the historical unfolding of three cleavages, traced from the liberation to the present, this chapter analyzes the conflictual relationship between the state and civil society in South Korea. From this history, we have seen that the South Korean state has maintained a dominant position over civil society. But in recent years, especially after the political transition of 1987, the state–civil society relationship has been substantially changing, allowing the vigorous expansion of civil society.

State power grew during three historical periods. The first period began directly after the liberation and ended in the late 1950s. During this interval, the South Korean state was challenged first internally by leftist nationalist forces and then by the Korean War. Externally, the South Korean state was challenged by the military standoff with North Korea. By the

39. The government policy during Cho Soon's tenure as EPB chief in 1989–90 can be referred to as reformist, with an emphasis on stabilization, balanced growth, and equity, which sought to curb the monopoly power of the chaebols by means of reform of the land tax system, strict control on bank credits, introduction of the "real name financial transactions system," tougher taxes on inheritance and allowance, and so on. Throughout the early 1990s this reformist policy line has been pushed back and reappeared.

circumstances of its inception, and in the course of meeting subsequent challenges, the South Korean state became "overdeveloped."

The second period was the 1960s under the Park Chung Hee regime. The state was able to increase its power by extracting increasing amounts of material resources from the socioeconomic sphere, resources that were greatly augmented because of accelerated economic growth. State power that functions to demobilize and disarm the radical opposition movement must be characterized as a negative power. But it was the Park regime that, throughout the 1960s and 1970s, transformed state power into a catalyst for economic development.

During this period, however, the power of civil society expanded proportionately more than that of the state. How much civil society has matured is reflected in the proliferation of political issues, and in the intensification and inter-linking of conflicts along the three cleavages. The escalation of political conflicts, then, has to be attributed to the collisions between the state and civil society as they both grew. Even though the socioeconomic conditions for democratization exist in South Korea today, the state's leading role in capitalist industrialization has had a boomerang effect on the process of democratization. In the course of allocating capital for industrialization, the state's economic management structure developed tremendously, but so did the repressive state apparatus often mobilized to control labor. As a consequence, the coalition between state elites and capitalists has been maintained. Thus the Korean bourgeoisie was unable to play the historically progressive role played by the Western bourgeoisie. Moreover, in this process of state-led industrialization, the middle class was also incorporated into the power bloc's political, economic, and ideological hegemony.

The third period covered the transition to democracy since the mid-1980s, which witnessed an explosion of civil society that both caused the democratic political change and was made possible by it. The factor that contributed the most energy and vigor to democratization and reunification efforts has been the growth of popular democratic forces. The state has been the most hegemonic with regard to reunification. Along this cleavage, the state could mobilize all its potential resources, and this is why of the three struggles the populist nationalist struggle for reunification is the most difficult. The vigor and energy for reunification, which came from the bottom, has been continuously co-opted from above by the state elites. Although the reunification issue is very important, it seems unlikely that this issue by itself will decisively influence the process and direction of democratization.

In the final analysis, the most critical variable is the balance of power between contending classes within civil society, that is, how effectively the populist democratic forces can mobilize and organize their strength vis-à-vis the ruling power bloc within civil society, and whether they can outmaneuver and neutralize the power of the state. If the counterhegemonic forces weaken, or are outmaneuvered, the course of history is quite predictable—the most we can hope for is Gramsci's passive revolution, that is, limited gains within the existing power structure.[40]

40. On this notion, see Gramsci, *Selections from the Prison Notebooks,* pp. 59, 105–20, 206.

2

The State, Politics, and Economic Development in Postwar South Korea

Stephan Haggard and Chung-in Moon

There have been two central debates about the role of the state in South Korea's rapid development. The first concerns the relationship between policy and economic outcomes, and pits market-oriented, neoclassical interpretations against statist alternatives. The central issue in this debate is the extent to which direct state intervention in markets contributed to this rapid growth.

Neoclassical interpretations identify the crucial turning point in South Korea's economic growth in the transition to an export-oriented growth strategy in the early 1960s.[1] The South Korean state continued to intervene

This chapter draws on Stephan Haggard, *Pathways from the Periphery* (Ithaca: Cornell University Press, 1990), chap. 3; Stephan Haggard and Chung-in Moon, "Institutions and Economic Growth: Theory and a Korean Case Study," *World Politics* 42 (January 1990): 210–37; Chung-in Moon, "The Demise of a Developmentalist State?: Neoconservative Reforms and Political Consequences in South Korea," *Journal of Developing Societies* 6:1 (1988): 67–84; Stephan Haggard, Byung-kuk Kim, and Chung-in Moon, "The Transition to Export-led Growth in South Korea: 1954–1966," *Journal of Asian Studies* 50 (November 1991): 850–73.

1. Prominent neoclassical interpretations of South Korean economic growth can be found in Anne O. Krueger, *The Development of the Foreign Sector and Aid* (Cambridge: Harvard

in the economy, but compared with other developing countries and with the economic policy of the 1950s, these 1960s reforms were market-oriented. The pursuit of a stable macroeconomic policy, realistic exchange rate policy, and selective trade liberalization signaled domestic firms of their comparative advantage and allowed South Korea to exploit its comparative advantage in the export of light, labor-intensive manufactures. Positive real interest rates mobilized savings, and the business climate encouraged direct foreign investment.

Alternative interpretations of South Korea's economic development place greater emphasis on institutional setting and strategic action by the state.[2] Exports did not increase as a result of "getting the prices right," but from a subtle interplay among arm's-length incentives, an interventionist industrial policy, and a particularly close relationship between the state and the private sector. Under this interpretation, there is greater continuity in Korean economic policy than is suggested in the neoclassical account, extending back not only to the 1950s, but to the interwar period when basic modes of economic intervention were forged under Japanese colonial rule.

As will become clear, we are more sympathetic to the second account than to the first. But this chapter is concerned with a second political question that is of central importance to the study of state-society relations in South Korea: why political elites and their technocratic allies chose the economic policies they did. Economic policy not only affects aggregate growth, but has distributional consequences for different social groups. The very shape of the South Korean social fabric—from the nature of agriculture land holdings, to the size and structure of the *chaebŏl,* to the sectoral composition of the working class—has been shaped in myriad ways by government policy and the intervention of the state in markets.

We focus on industrial policy as broadly conceived: the trade, exchange rate, and sectoral policies that have influenced the evolution of South Korea's industrial structure and defined the country's relationship with

---

University Press, 1979); and the contributions to *World Development* 16 (January 1988), a special issue on Korea.

2. Statist interpretations of South Korea's growth include Leroy Jones and Il Sakong, *Government, Business and Entrepreneurship in Economic Development: The Korean Case* (Cambridge: Harvard University Press, 1980); Shahid Yusuf and R. Kyle Peters, "Capital Accumulation and Economic Growth: The Korean Paradigm" (Washington, D.C.: World Bank Staff Working Paper no. 712, 1985). Yung Whee Rhee, B. Ross-Larson, and G. Pursell, *Korea's Competitive Edge* (Baltimore: Johns Hopkins University Press, 1984), operates broadly in a neoclassical framework, but gives greater weight to the institutional setting.

world markets. As Table 2.1 outlines, these policies have gone through a distinct evolution, from an inward-oriented strategy in the 1950s, to the export-oriented strategy that remains the hallmark of South Korea's growth, through an exercise in industrial deepening in the 1970s, to the efforts to reduce government intervention that constituted a leitmotif of government policy in the 1980s. The question for positive political economy is to understand the social, political, and economic factors that impinge on state action, particularly at critical junctures when new economic strategies are considered, adopted, and implemented.

The debate on these issues has centered on three clusters of explanatory variables; different theoretical accounts can be sorted by the relative primacy given to each. The first are international political and economic constraints. The second cluster of variables center on the state's relations with organized social groups, particularly urban labor and big business. Finally, institutional characteristics of the state itself, including the broad rules of the political game and the internal decision-making structure, can play an important role in explaining Korean economic policy. These broad relationships are summarized in Table 2.1; we discuss each of these three clusters of variables in turn.

Dependency, external constraints, and economic policy. As a small, strategically significant country, South Korea has been exposed to overwhelming external constraints throughout its modern history. As Bruce Cumings has emphasized, the structure of the contemporary South Korean state and crucial elements of the social structure can be traced to the Japanese occupation.[3] Dal-joong Chang, among others, has underlined continuities between Korea's pre- and postindependence relations with Japan.[4] Ezra Vogel emphasizes the crucial role of Japan as a model for South Korea.[5]

3. See Bruce Cumings, "The Origins and the Development of the Northeast Asian Political Economy," *International Organization* 38 (Winter 1981): 1–40, and *The Origins of the Korean War* (Princeton: Princeton University Press, 1981).

4. Dal-Choong Chang, "Japan's Transnational Corporations and the Political Economy of the Relationship between South Korea and Japan," Ph.D. diss., University of California at Berkeley, 1982.

5. Ezra Vogel, *The Four Dragons: The Spread of Industrialization in East Asia* (Cambridge: Harvard University Press, 1991), pp. 90–91.

Table 2.1. State, society, and international systems: An overview

	1953–60	1961–72	1973–79	1981–85	1986–present
Development strategy	Import-substitution industrialization	Labor-intensive export promotion	Industrial deepening	Stabilization and structural adjustment	Adjustment to surplus
International environment	Aid and U.S. policy intervention	U.S. pressure/ normalization with Japan	Protectionism/ oil crisis	Protectionism/oil crisis/debt crisis/ interest rate shock/ pressure for market opening	Protectionism/ won appreciation/ pressure for market opening
State-society relations	Symbiosis with business/ mobilizational co-optation of labor/neglect of the rural sector	Mobilizational co-optation of business/exclusion of labor and rural sector	Selective co-optation of big business and the rural sector/ exclusion of labor	Exclusion of labor and farmers/structural dependency on big business/co-optation of middle class	Decreasing insulative capacity/ increasing power of civil society
Regime type	Autocratic	Revolutionary/ mild authoritarian	Authoritarian	Quasi-revolutionary/ authoritarian	Increasingly pluralist
Bureaucrats	Weak, politicized	Reformed bureaucracy	Bureaucratic autonomy from society, but executive dominance	Relatively high degree of autonomy	Decreasing bureaucratic insulation

Since 1945, however, the strategic and economic relationship with the United States had been of much more central importance, particularly through the mid-1960s, when dependence on U.S. aid was high.[6] Yet the dynamics of this influence are often misunderstood. Critics of U.S. aid have argued both that Americans wielded substantial influence through the aid relationship and that overall development policy was ineffective. A closer examination of the relationship reveals a surprising ability on the part of Syngman Rhee to evade American conditions, an interesting example of the large influence of small allies. The impending termination of aid, however, played a crucial role in economic policy, since it changed the incentive for policy reforms that increased the availability of foreign exchange. These included greater commercial borrowing, a more open policy toward foreign investment, but above all the strong emphasis given to exports.

Peter Evans's model of "dependent development" based on the collusion of state, local, and foreign capital enjoyed a period of popularity in Korean social science in the 1980s.[7] South Korea's dependence on direct foreign investment was always relatively slight, however. Once South Korea initiated its export drive, it was the high dependence on international markets, rather than the penetration of foreign firms, that constituted the more important consideration in debates over industrial strategy. Concerns over maintaining competitiveness influenced policies ranging from the system of labor relations to the recurrent efforts to upgrade the industrial and export structure. By the 1980s, South Korea's very success, reflected in the accumulation of large current account surpluses in the mid-1980s, subjected the country to strong external political pressure to liberalize its domestic markets.

State-society relations: Business, labor, and government strategy. The close relationship between business and government and state control over labor have constituted recurrent themes in both American and Korean

6. For overview of the aid relationship, see Krueger, *The Development of the Foreign Sector;* David Cole, "Foreign Assistance and Korean Development," in *The Korean Economy: Issues of Development,* ed. Cole, Youngil Lim, and Paul W. Kuznets (Berkeley: Institute of East Asian Studies, 1980); Wan Hyok Pu, "The History of American Aid to Korea," *Korean Quarterly* 3 (Summer 1961): 71–96; Sŏng-Yu Hong, *Han'guk kyŏngje wa miguk wŏncho* [The Korean economy and American aid] (Seoul: Pakyungsa, 1962).

7. Peter Evans, *Dependent Development* (Princeton: Princeton University Press, 1979).

scholarship on the country's economic development.[8] The argument linking these political relationships to South Korea's industrialization strategy has a simple logic. The state has acted largely as the agent for large industrial firms, favoring capital both to promote aggregate growth and to secure financial support for political objectives. The rural sector and portions of the emerging middle class provided a conservative base of support for the regime, solidified in the case of farmers through various subsidies, price supports, and substantial protection from international competition. The government consistently tried to block the formation of an independent Left or union movement, securing working-class acquiescence, if not support, for rapidly rising real wages and a distribution of income that was—at least until the 1970s—relatively egalitarian.

Though compelling in its broad strokes, elements of this picture demand amendment. Some government controls on the labor movement predated the export-led growth strategy. Though new restrictions first emerged in the late 1960s in response to labor disputes with foreign firms—clearly an economic motivation—the main factor behind new controls on both the Left and labor were political and centered on the initiation of the authoritarian Yushin constitution. Moreover, it is not clear that the government had control over wages, particularly given rapid growth and the attendant strong demand for workers.

Nonetheless, South Korean firms undeniably benefited from minimal union "interference" in either wage-setting or other aspects of industrial relations and have consistently backed authoritarian controls on the labor movement. Conversely, dramatic increases in labor activism accompanied all periods of political liberalization: in 1960, in 1980, and finally in 1987.

Yet this raises the crucial question of the influence of business on the country's industrial strategy. At critical moments, including the immediate postwar period, following the military takeover in 1961, at the initiation

8. Jang Jip Choi, *Labor and the Authoritarian State: Labor Unions in South Korean Manufacturing Industries, 1960–1980* (Seoul: Korea University Press, 1989); Frederick Deyo, *Beneath the Miracle: Labor Subordination in the New Asian Industrialism* (Berkeley: University of California Press, 1989). For debates on the nature of the South Korean state and capitalism, see Taekŭn Yi and Unyong Chŏng, eds., *Han'guk Chabonchuŭiron* [Thesis on Korean capitalism] (Seoul: Kkach'isa, 1984); Hyŏnch'ae Pak and Huiyŏn Cho, eds., *Han'guk sahoe kusŏngch'e nonchaeng* [The debate on social formation in Korea], vol. 1 (Seoul: Chuksan 1989); Jang Jip Choi, ed., *Han'guk chabonchuŭi wa kukga* [Korean capitalism and the state] (Seoul: Hanul, 1985); Study Group of Korean Industrial Society, ed., *Onŭl uri han'guk chabonchuŭi wa kukga* [Today's Korean capitalism and the state] (Seoul: Han'gilsa, 1988).

of the heavy-industry drive in the mid-1970s, and in the restructuring of industry in the early 1980s, the government has exhibited substantial independence from the private sector. Though government-business relations have been close, the definition of industrial strategy did not necessarily originate with the private sector. Rather, private sector groups often opposed policies—including the transition to an export-oriented strategy—that ultimately favored them.

It is also important to note changes in business power. Largely as a result of government policy, the industrial structure became increasingly concentrated in the 1970s. The very size of the large industrial groups gave them bargaining leverage over the state in several policy areas, such as the allocation of preferential credit. Efforts to liberalize the style of economic management in the 1980s, however gradual, somewhat reduced the instruments available to the government to control business activities.

The "strong state" paradigm. Many developing countries face international constraints and fail to respond. Close business-government relations are common across most of the developing world, and labor movements are weak in many Third World countries. In the quest to isolate features that distinguish South Korean economic policy-making from that in other countries, particular attention has been focused on the nature of state institutions. Chalmers Johnson pioneered this perspective in his well-known book on *MITI and the Japanese Miracle.*[9] This statist or institutionalist perspective rests on a view of economic development in which problems of collective action abound. Rapid capital accumulation and efficient economic policy-making "require" limits on social demands, not only from labor or popular sector forces, but from the rent-seeking demands of business groups. As Alice Amsden argues, the crucial feature of business-government relations in Korea was not their closeness, but the particular

9. Chalmers Johnson, *MITI and the Japanese Miracle* (Stanford: Stanford University Press, 1981). Other analyses stressing the political strength of the state in Korea's economic development are Stephan Haggard and Chung-in Moon, "Liberal, Dependent or Mercantile?: The South Korean State in the International System," in *Antinomies of Interdependence,* ed. John Ruggie (New York: Columbia University Press, 1983); Robert Wade, *Governing the Market* (Princeton: Princeton University Press, 1990). On the debate on the role of the state in South Korea, see Sang Ryong Ch'oe, ed., *Hyŏndae Han'guk Chŏngch'i wa Kukga* [Contemporary Korean politics and the state] (Seoul: Pŏpmunsa, 1986); and Min Kang et al., *Kukga wa kongkong chŏngch'aek* [The state and public policy] (Seoul: Pŏbmunsa, 1991).

discipline that was exercised by the state over business activities: favors were granted, but only in exchange for performance.[10]

Clearly, authoritarian restrictions on political activity, corporatist organization and disorganization of interests, and ultimately coercion can expand the freedom and maneuver of political elites. But the strong state perspective is not limited to the broad characteristics of the regime alone; many developing country dictatorships pursue disastrous policies. Rather, the critical feature of the archetypal strong state resides in organizational features of the state itself, including efficient, meritocratic bureaucracies, centralized decision-making structures, and control over a large repertoire of policy instruments. These features contribute to the coherence and consistency of policy.

This institutional perspective naturally focuses on the crucial role of the military in transforming the South Korean economy. Despite Syngman Rhee's autocratic political style, the state was "weak" during the 1950s. Business interests established close rent-seeking relationships with political elites and technocratic forces within the bureaucracy were marginalized. The military made a difference not only in reorienting economic policy but in restructuring basic political and administrative institutions; these changes were a crucial prerequisite for subsequent policy reforms.

Japanese and American Legacies

Any discussion of Korea's economic development must begin with the Japanese occupation (see Chapter 3 by Carter Eckert in this volume). During the interwar period, the Japanese colonial bureaucracy oversaw Korea's position as a rice producer in a regional division of labor. Japan invested heavily in infrastructure and "rationalized" traditional land relationships through the fixing of property rights. These "reforms" increased Japan's ability to extract food surpluses from the colony, though they also increased tenancy and polarized the countryside.

Unlike European imperialism, however, the colonial bureaucracy also fostered industrial expansion. Light manufacturing proliferated in the 1920s, primarily under Japanese auspices, though important Korean business groups can be traced to the period. After 1931, and particularly after the attack on China in 1937, Korea became a supply and production base

10. Alice Amsden, *Asia's Next Giant* (New York: Oxford University Press, 1989).

for Japan's expansion into Manchuria. Heavy industries were established under the auspices of state-designated companies.

The significance of this period for subsequent development remains a controversial topic. Nationalist historiography has tended to downplay the developmental role of the Japanese, in part because of the extensive collaboration that existed between Korean capitalists and the Japanese. Nonetheless, it seems incontrovertible that the Japanese occupation expanded Korea's infrastructure, contributed to a wider commercialization of agriculture, and established the beginnings of modern capitalist enterprises.[11]

The Japanese occupation was important not only for its direct economic consequences, but for its effects on political development. On Japan's defeat, organizations of workers, peasants and youth emerged throughout the country in a burst of political activity in the fall of 1945.[12] The U.S. military government supported the Right, gathered around nationalist leader Syngman Rhee, and bolstered the bureaucracy, police, and military. These organizations provided Rhee with the tools for controlling opposition, despite the government's nominally democratic form.

The Left, meanwhile, saw its base of political support in the countryside and labor movement whittled away. The power of the rural "people's committees," which had assumed governmental functions after the war in some areas, and of leftist labor unions was largely broken by 1947. The U.S. occupation and the weakening of the Left guaranteed that South Korea would follow a broadly capitalist development path. In its details, however, government policy was ultimately dictated more by severe external economic constraints. The partitioning of the country left the South largely without electricity and a number of raw materials and intermediate goods. The departure of the Japanese created a vacuum in external economic relations and domestic management. Between 1944 and the end of 1946, manufacturing employment fell by nearly 60 percent, and by 1948 total

11. See Peter Duus, "Economic Dimensions of Meiji Imperialism: The Case of Korea, 1985–1910," in *The Japanese Colonial Empire: 1895–1945,* ed. Ramon Myers and Mark Peattie (Princeton: Princeton University Press, 1984); Sang-Chul Suh, *Growth and Structural Change in the Korean Economy* (Cambridge: Harvard University Press, 1978); Daniel Sungil Juhn, "Korean Industrial Entrepreneurship 1924–1940," in *Korea's Response to the West,* ed. Young Whan Jo (Kalamazoo, Mich.: Korean Research and Publications, Inc., 1971). For a contrasting view, see Hyŏnch'ae Pak, *Minjok kyŏngjeron* [Thesis on the national economy] (Seoul: Han'gilsa, 1978), pp. 41–102.

12. Cumings, *The Origins of the Korean War,* chap. 4; Gregory Henderson, *Korea: The Politics of Vortex* (Cambridge: Harvard University Press, 1969), chap. 5.

industrial output was a fifth of the 1940 level. Inflation was extremely high. Postwar trade dwindled to very low levels. As in Latin America in the 1930s, an inward-looking course was neither chosen nor imposed by American pressure, but resulted from the severe balance of payments difficulties the country faced.

Syngman Rhee and the Political Bases of Korean Import Substitution (1954–1960)

Assuming office against a backdrop of political and economic turmoil, the police, the bureaucracy, and the Liberal Party became the main bases of Rhee's political power. The Liberal Party and security apparatus gave Rhee increased control over potential opposition. Rhee's apparent political autonomy was partly checked by the Korean Democratic Party (KDP) in the National Assembly, the core of which was absentee landlords and a group of industrialists who opposed Rhee's control of the bureaucracy. Through a series of political maneuvers, Rhee forced constitutional amendments in 1952 that weakened the legislature and strengthened the executive.[13]

The land reforms of this period remain an underresearched topic. Limited reforms had begun under the military government with the sale of Japanese properties to tenants, but the American reforms had not touched Korean holdings. The postindependence reforms allowed Rhee to undercut the local power of the landlords in the assembly, who were lured by the vested properties used to compensate for distributed holdings. The KDP had little choice but to support reform, though actual transfers of property did not take place until the war itself. The reforms were not followed by a political commitment to rural development; Rhee gave greater emphasis to industry and the urban areas than the Kuomintang (Nationalist Party) on Taiwan.

Even before domestic political and economic stability was restored, the Korean War broke out in June 25, 1950. By the time the armistice was declared in July 1953 the national economy was virtually paralyzed. Major industrial facilities were destroyed, and about 43 percent of production facilities in the manufacturing sector was damaged. Inflation emerged as a crucial problem. In order to finance the war, the government rapidly in-

13. On the weakening of the legislature and the trend to autocracy, see Henderson, *Korea,* pp. 162–74.

creased the money supply, and a poor harvest in 1952 worsened economic conditions.

Given the devastation of the Korean War, the significance of U.S. support for the Rhee government can hardly be overstated. Aid financed nearly 70 percent of total imports between 1953 and 1961 and 75 percent of total fixed capital formation.[14] In return for aid, the United States sought economic reforms, including privatization and conservative fiscal and monetary policies. These reforms cut directly against Rhee's political interests, however, since Rhee and his Liberal Party financed their political activities through the distribution of patronage. Rhee proved skillful at manipulating South Korea's strategic significance to maintain the flow of economic and military support, however, a relationship U.S. President Dwight Eisenhower privately called "blackmail."[15]

The United States effectively took over responsibility for South Korea's reconstruction from the multilateral agencies in 1953. Eisenhower's plan for an additional $200 million for this reconstruction was politically motivated to overcome Rhee's vehement opposition to the signing of an armistice.[16] Rhee complained publicly about the slowness of aid deliveries, the lack of attention to new investment, and the emphasis given to commodity imports, which accounted for about three-quarters of all aid between 1953 and 1960. Half of this was agricultural commodities, with the rest going primarily to fertilizer and petroleum products.

Of the remaining project-related aid, only 16.5 percent went directly to manufacturing, but imported commodities were distributed to local firms for processing and industry did quite well. Growth of the gross domestic product (GDP) averaged 3.9 percent between 1953–55 and 1960–62, but manufacturing grew at 11.2 percent a year. The Korean War had produced a new commercial class, which grew rapidly from the supply shortages of

14. See Krueger, *The Development of the Foreign Sector;* Cole, "Foreign Assistance"; and Pu, "The History of American Aid."

15. "Memorandum: Discussion at the 311th Meeting of the National Security Council, January 31, 1957," Papers of D. D. Eisenhower (DDE), NSC Series, DDE Library.

16. See Pu, "The History of American Aid," pp. 82–90, on the political motivations behind the Tasca mission and subsequent aid. See John P. Lewis, *Reconstruction and Development in South Korea* (Washington, D.C.: National Planning Association, 1955); see also David Cole and Princeton Lyman, *Korean Development: Interplay of Politics and Economics* (Cambridge: Harvard University Press, 1971), p. 210, for a critique of the Nathan Plan. For a criticism of U.S. aid, see Sock Kyun Chu, "Why American Aid Failed," *Korean Quarterly* (Autumn 1962): 81–93.

the war economy and increased foreign trade.[17] A more important development was the transformation of both new and older commercial capitalists into manufacturing activities and the growth of older manufacturing firms. Local firms entered the intermediate and consumer goods sectors, including sectors such as cement and textiles.

When Rhee visited Washington, D.C., in July 1954, the United States outlined the economic and political quid pro quo for assistance. Rhee would recognize the authority of the United Nations Command over the South Korean armed forces and accept ceilings on the size of those forces. The government would also privatize state-owned properties and encourage private investment, allow close U.S. monitoring of the use of aid funds, maintain a realistic exchange rate through an auction system, and import aid commodities from those non-Communist areas where the lowest prices were offered, in effect, a demand that economic relations with Japan be normalized. Under U.S. pressure, the Ministry of Finance developed a financial stabilization program in 1956.[18] The stabilization programs were successful at slowing inflation, but GNP growth peaked at 7.7 percent in 1957, declined to 5.2 percent in 1958, 3.9 percent in 1959, and 1.9 percent in 1960.

As soon as the war ended, Rhee began to face more intense political competition. Rhee ran unopposed in the 1956 election, because of the sudden death of his major opponent, but managed to capture only 55 percent of the popular vote, down from 72 percent in 1952. One obvious way of mobilizing funds to finance elections and other party activities was to forge a closer alliance with the new group of businessmen that had arisen in the post–World War II period. The grant of various privileges generated rents that could be recycled back to government officials, to the party, and to individual legislators.

Estimating the aggregate size and composition of what might be called the rent-seeking sector would be impossible, but evidence from a variety of sources suggests that corruption was widespread. The greatest opportu-

17. On the rise of commercial capital after the Korean War, see Taehwan Kim, "Osipnyŏn dae ŭi han'guk kyŏngje yŏn gu" [A study of the Korean economy in the 1950s], in *1950 yŏn dae ŭi insik* [Assessment of the 1950s], ed. Hyŏnchae Pak et al. (Seoul: Han'gilsa, 1984); Daekŭn Lee, *Han'guk chŏnchaeng kwa 1950 yŏn dae chapon ch'uk'chŏk* [The Korean War and capital accumulation in the 1950s] (Seoul: Kkachisa, 1987).

18. Ch'ŏl Gyu Im, "Yusŏm" [United States Operations Mission], *Sindonga* (May 1965): 168–69.

nities were provided by the overvalued exchange rate, which was linked to a complex licensing system for imports that provided new opportunities for profit in a range of processing industries, including the famous "three whites," wheat flour, sugar, and cotton yarn.

Another controversial element of economic management under the Rhee regime was the allocation of bank loans. In the 1950s, capital was scarce and inflation relatively high. Government ceilings on loan rates meant windfalls for those firms gaining access to finance, who then paid "commissions" for their privilege. Privatization of state-owned enterprises and banks, government contracting, and investments by the party provided additional opportunities for graft.[19]

This political structure naturally had consequences for the autonomy of the bureaucracy. The staffing of the bureaucracy not only was a form of direct patronage, but facilitated the use of government resources for political ends.[20] In 1955, Rhee established the Ministry of Reconstruction (MOP) to develop plans that could be used to nail down U.S. aid commitments over a longer time horizon. As a new ministry with no set constituency and close ties with the United States, the MOR developed a significant cadre of trained administrators relatively insulated from Liberal Party pressures,

19. By one estimate, the Liberal Party had a substantial interest in at least 50 percent of the private projects receiving American aid in 1960. Joungwon A. Kim, *Divided Korea: The Politics of Development 1945–1972* (Cambridge: Harvard University Press, 1975), p. 152. Among the sources we have used in examining the rent-seeking sector are U.S. General Accounting Office, Report on Examination at Economic and Technical Assistance Program for Korea, International Cooperation Administration, Department of State, Fiscal year 1957–1961, Part I (B-125080), September 21, 1961. E. Grant Meade, *American Military Government in Korea* (New York: Columbia University Press, 1951), pp. 203–12; "Policies and Actions of ROK Government in Economic Field," Foreign Service Dispatch, U.S. Embassy to State, February 18, 1954, RG 895.00/2-1854, National Archives; Jinhyŏn Kim, "Pujŏng ch'ukchae ch'ŏri chŏnmalsŏ" [From A to Z of illicit wealth accumulation], *Sindonga* (November 1, 1964): 160–61; Kyŏngnam Yi, "Hae bang hu kwŏllyŏkhyŏng pujŏng ch'ukchae" [Cases of illicit wealth accumulation through power connections], *Sindonga* (April 1985): 301–2; Pyŏng Yun Pak, *Chaebŏl kwa chŏngch'i* [Chaebŏl and politics] (Seoul: Han'guk Yangso, 1982); Hangminsa, ed., *Hyŏkmyŏng chaep an: Kirok* [Revolutionary trial: Records] (Seoul: Hangminsa, 1985).

20. Cumings, *The Origin of the Korean War,* pp. 151–58; Dongsoh Pak, *Historical Development of Korea's Bureaucratic System* (Seoul: Han'guk Yŏngusa, 1961). See also Wŏnyŏng Song, "Kyŏngmudae ŭi inŭi changmak" [Human curtain of Presidential Palace], *Sasang gye* (June 1960); Munyŏng Yi, "Kongmuwŏn pup'ae isipnyŏnsa" [Corruption of public servants: Twenty years history), *Sasang gye* (March 1966); Bark Dong Suh, "Public Personnel Administration," Ph.D. diss., University of Minnesota, 1967, pp. 221–22.

supported by the Bureau of the Budget within the Ministry of Finance.[21] In April 1959, MOR economists drafted a Three-Year Plan, but the economic bureaucracy as a whole had little autonomy from pressures emanating from the party, the private sector, and the executive itself. Besieged by political difficulties in 1959, the Liberal Party approved the plan only a few days before the student revolution that ended Liberal Party rule.

In sum, South Korea in the 1950s exhibited political characteristics inimical to development planning of any sort. The government was poorly insulated from the demands of the private sector, leading to a particularly unsystemmatic approach to import-substitution industrialization. The economic bureaucracy was subject to political interference from both the executive and the ruling party. Aid financed a triangular political alliance between Rhee and the Liberal Party, the bureaucracy, and a new manufacturing class.

The Second Republic (April 1960–May 1961)

The Second Republic was born after the "student revolution" in April 1960. Economic development and the elimination of corruption were the top political priorities of the Chang Myon government that took office in July. The government took the initiative in devaluing the exchange rate in February 1961 and rationalizing public enterprises. In November, the Ministry of Reconstruction (MOR) was instructed to draft a new five-year development plan that would improve on and supersede previous efforts.

Work was also begun on restructuring the economic bureaucracy itself. Reformers pieced together an intrabureaucratic coalition in favor of a "super ministry," later to become the Economic Planning Board. The key innovation was to combine planning powers with control over the budget and inflows of foreign capital. The new ministry was to be built around the planning offices of MOR, but was also to absorb the Bureau of the Budget and control over the allocation of aid funds that had been with the Ministry of Finance. The plan was unveiled days before the military government took power.

The larger political context was not favorable to reform. Part of the problem lay with short-term economic conditions: an ill-timed devaluation,

21. For a discussion of the reforms at the Bureau of the Budget, see Hahn Been Lee, *Future, Innovation and Development* (Seoul: Panmun Book Co., 1982), pp. 172–77.

an increase in rates for government-subsidized services, and food shortages. Economic problems were not the only difficulties facing the new regime, however. Chang Myon suffered broader political weaknesses, including factional division of the Democratic Party and corruption among his supporters. Reform of the military, purge of corrupt officials, confiscation of illicitly accumulated wealth, and unification with the North became highly divisive and politically charged issues. The government was unable to reconcile the conflicting demands placed on it from the Left and the Right, and finally proved incapable of maintaining order.

Military Interregnum (May 1961–December 1964)

The military coup of May 16, 1961, had three consequences for economic policy. First, the military broke the political networks of the Rhee period by centralizing power in the executive. A second major change was the restructuring of business-state relations. Park Chung Hee forged a new alliance with the private sector, but one in which the opportunities of rent-seeking were reduced. Finally, the centralization of political authority was matched by a centralization of economic decision-making in a powerful Economic Planning Board.

The early actions of the military government had a strong puritanical and antiurban tone that reflected the rural origins of the coup leaders.[22] After the coup, all political parties and organizations and unions were banned and the press was subjected to censorship. A revolutionary court was established in July to try those accused of various crimes, including the illicit accumulation of wealth, corruption, and "hooliganism." One of the first tasks of the newly formed Korean Central Intelligence Agency (KCIA) was the screening of 41,000 government employees, 1,863 of which were found to have been involved in corruption and "antirevolutionary" activities.

In August 1961, Park promised a return to civilian government in May 1963. Hoping to capitalize on the opposition's disarray, the junta announced an early election. The younger officers wanted an extension of military rule to carry out a wide-ranging transformation of society and

22. Cole and Lyman, *Korean Development,* p. 274, for data on the rural origins of the coup leaders. Also see John Kie-chang Oh, *Korea: Democracy on Trial* (Ithaca: Cornell University Press, 1968), pp. 157–64.

economy. When Park sought to heal the split within the military by announcing that he would hold a national referendum on continued military rule, he precipitated a broader political crisis and strong protests from the United States. Even with a fragmented and politically tainted opposition, Park's Democratic Republican Party (DRP) won only a narrow victory in 1963 amidst charges of election fraud. Once ensconced, however, Park skillfully used the powers of incumbency and the newly centralized economic bureaucracy for building networks of political support.

The link between state power and development strategy is also visible in the restructuring of state-business relations. Two weeks after the coup, thirteen prominent businessmen were arrested, and an investigation was launched into the activities of another hundred and twenty. Initially, radical members of the junta argued that all illegally accumulated fortunes should be confiscated outright and the profiteers executed. The government did seize all outstanding shares of commercial bank stocks, thus gaining control of a powerful policy instrument. They compromised with large manufacturing and construction firms, however. In order to revive the economy, the primary task of the military junta, they needed to co-opt rather than punish them. In return for the pledge of collaboration, the military government released the business leaders. On their release, the members of the newly formed Federation of Korean Industries submitted a plan to the Supreme Council identifying fourteen key industrial plants, including cement, steel, and fertilizer, in which they were interested in investing. The key issue was access to investment capital. The new business organization called for easier access to foreign capital, which demanded government guarantees. This became a central feature of government credit policy over the 1960s and 1970s, and foreign borrowing increased dramatically.

The "illegal wealth accumulation" episode is the subject of some controversy. Some accounts stress the continuity with past practice and the structural power of business.[23] The military was forced to make peace with the newly organized private sector, and the practice of "political taxation" of the private sector was an open secret.[24] But the thesis of continuity overlooks important changes in the nature of business-government relations. The economic reforms launched by the military significantly reduced the

23. Kyong-dong Kim, "Political Factors In the Formation of the Entrepreneurial Elite in South Korea," *Asian Survey* 16 (April 1976): 465–71.

24. See the statement on preferential loans by the Korean Businessman's Association in *Tonga ilbo*, February 18, 1965; "Taedam: T'ŭkhye kŭmyung ch'anban nonjaeng" [Roundta-

opportunities for the unproductive profit-making activities that had existed under the Rhee government. Devaluation provided new incentives to export. The government retained a high level of discretion over some policy instruments, but others, such as loans to exporters and access to imported inputs, were given on a nondiscretionary basis. Even where discretionary favors were extended to larger firms, they were generally tied to some developmental purpose.

The change of government provided an auspicious opening for reformers within the bureaucracy. The new Economic Planning Board had a powerful say over other ministries through the budget and controlled access to foreign exchange. The Bureau of International Cooperation, which oversaw aid relations and was the dominant bureau throughout the early 1960s, persuaded Park to establish more extensive controls on the import of foreign capital. In July 1962 the bureau was given the power to extend government guarantees to loans and to oversee the activities of the borrowing firms. When coupled with the power to approve and extend incentives to foreign direct investment, the new ministry had complete control over Korea's import of foreign capital.

The changes in the South Korean political system under the military proved important for the adoption and implementation of a coherent economic strategy. The political "reforms" enhanced the freedom of maneuver of the executive vis-à-vis the legislature, the ruling party and rent-seeking groups. The administrative reforms elevated the technocrats within the bureaucracy and expanded the instruments at their disposal. However, these changes did not in themselves constitute an economic program. Understanding the economic reform demands exploring in closer detail the interests of three sets of actors: the technocrats, the military, and the United States.

On coming to power, the junta assigned the EPB the task of drafting a new plan. The junta outlined a series of quantitative objectives, including growth rates and targets for the principal macroeconomic variables that were artificially inflated to distinguish the new plan from its predecessor.[25] The overall philosophy was "a form of 'guided capitalism' in which the

ble: Pros and Cons of Preferential Financing], *Sindonga* (April 1965); Pyŏng Yun Pak, *Chaebŏl kwa chŏng ch'i*, pp. 198–200, 209–13; Chin Bae Kim and Ch'an Nae Pak, "Cha'kwan" [Foreign Loans], *Sindonga* (December 1968).

25. Interview with Ducksoo Lee, World Bank, Washington, D.C., September 1985.

principle of free enterprise and respect for the freedom and initiative of private enterprise will be observed, but in which the government will either directly participate in or indirectly render guidance to the basic industries and other important fields."[26]

The more conservative approach of the planners did not fit with the political interests of the military. Initial policy actions reflected a populist thrust. The junta decreed the abolition of all "usurious" debts to farmers and fishermen, guaranteed government repayment of those debts that were within legal interest rate limits, and moved to guarantee high and stable prices to farmers through subsidies. The government created a Medium and Small Industry Bank. These policies were coupled with a highly expansionist monetary policy and large budget deficits driven by the ambitious investment demands of the plan and pay increases to public servants.

The United States initially signaled its displeasure at the intervention of the military. By June, though, a Presidential Task Force on Korea argued that the United States should establish ties with the "moderate" elements of the regime to push reforms. Support would also be extended for private efforts to encourage direct investment. The need to exert pressure to achieve reform was explicitly recognized: "experience has shown the effectiveness of sanctions, based upon withholding of inducements of economic aid, as a means of ensuring Korean performance."[27]

By August 1961 cables from Seoul and internal documents showed a grudging admiration for the military government's ability to get things done.[28] In addition, there were reasons for not leaning on the government too hard. Until Park's announcement of March 1963 that military rule might be extended, the United States was constrained by the fear that Kim Jong Pil and other younger colonels would gain in power. In January 1963 the U.S. embassy went so far as to argue that the military's complete withdrawal from politics was neither "feasible nor desirable."[29]

26. Economic Planning Board, *Summary of the First Five Year Economic Plan, 1962–1966* (Seoul: EPB, 1962), hereafter cited as First Plan Summary, p. 28.

27. Report to National Security Council, "Presidential Task Force on Korea," June 5, 1961, Presidential Papers of John F. Kennedy, National Security Files, JFK Library.

28. For example, telegram #293, U.S. Embassy to State, August 12, 1961, Presidential Papers of JFK, National Security Files, JFK Library.

29. Telegram, U.S. Embassy (Berger) to State, January 8, 1963, which reports on a long meeting with Park (Presidential Papers of JFK, National Security Files, JFK Library).

A badly bungled currency conversion plan in June 1962, revelations of corruption and KCIA malfeasance, and the inflationary consequences of the military's economic policies gradually moved the U.S. Agency for International Development mission to adopt a tougher position. The director of the AID mission withheld portions of U.S. aid, including food assistance through the PL480 program, with the purpose of forcing the South Korean government to adopt a stabilization plan.[30] This pressure came at a decisive moment of particularly poor harvests in the fall of 1962 and the spring of 1963. The expectation of devaluation and rumors of a U.S. aid cutoff pushed grain prices up dramatically, worsening the usual "spring famine."

The pressures exerted on the economic front by the United States came to overlap with growing concern in Washington about the country's political direction. Park's announcement in March that military rule might be extended was met by an extremely tough American response. U.S. President John F. Kennedy sent a personal note of protest to the junta and the State Department announced that $25 million in economic aid to assist the Five-Year Plan was being withheld.

The U.S. pressure appeared to work. Park agreed to elections in the fall as well as to a stabilization plan. The object of the stabilization was to persuade the South Korean government to "adopt basically new fiscal and foreign exchange policies in order to meet program goals."[31] Some accommodation was made in the implementation of the plan to ease the ruling party's electoral concerns, but the United States basically stood firm, fearing that the government would "react to their plight by putting pressure on [the] U.S. to provide more aid."[32]

30. See telegrams #1237, #1246, and #1251, U.S. Embassy to State, all June 8, 1962, Presidential Papers of JFK, National Security Files, JFK Library. The issue of aid manipulation remains, of course, an extremely sensitive issue. In an interview, Gilbert Brown, who was sent to South Korea to investigate the discrepancy, claims that the manipulation of aid was even being kept out of the cable traffic. See, however, telegram #90, U.S. Embassy to State, July 22, 1963.

31. Telegram #690, U.S. Embassy to State, November 17, 1963, which contains a detailed summary of the agreements of the stabilization plan (Presidential Papers of JFK, National Security Files, JFK Library).

32. Compare telegram #838, U.S. Embassy to State, April 29, 1963, with telegram #690, U.S. Embassy to State, November 17, 1963 (Presidential Papers of JFK, National Security Files, JFK Library).

The Emergence of Export-Led Growth, 1964–1970

The 1963 election by no means marked the end of opposition to Park's rule, and the country experienced political crises in 1964 and 1965 over the ratification of the treaty normalizing diplomatic relations with Japan.[33] In using martial law to manage protest, the crisis demonstrated Park's power over political life. The years from 1964 to 1966 witnessed remarkable economic policy reforms—devaluation, tax and interest rate reforms, an opening to foreign capital, and the drive to expand exports—many of which centered on the mobilization of resources, a crucial selling point given that the United States intended to reduce its aid commitment. Allegations followed that newly mobilized resources were being tapped for political purposes. Increased tax collection, the expanded role of state-owned banks in financial intermediation, government control over the allocation of foreign loans were all surrounded by allegations of corruption. While no doubt true, the very nature of the reforms reduced discretionary control in some areas, including trade finance and access to imported inputs for exporters.

The new wave of reforms unfolded in a particular sequence. In 1964, the AID mission shifted its emphasis from stabilization to devaluation.[34] Despite strong protests from the private sector, which feared higher import costs, the United States insisted on a large devaluation, and in May 1964 the official rate was devalued from 130 wŏn to the dollar to 255. In that same month, Chang Key Young took over as deputy prime minister and head of the EPB, where he stayed until 1967. A new American team believed that it was counterproductive to push strict monetary targets while simultaneously undertaking difficult reforms of the fiscal and financial systems. The issue was not "getting the prices right," but getting them "overright" in order to give the economy a push: a low exchange rate, cheap credit for productive activities and exports, and high interest rates for savers. The inflationary consequences of such a policy course would be partly offset by the mobilization of new resources, but some inflation was seen as tolerable.

33. See Kwan Bong Kim, *The Korean-Japan Treaty Crisis and the Instability of the Korean Political System* (New York: Praeger, 1971).

34. The following draws on an interview with Gilbert Brown, September 1985, Washington, D.C.

The improvement in tax collection is a clear example of the link between administrative reform and the extractive capability of the state. In March 1966, under the direction of a close military associate of Park Chung Hee's, a sweeping reorganization of the Taxation Bureau was launched. Tax collections increased 18.6 percent in 1964, 44.5 percent in 1965, and 68.7 percent in 1966 with little change in the tax structure or rates.[35] A concern with domestic resource mobilization was also behind the interest rate reform of late 1965. Park pushed a doubling of interest rate ceilings through the National Assembly in September 1965 with U.S. prodding.[36]

While these reforms have deservedly attracted attention, two policy initiatives defined the new course: the single-minded emphasis placed on exports and the effort to induce foreign capital inflows. The neoclassical interpretation of the success of the export effort was that it hinged on the devaluation and the selective liberalization of imports. But the export drive also entailed the development of a particular institutional structure that mobilized support for the export sector across normal bureaucratic lines by engaging the power of the president. The program linked the public and the private sectors, provided channels for the exchange of information between them, and disseminated technical and market information that was critical for establishing effective market links between South Korea and the rest of the world.

In late 1964, while AID was preoccupied with developing a new stabilization program for 1965, a program for export expansion was formulated within the Ministry of Commerce and Industry.[37] In March 1965, an Export Promotion Subcommittee (EPSC) was formed. The EPSC consisted of the vice-ministers of the economic ministries and relevant agencies and representatives from private sector peak associations. The sectoral focus of the export program is clear in the setting of export targets by region, industry, and in some cases, by individual firm. At the beginning of the export drive targets were command in nature, but gradually the target setting

35. Frank M. Landers, *Technical Assistance in Public Administration: USOM/Korea, 1955–1967* (Seoul: USOM/Korea, 1967), p. 133.

36. On the interest rate reforms, see the somewhat different assessments in David Cole and Yung Chul Park, *Financial Development in Korea 1945–1978* (Cambridge: Harvard University Press, 1983), pp. 163–65; and Ronald McKinnon, *Money and Capital in Economic Development* (Washington, D.C.: Brookings Institution, 1973).

37. The following section draws on Amicus Most, *Expanding Exports: A Case Study of the Korean Experience* (Washington, D.C.: USAID, 1969).

exercise became a way to identify policy barriers to expanded exports. In one survey, only one firm claimed that it had been penalized for failing to meet an export target. Nonetheless, of eighty-five firms polled, fifty-eight mentioned that the rigor of tax collection was linked to export performance. Export promotion efforts extended up to the president. Through monthly National Export Promotion meetings, Park could act directly on problems that individual industries were facing, often by simply issuing directives on the spot.[38]

Probably the most important way in which the government enhanced the profitability of exporting was through its control of credit, a set of policies that reveal the odd mix of market-oriented and statist approaches.[39] Short-term, low-interest loans were extended without limit against any letter of credit. These loans were made at 6.5 percent, compared to discounts on commercial bills that were 24 percent after the interest rate reform.

Neoclassical interpretations argue that the 1960s was a decade of liberalization.[40] They also note, however, that after the 1964 devaluation, a temporary special tariff law was enacted to capture windfalls on restricted import items, with tariffs up to 90 percent being applied, and that an import prepayment deposit was frequently required of 100 percent of import value. Even after 1965 a number of policies continued to affect the ability to import.[41] The switch from a positive list system, in which only listed goods are permitted entry, to a negative list system, in which all goods are permitted entry unless specifically listed, did not come until July 1967, and even then, the new system restricted 42.9 percent of all import categories. Gilbert Brown, a champion of the neoclassical interpretation of South Korea's takeoff, states bluntly that "no major industries were left

38. Ibid., p. 118.

39. Cole and Park, *Financial Development in Korea,* chap. 6; Wontack Hong and Yung Chul Park, "The Financing of Export-Oriented Growth in Korea," in *Pacific Growth and Financial Interdependence,* ed. Augustine H. H. Tan and Basant Kapur (Sydney: Allen and Unwin, 1986).

40. Charles Frank, Kwang Suk Kim, and Larry Westphal, *Foreign Trade Regimes and Economic Development: South Korea* (New York: National Bureau of Economic Research, 1975); Krueger, *The Development of the Foreign Sector.*

41. They included the obligation to surrender foreign exchange in exchange for certificates, advance deposit requirements, the licensing of traders, and minimum export requirements for importers. Import quotas of individual items were abolished only at the end of 1966, but the quantitative restrictions were replaced by a system under which items could be imported only by manufacturers of related products.

without either quantitative restrictions or tariff protection adequate to maintain strong domestic market positions."[42]

In sum, Korea's strategy followed a particular policy sequence. First, stabilization allowed a significant devaluation, undertaken over strong business protests. Shortly thereafter, a wide-ranging program of subsidies and supports to exporters was also launched, but protection of the domestic market remained in place. These actions dramatically enhanced profitability, established export-oriented firms in light manufacturing as the "leading sector," and cemented a close business-government alliance.

The Yushin Regime and Industrial Deepening (1971–1979)

The transition to export-led growth was followed by remarkable economic performance and rapid structural change. Between 1966 and 1969 annual real growth averaged over 10 percent. Exports were on the rise, and the balance of payments situation improved. International competitiveness in labor-intensive industries, devaluation, the upswing of the world economy, and the Vietnam boom contributed to rapid growth and export expansion.

By the end of the decade, however, the South Korean economy encountered new difficulties. The GNP growth rate declined from 15 percent in 1969 to 7.9 percent in 1970, and inflation accelerated. Despite rapid export growth, the current accounts deficit increased from $103 million in 1965 to $847 million in 1971, reflecting consistently high levels of investment relative to savings and an expansionist macroeconomic policy.[43] The debt-service ratio on long-term debt jumped from 7.8 percent in 1969 to 18.2 percent in 1970. South Korea's problems were also related to wage and exchange rate developments. Real wages rose rapidly between 1966 and 1970, weakening international competitiveness, and slowing export growth.

Economic difficulties exacerbated the regime's political problems. Park's decision to amend the constitution to allow for a third presidential term generated immense political opposition in 1969. A national referendum

42. Gilbert Brown, *Korean Pricing Policies and Economic Development in the 1960s* (Baltimore: Johns Hopkins University Press, 1973), p. 167; Wontack Hong, *Trade, Distortions and Growth in Korea* (Seoul: Korea Development Institute, 1979), p. 107.

43. Data are obtained from Economic Planning Board, *Economic Handbook of Korea* (Seoul: EPB, 1978).

passed the amendment, with the help of dramatic increases in government spending, but it undermined Park's political legitimacy. The increasing politicization of class and sectoral cleavages, a by-product of rapid industrialization, contributed to the political crisis. The labor-intensive export drive led to the dramatic expansion of the total labor force. As real wage growth slowed and inflation increased in 1970, labor militancy increased. The Protestant-backed Urban Industrial Mission and the Catholic Young Workers Association, both influenced by Liberation Theology, were instrumental in organizing the efforts of workers.[44] Two highly visible disputes with foreign-invested electronic firms occurred in 1968, and important strikes followed in 1969 and 1970. Most dramatically, a textile worker named Chun Tae Il immolated himself in November 1970 to protest poor working conditions in the small factories in Seoul (see Chapter 4 by Hagen Koo in this volume).

Another significant development was the rising gap in incomes between the rural and urban areas. Poor agricultural performance, declining rural income, and new job opportunities in urban areas fostered rapid internal migration and created a class of urban marginals and squatters. In August 1971 about 30,000 urban poor in the Kwangju complex, a southern suburb of Seoul, staged a violent riot attacking police stations and government buildings. The Kwangju riot marked the first episode of violence by the urban poor and appeared to sum up the underside of export-led economic growth: an explosion of urban migration, poor housing, and uneven employment opportunities.

Growing political and economic grievances were exploited by Kim Dae Jung in his bid for the presidency in 1971. Appealing to populist sentiment and resentment over regional disparities, Kim attacked Park and his economic policies and nearly defeated him. The National Assembly elections in May proved a further setback to the government. Despite the financial and organizational weakness of the opposition New Democratic Party, it managed to capture all but one seat in the Seoul area and showed a strong performance nationwide.

Finally, the role of external security threats must be addressed. Critics

44. On state-labor relations in the 1970s, see Jang Jip Choi, "Interest Conflict and Political Control in South Korea," Ph.D. diss., University of Chicago, 1983; Chun Sik Pak, "1980 yŏndae ŭi no dong undongkwa kukga kaeip" [Labor movement and state intervention around the 1980s], in Study Group on Korean Industrial Society, *Ouŭl uri han'guk chabonchuŭi wa kukga*, pp. 320–50.

downplay security challenges, arguing rightfully that they do not necessitate authoritarian politics. Nonetheless, South Korea did face substantial uncertainty in its external military setting. On January 21, 1968, North Korean commandos raided the Blue House (South Korea's equivalent of the White House). Two days later, North Korea seized the USS *Pueblo* and its eighty-two crew members. A year later, North Korea shot down a U.S. E-121 reconnaissance plane with thirty-one crew members. While North Korean belligerence was on the rise, the U.S. security commitment appeared to be weakening. The U.S. response to these hostile events was relaxed, and in July 1969, the United States announced the Nixon Doctrine: Under the slogan of "Asian hands must shape the Asian future," the administration of Richard Nixon decided to withdraw an entire combat division (the Seventh Division, with a force of twenty-four thousand) from South Korea. The perception of a security crisis, even if magnified by the regime, provided an opportunity for Park to act.[45]

The initial response to the economic difficulties of the late 1960s was quite orthodox, however. Stabilization measures were introduced in 1970 and a standby loan agreement with the International Monetary Fund was signed for 1971, as the government tried to reverse the expansion of credit and money that had accompanied the 1969 referendum. Real growth rates declined, investment slowed, and export growth dropped. For Park, who equated economic growth with political legitimacy and national security and faced severe electoral and non-electoral challenges, these developments were intolerable. Park had made a costly commitment to the rural sector by announcing his intention to pursue a high rice price policy. Increasing grain subsidies in the wake of poor harvests between 1970 and 1973 undercut the commitment to fiscal austerity. The combination of stabilization efforts and devaluation forced firms with foreign debts close to bankruptcy generating strong business pressures on the government. Uncertainty was compounded by the "Nixon Shock" of August 15, 1971—new American restraints on East Asian textiles exports and declining receipts from South Korean troops in Vietnam.

On December 6, 1971, the government declared a state of emergency

45. See Chae-jin Lee and Hideo Sato, *U.S. Policy toward Japan and Korea* (New York: Praeger, 1982), pp. 42–48. Kyŏng Hyon Yu's "Chuhan mikun ch'ŏlsu ŭi P'ajang" [Impacts of U.S. announcement of troop withdrawal], *Sindonga* (August 1970), neatly elucidates the domestic effects of the security crisis.

and closed the universities. A year later, the government imposed martial law, paving the way for the institution of the authoritarian Yushin constitution. Under the Yushin regime, executive authority was further consolidated, and opposition forces were either co-opted or neutralized, insulating the economic domain from social protest. A realignment of power also took place in the ruling circle. The ruling Democratic Republican Party was transformed into a mere appendage of the executive. Park's personal power was strengthened, the political and administrative role of the Blue House dramatically increased, and bureaucrats gained unprecedented power as the National Assembly was marginalized. The Yushin regime opened a new era of state-society relations in which state dominance was increased through new legal-institutional arrangements.[46] (See Chapter 1 by Jang Jip Choi in this volume.)

The "big push" toward heavy industrialization, which characterized the direction of economic development in South Korea between 1972 and 1979, developed in this political context. "Industrial deepening" through the promotion of heavy and chemical industries appeared to solve several problems simultaneously. Heavy industry would provide an engine of rapid economic growth and export expansion to counter eroding international competitiveness and growing protectionism among light, labor-intensive manufacturers in the United States. The heavy industry drive would legitimate Park's Yushin system. It would also increase military self-reliance by creating a defense-industrial complex; this was in fact the major motive behind the heavy industry push. In his New Year's address in January 1973, typically a major political statement, Park outlined an ambitious vision for the Yushin regime: $10 billion in exports and a per capita income of $1000 by the early 1980s. The key to the new phase of growth was an emphasis on heavy and chemical industries: iron and steel, machinery, nonferrous metals, electronics, shipbuilding, and petrochemicals.[47]

46. For the pattern of power consolidation under the Yushin regime, see Hyug Baeg Im, "The Rise of Bureaucratic-Authoritarianism in South Korea," *World Politics* 39 (1987): 231–57; Sae Jung Kim, "Political Economy of Authoritarianism: State Propelled Industrialization and Persistent Authoritarian State in South Korea 1961–1979," Ph.D. diss., McGill University, 1986; Hak-Fyu Sohn, *Authoritarianism and Opposition in South Korea* (London: Routledge, 1989).

47. For an overview of the heavy and chemical industrial plan, see The Planning Council of the Commission for the Promotion of Heavy and Chemical industry, *Chunghwahak kongŏp ch'ujin kyehoek* [The plan for the promotion of the heavy and chemical industry] (Seoul: EPB, 1973).

Instruments deployed in support of heavy industrialization included tax incentives, protection, and tariff exemptions for the imports of capital goods. The central policy instrument for supporting plan goals, however, was preferential credit. Numerous funds developed over the 1970s to advance particular industrial purposes. The allocation of funds was largely in the hands of a newly established and independent planning council, but ultimately, with the president himself, who exercised final approval over major projects.[48] The plan also called for massive increases in foreign borrowing. During the Fourth Five-Year Plan, 70 percent of financing of government identified projects, such as the petrochemical facilities, steel mill expansion, and oil refineries, was to come from foreign loans, while 60 percent of total heavy and chemical investment was to be financed by foreign loans and direct investment in joint ventures. For the larger projects, the government also greatly expanded its direct role in production, most dramatically via the Pohang Iron and Steel Company and the Korean Heavy Machinery Company.[49]

The first oil shock and global recession temporarily halted the heavy industry drive. Rather than maintaining a fixed exchange rate, compressing imports, and deflating, as Taiwan did, South Korea devalued and launched an aggressive export drive.[50] But the resumption of the heavy industry drive produced a new round of economic problems. Contrary to the initial conception, the heavy industry drive did not improve international competitiveness. Investments were duplicative, resulting in surplus capacity in key sectors. Industry was also extremely dependent on foreign technology, industrial raw materials, and parts and components. The import intensity of the new industries undermined price competitiveness. At the same time, new industries demanded skilled labor, placing pressure on tight labor mar-

48. For overviews of decision-making processes involving heavy-chemical industrialization, see the Planning Council, *Han'guk kongŏpphwa palchŏne kwanhan chosa yŏn'gu III: chongchaek kyolchong imyonsa* [A study of Korea's industrial development: Behind story of policy-making] (Seoul: Office of Prime Minister, 1979); Kwan Yong Chong, "Chunghwahak Kongŏphwa chŏngchaekŭl tonghae bon han'gukŭi kukga sŏngkyŏk" [The character of the Korean state through the heavy and chemical industrial policy] in Study Group of Korean Industrial Society, *Onŭl uri han'guk chabon chuŭi wa kukga*, pp. 90–129; Byŏng Yun Pak, "Chunghwahak kongŏp'gye ŭi naemak" [Hidden story of the heavy and chemical industry], *Sindonga* (May 1980).

49. Leroy Jones, *Public Enterprises and Economic Development: The Case of Korea* (Seoul: Korea Development Institute, 1978).

50. World Bank, *Korea: Current Developments and Policy Issues* (Washington, D.C.: World Bank, Report #3005-Ko, 1980).

kets and leading to rapid wage increases. The rapid pace of investment and inflows of foreign exchange from Korean firms engaged in construction in the Middle East contributed to strong inflationary pressures in the economy. Finally, the reliance on debt, both domestic and foreign, weakened the financial structure of many firms. By 1979 firms were forced to resort to borrowing to repay loan principal and interest at a time when the government was seeking to slow inflation by tightening credit.[51]

Industrial deepening also had social and economic consequences that were to become politically salient. The bias toward heavy industry and the creation of general trading companies as legal entities produced a high level of business concentration. Small- and medium-size firms gradually lost their financial independence, either going bankrupt or becoming subcontractors of big business conglomerates (chaebŏls). Despite the government's strong efforts to improve the rural sector, the income gap between the rural and urban sectors widened.

There is also some question about the gains to workers. Government data show rapid wage increases, but the consumer price index probably understates inflation, particularly in the large urban centers, where food and real estate prices rose sharply during the late 1970s. Demands for welfare and redistribution became more widespread, and a populist "horizontal alliance" involving students, labor, farmers, church leaders, and dissident intellectuals began to take a shape. The pattern of development resulting from the industrial deepening effort eventually contributed to Park's other political difficulties. The Yushin regime collapsed with Park's assassination on October 26, 1979, triggered by debates within the leadership over how to manage the opposition.

The Yushin era marked a realignment of state-society relations. State power was substantially increased through the authoritarian Yushin constitution, the consolidation of executive power and centralization of decision-making. In the name of national security, Park placed tight controls on labor, students, and dissident activity.

The exclusion of labor was particularly clear, though its origins predated

51. On the negative effects of the heavy industrial drive, see Korean Development Institute, *Kyŏngje anchŏnghwa sichaek charyochip* [Collection of materials on stabilization], vol. 2 (Seoul: KDI), pp. 1175–90; Kyŏn Kim, "Han'guk ŭi chunghwahak kongŏphwa kwachŏng esŏŭi kukga kaeip yangsang kwa kwigyŏl" [Patterns of state intervention and outcomes in Korea's heavy and chemical industrialization], in Study Group of Korean Industrial Society, *Onŭl uri han'guk chabonchuŭi wa kukga,* pp. 130–83.

the Yushin system. In December 1971, the government enacted the Special Law Concerning National Security and blocked workers' rights to collective bargaining and action in all industries. The government also systematically penetrated labor organizations to weaken their political voice and organizational strength. The Federation of Korean Trade Unions (Noch'ong), the umbrella organization of all labor unions in South Korea, was placed under tight corporatist control. By the end of the 1970s, its membership was only 24.4 percent of the total work force.

Through material incentives and political support extended through the New Village (Saemaŭl) Program, the government attempted to reorganize and co-opt the rural sector. Generous grain and fertilizer subsidies throughout the decade sought to tie the countryside closer to the regime while reversing the perception of rural neglect. Although the magnitude of actual benefits to the rural sector is a matter of debate, pro-rural political symbolism consolidated a base of rural support.[52]

There is no doubt that big business was the principal beneficiary of the industrial deepening strategy. The freeze on private debt through the August 3 measure in 1972 relieved the private sector, especially big business, of curb market debts.[53] The measure of May 29, 1973, established the secondary financial institutions, a new area of expansion for big business. Furthermore, the introduction of the general trading company (GTC) system allowed big business to secure numerous privileges—guaranteed letters of credit, loosened foreign exchange regulations, and further liberalization of import duties—and ensured the virtual monopoly of the chaebŏl in international trade. The most lucrative benefits to business were the preferential allocation of credit. Between 1972 and 1979 more than 60 percent of policy loans and 50 percent of general bank loans went to one hundred business groups. Heavily subsidized credit, monopoly or oligopoly positions in the domestic market, extensive protection in the heavy and chemical sectors, and guaranteed sales through government procurement fostered a conglom-

52. By the mid-1970s, the South Korean government claimed that the average rural income was higher than the average urban workers' income as a result of the New Village Movement. But this claim has been challenged by many. See Hyŏn Chae Pak et al., *Han'guk nongŏp munje ŭi saeroun insik* [New understanding of Korean agricultural problems] (Seoul: Dolbege, 1984).

53. For an excellent analysis of the August 3, 1972, measure, see Sŏng hyŏng Yi, "Kukga, kyegŭp mitt chabon ch'uch'ŏk: 8.3. choch'i rŭl chungsim ŭro" [The state, class and capital accumulation: The case of the August 3 measure], in Jant Jip Choi, *Han'guk chabonchuŭi wa kukga*, pp. 261–80.

erate movement. By the end of the 1970s, a handful of the largest chaebŏls dominated the economy. Total production of the top fifty conglomerates on a valued-added basis accounted for 43 percent of GDP in 1978.[54] The "business-government nexus" *(chungkyung yuchak)* peaked during the period of industrial deepening and created particular political problems for the government in the early 1980s.

South Korea thus continued to pursue an outward orientation in the 1970s, but with a new emphasis on heavy and chemical industrialization and on the basis of a more openly authoritarian politics. A new developmentalist coalition was formed around an increasingly dirigist state favoring big business with selective co-optation at the rural sector. But this coalition did not prove either economically or politically stable.

Regime Change and Neoconservative Reforms: Stabilization and Structural Adjustment (1980–1987)

Despite the structural problems outlined above, the South Korean economy enjoyed an unprecedented economic boom during the 1977–78 period, partly because of the export drive, massive foreign exchange earnings from construction projects in the Middle East, and expansionary macroeconomic policies associated with the heavy industrial drive. Starting in 1979, however, the underlying difficulties became manifest and the economy began to falter. Growth rates averaging 9.9 percent from 1962 to 1978 fell to 2.2 percent in 1979–81, and inflation soared to 26.4 percent from an annual average 16.1 percent between 1962 and 1978. Real growth in exports fell from 27.4 percent annual average between 1962 and 1978 to 7.5 percent between 1979 and 1982. The current accounts deficit balooned from $1.1 billion in 1978 to $4.4 billion in 1981. Both internal and external factors contributed to this economic downturn; while such external factors as the second oil shock and the sharp rise in international interest rates accelerated inflation and balance of payments deficits, surplus capacity resulting from the heavy industry drive and a major crop failure in 1980 aggravated the overall economic outlook.[55]

54. *Hanguk ilbo,* September 29, 1981. Il Sakong's "Economic Growth and Economic Concentration," *Korea Development Study* (1980), provides an excellent analysis of business concentration in the 1970s.

55. EPB, *Economic Indicators* (Seoul: EPB, 1986); "Uri kyŏngje ŭi hyŏnhwang kwa kwalli pangan" [Present status of our economy and management policies] (Seoul: EPB, 1982), pp.

The appearance of economic difficulties in the late 1970s precipitated an intense debate inside and outside the government. Initially, inflation and slowed export growth were explained in cyclical terms, and prescriptions focused on demand management. However, several technocrats argued that the crisis emanated from structural problems associated with industrial deepening. As inflation increased in late 1978, those proposing a structural analysis gained ground within the government. The stabilization measures announced on April 17, 1979, reflected their ascent and a new emphasis not only on macroeconomic stabilization but on industrial strategy and the style of economic policy-making as well.

Before the measures could be fully implemented, however, South Korea went through a series of traumatic political changes: the assassination of President Park, a brief political opening, followed by the seizure of political power by Chun Doo Hwan in June 1981, and the launching of a new Fifth Republic. Seeking both to distance himself from Park's policies and to address the crisis, Chun turned to technocratic reformers, who had been a minority under the previous regime, and elevated them to positions of importance in the new government.

Restoring macroeconomic stability emerged as the primary task under the new regime: the conventional policy tools of fiscal restraint, monetary control, and a freeze on wages were used to that end. Fiscal discipline, a central component of the stabilization effort, was stringent. The rate of increase in government expenditure dropped from 21.9 percent in 1981 to zero in 1984. These figures are quite impressive when compared to average annual growth rates of government spending of 28.9 percent between 1962 and 1969, and 28.1 percent between 1970 and 1979.[56]

Traditionally, South Korea's fiscal structure has been quite rigid, with about 70 percent of the entire budget declared "untouchable." A bilateral defense burden sharing agreement with the United States stipulates that 6 percent of South Korea's GNP be allocated for defense. This normally accounts for over 30 percent of the budget. Debt service, grants to local governments, educational financing, and wages for public servants account for another 40 percent, leaving 30 percent of the budget adjustable. Given these rigidities, budget cutting involved severe reductions in expenditures

5–7. See Chung-in Moon, "The Demise of the Developmentalist State: Neoconservative Reforms and Political Consequences," *Journal of Developing Societies* 4 (1988): 68–70.

56. EPB, *Economic Indicators* (1986).

for social and economic development as well as general administration. The most noticeable squeeze came from the general administrative sector through a wage freeze and early retirement of public employees. In addition, a massive organizational reform of the government sector was implemented, under which redundant and overlapping government agencies were either eliminated or merged. Even the "untouchable" defense budget was subject to incremental trimming.

More substantial fiscal cuts were realized in special account items, primarily government subsidies. Cutting subsidies is often a major stumbling block to successful stabilization efforts. In South Korea, however, the Grain Management Fund, by which farmers received average annual grain price increases of 20 percent during the 1970s, was cut to 14 percent in 1981 and frozen in 1982. A similar cut was also made in the Fertilizer Account, which subsidized fertilizer prices.[57] The private sector was not immune to the effects of fiscal discipline. Over thirty public funds established to finance government sponsored projects were either eliminated or transferred to state-owned financial institutions. The public enterprises also experienced tighter government scrutiny. Fiscal restraint was accompanied by tight monetary and credit controls.

The stabilization had also reversed the trend of rapidly rising real wages. In curbing wage growth, the government relied on various controls as well as directly repressive state intervention aimed at limiting labor's political power. The government first announced an annual wage policy in 1981. Government action was not limited to checking wage increases, however: broader actions were aimed at the structure of the labor movement itself and the government's capacity to intervene to manage labor disputes. Through amendments to the Trade Union Law, the government altered the existing union structure, decentralizing the union movement to the company level. A new Labor Dispute Law increased the government's power in the mediation of disputes, subjected collective action to prior government approval, and prohibited the involvement of outside groups—grass-roots church organizations and students, in particular—in labor disputes.[58]

57. Son Yi, "Piryo kyejong unyŏng e kwanhan punsŏk" [Analysis of the fertilizer account operation], in *Kukga yesan kwa chŏngch'aek mokp'yo* [National budget and policy objectives] ed. Kwang Choi (Seoul: KDI, 1983).

58. Michael Launius, "The State and Labor in South Korea," *Bulletin of Concerned Asian Scholars* 16 (1984); *Monthly Review of Korean Affairs* (June 1984); Korean Christian Re-

The long-term program of the reformers was not limited to stabilization. More fundamental was the effort to realign the state's role in the economy by pursuing both extensive structural reform of the national economy and a more market-oriented style of economic management. Structural adjustment entailed three sets of reforms: industrial restructuring, financial reforms, and liberalization of the domestic market. Each involved a restructuring of the government's political relationship with key social groups.

One factor in the crisis of 1979–80 was the industrial policy associated with the heavy industry drive. The availability of concessional loans led to excessive and duplicative investment, surplus capacity, and business concentration. Two principles guided the government's effort to restructure the heavy industry sector: "rationalization" and a reduction of industrial concentration.[59] The first task was to reorganize six problem sectors, including automobiles and power-generating equipment, in which problems of surplus capacity had emerged. Business lines were consolidated by merger, particular products were assigned to specific firms, and foreign participation was invited. Support was extended to a new range of "strategic" high-technology industries, such as semiconductors, computers, telecommunications, and aerospace, that seemed more suited to South Korea's changing comparative advantage, and more emphasis was placed on indirect, nondiscretionary supports such as incentives for research and development and manpower training.[60]

At the same time, the government undertook to reduce the level of concentration in the manufacturing sector by giving greater attention to small and medium-size firms. Emphasis on heavy industry had led to a relative neglect of the small and medium-size firms that remained central to South Korea's exports of light manufactures. These firms had faced the most intense protectionist pressures, but they had also exhibited great flexibility in adjusting and upgrading in the face of market pressures even as credit was channeled to larger companies. Furthermore, small and medium-size

---

search Institute of Social Problems, *Han'guk sahoe ŭi nodong tongje* [Labor control in Korean society] (Seoul: Minjungsa, 1987), pp. 31–60.

59. EPB, "Che O ch'a okaenyŏn kyŏngje sahoe kaebal kyehoek: Suchŏng chich'im" [The fifth five year social and economic development plan: Guidelines for revision] (Seoul: EPB, 1983).

60. *Donga ilbo,* September 12, 1985; *Chosun ilbo,* May 7, 1986.

firms have emerged as a new alternative to reduce heavy dependence on Japan for parts and components for advanced industrial products such as automobiles, consumer electronics, and heavy machinery because their small size and flexibility constituted an advantage. Aware of their strategic importance, the government readjusted lending priorities to foster small and medium-size firms, and amended tax laws to boost the sector by reducing the preferences granted to the chaebŏls. The Ministry of Commerce and Trade also launched a plan to integrate the small parts and components manufacturers and large firms into closely knit production complexies in order to enhance linkages and flexibility.[61]

To erase the image of the state's discretionary protection of big business, more direct actions were also taken to reduce industrial concentration. In April 1981, the government enacted the Monopoly Regulation and Fair Trade Law. The law covered a wide range of issues, including supervision of the leading producers in each sector, regulation of business concentration, and protection of subcontractors. Special emphasis was placed on attempting to curb conglomerate concentration through cross-investment, reciprocal buying, and cross-subsidization among chaebŏl subsidaries.[62]

Reforming the financial sector involved liberalization, rationalization, and internationalization. Liberalization aimed at greater bank autonomy in determination of credit allocation, in part through the privatization of the state-owned commercial banks. Policy loans and administrative guidance over bank portfolios have been reduced, though the government still exercises influence over banks through its ability to appoint key personnel. Privatization also had its limits. The government relinquished its holdings in the five commercial banks in the country, but retained important oversight and regulatory powers. The new bank law limited the largest groups' holdings in the new banks, and their lending practices were monitored and regulated to avoid their capture by the chaebŏls.

Rationalization involved restructuring the financial sector to allow greater competition. The objective was to redress the imbalances in the financial sector, signaled by firms' dependence on debt and the rapid growth of the informal, or "curb," market. First, the government lifted restrictions limiting competition among different types of financial institutions, re-

61. *Business Korea,* December 1984, p. 28.

62. Chae Uk Yi, "Kongjŏngkŏrae'pŏp: Muŭssi chalmot toetna?" [The fair trade law: What went wrong?], *Sindonga* (November 1984): 430–42.

sulting in a dramatic upsurge in the nonbank private financial sector. This sector, which includes investment and insurance companies and direct credit markets for corporate bond and commercial paper, grew rapidly in the early 1980s and is not subjected to the restrictions governing commercial banks. As a result, the large groups have moved aggressively into this area.

Another significant measure was a failed attempt to enforce a "real name" deposit system, which prohibits by law any financial transactions under false names. This measure sought to restore public confidence in the integrity of the financial system in the wake of a series of financial scandals in the curb markets. Not only would the reform eliminate the dual structure of financial institutions, but it would also increase tax revenues through the effective detection of financial dealings under false names and illicit accumulation of wealth through curb market speculation.

The government also pursued plans to liberalize and internationalize the capital market. The major features of the plan included allowing investment in the secondary market; allowing corporations to raise funds directly through issues in foreign markets; the mutual listing of stocks on South Korean and overseas markets; and a greater volume of dealings between domestic and foreign securities companies. The South Korean market was also gradually opened to the operation of foreign banks, partly in response to an increase in U.S. pressure for national treatment. Initial steps were made toward granting national treatment for foreign banks, which previously faced a number of restrictions on their operations.[63]

Import liberalization and the easing of restrictions on foreign investment were an important component of the economic reforms, in part because of strong U.S. pressure. For example, the South Korean government was forced to liberalize a wide range of farm products and consumer goods manufactured by small and medium-size firms. South Korea has also sought to liberalize its policies on direct foreign investment, which have been the most restrictive of the four East Asian NICs (Newly Industrialized Countries). This has involved two policy thrusts: on the one hand, a commitment to easing entry, and on the other, a dismantling of some special incentives extended to foreign firms. Restrictions on the repatriation of principal and the remittance of dividends were lifted. To assist the recovery of the heavy

63. Sang-Myong Lee, "The Internationalization of Korea's Financial Markets," *Monthly Bulletin of Korean Exchange Bank* 14 (1986): 1–13.

and chemical sectors, measures were taken to ease the licensing of technology, mainly by limiting the reach of government review. At the same time, several extremely generous tax exemptions extended to foreign firms have been either abolished or scaled back in order to equalize the incentives facing foreign and local firms.

The long-term consequences of the structural adjustment measures remain to be seen, but the short-term results of the stabilization were remarkably successful: Growth quickly resumed and inflation dropped into the low single digits. The success must be attributed to a number of characteristics of the South Korean political system under the Fifth Republic—a new military leadership, the ascent of a new technocratic group, and the continuing insulation of economic decision-making from popular pressure through authoritarian controls.

Despite the program's economic success, the stabilization and structural adjustment did not result in increased political support for the government; indeed the ruling party was nearly defeated in the general election of February 1985. The election showed that the ruling Democratic Justice Party had lost support not only in the urban areas, but in the rural areas, the party's traditional support base. Public distrust and demands for democratization increased. Generally speaking, this phenomenon developed out of the overall legitimacy problems of the regime: its illegal seizure of power, military intervention, repression of human rights, and dictatorial rule. Nevertheless, the ruling regime calculated that successful economic reform would mitigate these negative legacies and eventually bring political payoffs. This did not prove to be the case.

The political problems resulted from several contradictions that emerged from the pursuit of the neoconservative reforms themselves. The first contradiction was the growing disjuncture between political power and social support. During the 1960s and 1970s, Park Chung Hee orchestrated export-led industrialization by forming a "developmentalist" coalition through the co-optation of big business, side payments to farmers and political controls on labor, which nonetheless benefited from rapid growth. The Chun regime adopted an economic strategy that undermined this coalition. The combination of stabilization and structural reform had distributional and thus political consequences for virtually every sector of society. Big business was consciously chosen as a prime target. Accusing the tight connection between big business and the government under the Yushin regime of being responsible for corruption and economic crisis, the Fifth

Republic attempted to squeeze the chaebŏls. Tight credit control hurt big business, the enactment of the Monopoly Regulation and Fair Trade law undercut the chaebŏls' domestic position, and the forced merger and consolidation of the heavy and chemical industries limited the range of chaebŏl activities. Both the Federation of Korean Industries (FKI), an umbrella organization of big business, and individual chaebŏls protested government policies, a stance that was rare under the previous regime.

At the same time, the Chun regime undermined the conservative coalition by alienating farmers. Fiscal restraint severely victimized farmers by shrinking the grain management fund and eliminating the fertilizer account. Import liberalization for farm products, hastily implemented under mounting pressure from the United States further undercut farm support. The deteriorating plight of farmers provided fertile ground for activist groups such as the Catholic Farmers' Association and the Federation of Christian Farmers, which sought to mobilize the farm sector and to link it with other opposition forces, including labor and students. Sporadic demonstrations protested import liberalization, subsidy cuts, and the escalating farm debt.[64]

Strained relations with big business and farmers posed a political dilemma for the regime, because they are the key social forces likely to support the conservative ideological line of the Chun regime. Other social groups, most notably, labor, increasingly opposed the government. While nominal wages began to grow again by 1982, real wages lagged behind labor productivity, and the labor movement was forced to undergo a restructuring that significantly weakened its political clout.

The Chun regime was obviously hoping for broad popular support from a "silent" majority of the middle class who benefited from improved economic conditions. The middle class (i.e., owners of small and medium-size firms, and professional, managerial, and technical workers) expanded rapidly through the 1960s and 1970s.[65] But these beneficiaries of the economic reform became strong opponents of the government on political grounds.

In the meantime, the traditional bases of support for the regime were

64. Radical farmers have recently formed Chŏnnongyŏn (National Federation of Farmers Organizations), which is horizontally tied to Chŏnminryŏn, an umbrella organization of radical social movement, and have engaged in violent political protests on import liberalization of farm products and other grievances.

65. Hagen Koo, "Middle Classes, Democratization, and Class Formation: The Case of South Korea," *Theory and Society* 20 (1991): 485–509.

evaporating. Stabilization succeeded in removing "public bads," such as inflation, and in reestablishing economic growth. Stabilization and structural adjustment measures undercut external benefits through the reduction of rents to favored groups—preferential credit, protection, and so forth. These sectoral rewards were the means through which political coalitions had been formed and sustained. The government's intention to co-opt small and medium-size firms through selective support did not prove successful. The readjustment of lending priorities favored only a portion of small and medium industry specializing in parts and component manufacturing. The import liberalization plan was originally designed to protect the interests of small and medium-size firms, while liberalizing monopoly and oligopoly items. The rate of liberalization of monopoly and oligopoly items was 62.4 percent in 1984, however, while that of manufactured goods from small and medium-size firms was 84.8 percent, a result opposite from that intended by the government.[66]

The neoconservative reforms, decentralized economic decision-making, sought to increase the role of market forces as the determinant of economic activity and resource allocation, and favored nondiscretionary interventions. As a result, the state was deprived of political resources and the instruments to control and coordinate the private sector. The liberalization of the banking and financial sector reflects this clearly. Tight credit control and elimination of policy loans dealt a blow to big business that had traditionally depended on access to highly concessional financing. But liberalization created secondary financial institutions through which big business could regain access to credit. Furthermore, the internationalization of banking and financial markets provided chaebŏls with additional sources of corporate financing. Because discretionary credit control was the key instrument for controlling the private sector, the decreased dependence of big business on the state shifted power toward the private sector. As the collapse of the Kukje Group illustrates, the state could still wield power over the private sector. The government also retained the authority to appoint key bank personnel. Nonetheless, the exercise of its power was structurally constrained by the very size of big business groups.

Finally, the reforms created a new tension between politicization and depoliticization of economic issues. Under the Park regime, economic issues

66. Sŏng Tae Chŏng, "Suip chayuhwa ŭi munjechŏm" [Problems of import liberalization], *Sindonga* (August 1984): 196.

were relatively detached from public attention. Corporatist co-optation, preferential treatment, and repression limited societal opposition. But the neoconservative reforms under Chun and the movement for democracy produced tense policy cleavages and increased public awareness of economic issues. This became clear in the 1985 general elections, when economic issues played an important role in the public debate. Decentralization of economic decision-making and new institutional arrangements such as public hearings on economic policies have facilitated this trend.

The Korean stabilization and structural reform effort thus was an economic success. Austerity measures curbed inflation and reestablished historically strong growth rates. Though limited, structural adjustment improved the international competitiveness of South Korean firms. Some of this success can be attributed to favorable international conditions, particularly declining costs of raw materials, low interest rates, and the depreciation of the South Korean currency against the rising yen and the falling dollar. To a large extent, however, state strength accounted for these policy successes. The Chun regime exhibited basic continuities with the authoritarian Yushin period and as a result was able to impose short-term adjustment costs on farmers, labor, and the bureaucracy, even though these measures had a political cost.

Conclusion:
Democratic Transition, Institutional Change and Economic Policy

A major theme of this chapter is that institutional characteristics of the state affect the ability of social groups and political elites to realize their objectives and the capacity of bureaucrats to formulate and implement consistent and coherent policies. The Rhee regime encouraged rent-seeking by the private sector, resulting in inconsistent and inefficient policy outcomes, while the Chang Myon government was wholly immobilized by political pressures. The early Park, Yushin, and early Chun regimes, by contrast, penetrated civil society to forge new growth coalitions, while coopting, controlling, or limiting potential opposition. However, the institutional continuity that ran from the military government through the Chun regime now appears to be undergoing a dramatic transformation.

Chun bowed to public pressure in the summer of 1987 and agreed to crucial constitutional revisions. A transition to democracy was carried out through the presidential election of December 1987 and the National Assembly election of April 1988. Roh Tae Woo was barely elected to the presidency, winning only 36 percent of the popular vote. Moreover, the three opposition parties formed the majority in the National Assembly, and this has fundamentally limited the new regime's political capability.

Equally important was the expansion of the political space in which a broader array of social groups could operate. New farm groups formed, and street protests by farmers increased dramatically around the issues of farm debt, taxes, and import liberalization. Rice pricing policy became subject to competitive bidding among the political parties for farm support. As a result, rice price increases in 1987 and 1988 far outstripped initial government proposals.

Labor's response to the new political climate was even more swift. In the two months from July 4 to September 4, 1987, there were more labor disputes than had taken place in the previous ten years, and over a thousand new unions were organized. Labor disputes became more violent, defying both corporate management and the government. Departing from the previous practice of exclusionary policies toward labor, the government initially sought to distance itself from management in labor disputes, at least until the Hyundai strike of 1989. The ruling Democratic Justice Party introduced amendments to the labor law that guaranteed collective bargaining, collective action, and the freedom to form new unions (see Chapter 4 by Hagen Koo in this volume).

Past patterns of state support for big business were also regarded as carrying a high political cost. Roh Tae Woo's campaign platform converged with the opposition's in calling for the elimination of policy loans, the progressive taxation of large landholders, the implementation of the real-name financial transaction system, and a general reduction of preferential treatment for big business.[67]

The Sixth Republic's progressive overture did not last more than a year, however. On the political front, Roh's efforts to differentiate himself from his predecessor failed completely. Opposition lawmakers as well as the student opposition pressed aggressively for an accounting of the various abuses that occurred during the Chun years, from his seizure of power and the Kwangju massacre to questions of personal corruption. These issues

67. Chae Wan Ch'oe, "Nambaltoen kyŏngje kongnyak: silhyŏn kanŭngsŏng huibakhada" [Overissued economic campaign promises: Dim feasibility], *Sindonga* (January 1988): 238–45.

and the minority status of the ruling party served to deadlock the legislature, at the same time that the government faced nonstop street demonstrations.

Though the political milieu was the major source of what Roh himself labeled a "total crisis," the economy was also a contributing factor. The years from 1986 through 1988 were boom times, with average annual growth of 12 percent. But this was accompanied by a rapid increase in asset and land prices. In 1989, growth slowed to 6.5 percent, but land prices continued to march upward at an annual rate of over 30 percent. The strong wŏn contributed to problems in the external sector: in 1989, exports actually fell.

Roh responded to the crisis in three ways. The first was a major political realignment through the formation of a grand conservative coalition in which two opposition parties (Kim Young Sam's Reunification Democratic Party and Kim Jong Pil's New Democratic Republican Party) were merged with the ruling party. The creation of the Democratic Liberal Party, modeled after the Japanese Liberal Democratic Party, reflected an ideological shift toward the Right. With this alignment, the "progressive" phase of the Roh administration slowed down substantially.

Second, the political realignment was followed by changes in the economic bureaucracy. Pro-business, expansionist technocrats replaced the economic cabinet led by Cho Soon and Moon Hi Gap, advocates of more progressive reforms aimed at economic stability and greater attention to equality. Along with this institutional shakeup, the government undertook measures to improve its relations with the private sector. The wŏn was depreciated after two years of steady appreciation. Credit controls eased and interest rates fell as the government managed the money supply in a more "flexible" manner. The implementation of the real name financial transaction system was indefinitely delayed, and comprehensive real-estate tax measures were weakened. Labor laws were relaxed to reflect business interests. The government adopted a much more repressive stance against the labor movement and demonstrators, including suppressing several major strikes through massive police force. The cool posture of the government toward business narrowed to a focus on the very largest of the chaebols. Thus, while seeking to reduce the degree of concentration among the fifty largest chaebols through various measures, the government simultaneously undertook policy measures to strengthen the private sector and respond to the slowdown in the economy that occurred in the second half of 1989.

These institutional and policy responses were not effective, however; indeed, the politically motivated effort to stimulate the economy was costly. The real GNP growth rate rose to 9.0 percent in 1990 and to 8.6 percent in 1991, but was accompanied by increasing inflation. The balance of payments deteriorated sharply, falling into deficit in 1990 after years of surplus; in 1991 the current accounts deficit reached $9.5 billion. The tight money and credit controls reinstated to manage inflation triggered rising bankruptcies, especially among small and medium-size firms and precipitated declining investment. Stock prices plunged to their lowest level since 1987, giving rise to substantial middle-class protest.

Equally problematic is the fact that the Roh's grand conservative coalition did not prove durable. The attempt to curb chaebŏl concentration contributed to a political showdown in the second half of 1991. Defying the government's anti-chaebŏl campaign, Chung Ju Yung, founder and chairman of the Hyundai Group, formed a new political party, the Unification National Party, a move that would have been unthinkable under the previous regimes. The hastily formed party emerged as the second major opposition party by winning 17 percent of the votes and 10 percent of the seats in the National Assembly in the March 1992 general election. Chung's party undercut the constituent base of the ruling party, demonstrating that big business could wield significant political leverage in a democratic context.

Economic policy under Roh was erratic. Initial efforts to court support and blunt the force of the opposition through "progressive" measures died quickly and were replaced by a more pro-business stance. Yet this effort was not effective either: business remained suspicious of the government and sought new channels for articulating its views, and the Left, labor, and certain provinces remained alienated from a regime still closely identified with the Chun era.

The period of political liberalization raises several issues about the relationship between democratization, state strength, and economic policy that can only be signaled here. First, the liberalization of politics has provided new channels for groups to air their grievances. Operating in a more open political context, opposition parties are exploiting economic issues to their political advantage. Second, liberalization is forcing a change in the relationship between politicians and bureaucrats. The ruling party's efforts to build political support through the manipulation of policy instruments have reduced the independence of the economic bureaucracy and forced the technocrats to navigate a more politicized policy-making process.

The more fundamental question is whether South Korean economic policy-making can break the government's reliance on an authoritarian style of rule. The return to an open politics of exclusion now appears extremely difficult because of the increasing constraints posed by electoral politics. Yet South Korea still lacks the institutions, political alignments, and particularly stable party structure capable of supporting other alternatives. On the one hand, the Left is too splintered and too radical, and lacks the single coherent party organization that would provide the basis for a social democratic political order and the economic policies such an order would imply. On the other hand, the experiment in mimicking Japan's system, in which a single conservative party dominates, has also failed. Until the new democratic order is more firmly consolidated, we can expect that the political conflicts over economic policy that characterized the Roh years will continue.

3

The South Korean Bourgeoisie: A Class in Search of Hegemony

Carter J. Eckert

> Our country's businessmen have not been able to acquire public esteem. On the contrary, [they] have been denounced or kept at a safe distance with feigned respect. There are, of course, a variety of reasons for this.
>
> *Kim Woo Choong*
> *Chairman of the Daewoo Group*

If Marx and Engels had ever turned their attention to Korea, they might well have characterized the contemporary Korean state of their time as a committee for managing the common affairs of the *yangban*. And with good reason. The *yangban* aristocracy exercised an extraordinary degree of influence over both their state and society. Not only did they own much of the land, the main form of wealth; through their control and manipulation of the state civil service examinations, strategic intermarriage (including the provision of royal consorts), and the formation of active *yangban* associations at the local level, they were also able to maintain a position of political power from one generation to the next that invariably rivaled, and not infrequently surpassed, the power of the Chosŏn kings. Such wealth and power, moreover, were sustained within the society as a

An earlier version of this chapter appeared in the *Journal of Korean Studies* 7 (1990): 115–48.

whole by occasional top-down marginal adjustments and reforms in the distribution system and by widely diffused neo-Confucian cultural and ideological norms articulated and propagated by the *yangban* themselves. This formidable array of economic, political, and normative resources made the *yangban* as a class virtually impervious to attack from either the state or other segments of society. In turn, the *yangban*'s deep penetration of both state and society contributed significantly to the remarkable political and social stability that characterized the five centuries of Chosŏn rule, one of the longest dynasties in East Asian history.[1]

In purely economic terms a native bourgeoisie now bids fair to be the historical successor to the *yangban* as South Korea's dominant class. But one wonders if Marx and Engels, were they still writing today, would not at least hesitate before describing the contemporary South Korean state as a committee in the service of the bourgeoisie. Bourgeois political power in South Korea, though clearly growing, is still a far cry in both scope and impact from that traditionally wielded by the *yangban*. In the social realm, moreover, one finds a striking contrast between the respective positions of the two classes. As the quotation at the beginning of this chapter suggests,[2] the Korean bourgeoisie remains, despite its wealth and increasing political influence, a decidedly unhegemonic class, estranged from the very society in which it continues to grow.[3] The origins of this problem are complex

1. See, for example, Edward Willett Wagner, "The Ladder of Success in Yi Dynasty Korea," *Occasional Papers on Korea* 1 (April 1974): 1–8, and *The Literati Purges: Political Conflict in Early Yi Korea* (Cambridge: East Asian Research Center, Harvard University, 1974). See also James B. Palais, *Politics and Policy in Traditional Korea* (Cambridge: Harvard University Press, 1975); "Stability in Yi Dynasty Korea: Equilibrium Systems and Marginal Adjustment," *Occasional Papers on Korea* 3 (June 1975): 1–18; "Han Yong-u's Studies of Early Chosen Intellectual History," *Journal of Korean Studies* 2 (1980): 199–224, especially 219–21. See also Fujiya Kawashima, "A Study of the Hyangan: Kin Groups and Aristocratic Localism in the Seventeenth- and Eighteenth-Century Korean Countryside," *Journal of Korean Studies* 5 (1984): 3–38.

2. Taken from Kim Ujung [Kim Woo-Choong], *Segye nŭn nŏlko, hal il ŭn mant'a* [The world is wide, and there's much to do] (Seoul: Kim Yŏngsa, 1989), pp. 16–17.

3. The concept of "hegemony" that provides the framework for this chapter is based on the work of Antonio Gramsci. See Gramsci's *Selections from the Prison Notebooks*, ed. and trans. Quintin Hoare and Geoffrey Nowell Smith (New York: International Publishers, 1971). I have also found the following works useful for understanding Gramsci's thought: Walter L. Adamson, *Hegemony and Revolution: A Study of Antonio Gramsci's Political and Cultural Theory* (Berkeley: University of California Press, 1980); Robert Bocock, *Hegemony* (Chichester: Ellis Horwood, 1986); Anne Showstack Sassoon, *Approaches to Gramsci* (London: Writers and Readers Publishing Cooperative Society, 1982); Jang Jip Choi, *Han'guk hyŏndae*

and historical, and they ultimately raise fundamental questions about the stability of the existing capitalist system in South Korea.

The Growth of Bourgeois Economic Power

Western social scientists, intrigued by South Korea's recent economic development, have tended to focus their studies of Korean capitalism on the period of rapid growth after 1961. Korean scholars, however, both North and South, have been inspired by nationalist sentiment to look for the "sprouts" *(maenga)* of Korean capitalism, including a nascent capitalist class, in the seventeenth and eighteenth centuries.[4] The truth is that capitalism in Korea is neither so new nor so old. To concentrate solely or even primarily on the period after 1961 would be profoundly ahistorical; yet, the claims of the nationalist historians are difficult to support.

Both logic and evidence suggest that capitalism as we know it today in South Korea did not really begin until the late nineteenth century. Only then, with the forced incorporation of the country into the existing international capitalist economy by Japan and the West, did Koreans have access to a market of sufficient size and dynamism to stimulate and support a process of sustained capital accumulation. Only then, moreover, were Koreans introduced to the knowledge and achievements of the Industrial Revolution, which provided the technological basis for modern capitalism, and to the various structural and organizational elements of capitalist civilization, including, for example, the joint-stock company. Although we now know that the Chŏson period was by no means a time of economic stagnation, there is no logical or empirical reason to assume that the signs of growth to which Korean scholars so frequently point—increasing monetization of the economy, the rise of a new group of merchants outside the officially sanctioned trade network, commercialization and rationalization of agriculture in the countryside, the appearance of free wage labor—were necessarily leading to a Korean version of Western industrial capitalism.[5] It is more likely that they were not. The development of industrial capitalism seems to have been an indigenous phenomenon only in the West, indeed, perhaps

chŏngch'i ŭi kujo wa pyŏnhwa [Structure and change in contemporary Korean politics] (Seoul: Tosŏ Ch'ulp'an Kkach'i, 1989), pp. 11–37.

4. See Carter J. Eckert, *Offspring of Empire: The Koch'ang Kims and the Colonial Origins of Korean Capitalism, 1876–1910* (Seattle: University of Washington Press, 1991), chap. 1.

5. Ibid.

only in England. In all other countries it has been to a greater or lesser extent imported and adapted; in the case of Korea, capitalism was both a product and a response to imperialism, an important point to which we shall return later.

Since the late nineteenth century, Korean entrepreneurs have been a regular and vital part of modern Korean history, skillfully taking advantage of every major economic opportunity. While the opening of the country to international trade after 1876 dealt a death blow to Korea's traditional merchant class, which was overly dependent on official patronage and too closely linked to the old network of trade in Korean goods and currency, more enterprising Koreans made fortunes in the new international commerce in export grains (especially rice) and imported manufactures. Two groups here were especially important. Agents called *kaekchu* or *yŏgak* acted as middlemen in the new trade, especially in the early years of the treaty ports, when foreigners were still either forbidden to travel to the interior of the country or too limited in their knowledge of Korean language and customs. Even more important in the process of capital accumulation during this period were the Korean landlords, who owned the land on which the rice for export was grown. As the price of rice rose during this period in response to the market, so too did the profits of the landlords, some of whom, like the Koch'ang Kims of north Chŏlla province, rose from very modest circumstances in the late nineteenth century to a position of great wealth by the time of the annexation in 1910.[6]

During the colonial era (1910–45), Japanese needs and interests were always given precedence over Korean, but the government-general did not completely block Korean entrepreneurship. The first decade of colonial rule was, to be sure, extremely difficult for Korean businessmen; Korea's first two governors-general, Terauchi Masatake and Hasegawa Yoshimichi, decided to treat the peninsula in classic colonial fashion as a granary of cheap rice for Japanese consumption and, conversely, as a market for Japanese manufactured goods, and both industrial development and Korean entrepreneurship were accordingly restricted by the so-called Company Law.

Later, however, as a result of the economic effects of World War I and massive Korean nationalist demonstrations against Japanese rule in 1919, the economic and political climate in Korea was liberalized, and the door was opened to wider Korean participation in the colonial economy. After

6. Ibid.

1919 many Koreans who had made money in the rice trade began to transfer some or all of their profits into a still small but growing industrial sector, and especially into textiles. In the 1930s and 1940s, as Japanese army conquests in Manchuria, China proper, and finally Southeast Asia turned much of continental Asia into a single imperial market and the demand for military goods escalated, Korea rapidly developed into the most industrialized country in Asia after Japan itself, and many Koreans made money as traders and manufacturers. For a few, like the Koch'ang Kims, who had established a large-scale spinning and weaving facility as early as 1919 and later expanded their operation into Manchuria and central China, the profits were spectacular. For most Koreans, however, the scale and gains of entrepreneurship were far more modest. Nevertheless, by the end of the colonial period, Korea had clearly seen the emergence of a true "sprout" of capitalism, a nascent bourgeoisie, a number of whose members, including the Koch'ang Kims, went on to become major business figures in South Korea. In fact, three of South Korea's top four business groups today, Samsung, Hyundai, and Lucky-Goldstar, were founded by men who began their entrepreneurial careers during the colonial period.[7]

In 1945, however, at the time of liberation, there was no clear assurance that Korea's new bourgeoisie would continue to expand and develop. Indeed, an impartial observer on the scene in late August of that year might well have predicted the quick triumph of an anticolonial revolution that would have purged Korea's capitalists, tainted by collaboration with the Japanese, and established a basically socialist economy. That, in fact, is essentially what happened in the northern half of the peninsula with Soviet approval and assistance. In the South, however, the U.S. Army set up a military government and carried out a counterrevolution against leftist forces that eventually led to the formation of the Republic of Korea as a so-called bulwark of communism in the Far East, a U.S. political commitment that was subsequently solidified by the Korean War.[8] The economic result of this commitment was the rescue of the Korean bourgeoisie and the development of a restructured capitalist economy in the South supported at first by U.S. aid, later by Japanese grants, loans, and commercial credits, and finally by South Korea's own success in the international export mar-

7. Ibid., chap. 2.

8. See Bruce Cumings, *Origins of the Korean War: Liberation and the Emergence of Separate Regimes* (Princeton: Princeton University Press, 1981).

ket. Land reform in the South, moreover, especially that executed by the North Korean occupation forces during the Korean War, also eliminated the Korean landlords as a class, thereby removing one of the major social obstacles to full industrialization and simultaneously enhancing the role of the bourgeoisie in South Korea's economy and society.[9]

As a result of these and other factors, capitalism in South Korea grew dramatically after 1945, especially after 1961. Although there has been considerable entrepreneurial continuity throughout the post-1945 period and even extending back into the colonial era, each new economic opportunity since 1945 has also tended to create new entrepreneurs, and some in each case have generally been able to achieve a more or less permanent place in the economy. In the 1950s the main economic opportunities included the gradual sale of former Japanese properties by the South Korean government; the demand for goods and services during the Korean War; and the political economy of aid dependency and import substitution under Syngman Rhee, when fortunes were made through the acquisition of foreign exchange at undervalued official rates, exclusive import licenses, public contracts, aid funds and materials, and inexpensive bank loans. Later, under Park Chung Hee's strategy of export-led development, entrepreneurs in officially targeted industries elevated Korean capitalism to international standards with the help of special licensing, tax, and financial privileges from the government. South Korea's participation in the Vietnam War also gave many entrepreneurs, especially in the transport and construction industries, a substantial boost in the late 1960s and early 1970s and helped

9. For a good overview of South Korean business development through the mid-1970s, see Leroy P. Jones and Il Sakong, *Government, Business, and Entrepreneurship in Economic Development: The Korean Case* (Cambridge: Council on East Asian Studies, Harvard University, 1980). On foreign assistance, see Anne O. Krueger, *The Developmental Role of the Foreign Sector and Aid* (Cambridge: Council on East Asian Studies, Harvard University, 1982); David C. Cole, "Foreign Assistance and Korean Development," in David C. Cole et al., *The Korean Economy—Issues of Development* (Berkeley: Institute of East Asian Studies, University of California, 1980), pp. 1–26; Chong-Sik Lee, *Japan and Korea: The Political Dimension* (Stanford: Hoover Institution Press, 1985), chap. 3. On land reform, see Jon Halliday and Bruce Cumings, *Korea: The Unknown War* (New York: Pantheon, 1988), p. 87. See also Bruce Cumings, *Origins of the Korean War,* Vol. 2: *The Roaring of the Cataract* (Princeton: Princeton University Press, 1990), pp. 471–72, 677–80. Sung Hwan Ban et al., *Rural Development* (Cambridge: Council on East Asian Studies, Harvard University, 1980), pp. 283–97; Jones and Sakong, pp. 35–36. The most comprehensive study of South Korean industrialization to date is Alice Amsden, *Asia's New Giant: South Korea and Late Industrialization* (New York: Oxford University Press, 1989).

pave the way for South Korean companies like Hyundai to capture almost 7 percent of the lucrative Middle East construction market after the first oil crisis in 1973. Today big business groups called *chaebŏl* dominate the South Korean economy, and at least two, Samsung and Hyundai, are among the fifty largest industrial firms in the world.[10]

Class and State

Great wealth invariably carries with it the potential for great political power, and capitalist societies by their very nature have tended historically to give their big business a preponderant share of political power and or influence. One thinks of the United States as perhaps a classic example, but even in Japan, where the state has played a far more interventionist role in the process of economic development, big business has more often than not been able to protest its interests against unwelcome state interference, even during periods of national crisis. T. A. Bisson has noted, for example, that even during World War II, Premier Tojo was forced to appoint a cabinet advisory board composed of financial and industrial magnates and to reshuffle the cabinet itself to appease business interests. Wartime controls in Japan, according to Bisson, "fell considerably short of applying a thorough scheme of state regimentation to the basic industries and the great business monopolies."[11] With respect to contemporary Japan, Richard Samuels has also stressed the importance of reciprocity within what he sees as a complex and dynamic process of government-business interaction.[12]

In general, Korea's particular form of capitalist development has militated against a powerful role for big business in the political sphere. As in Japan, the state, not the bourgeoisie, was historically the initiator and leader of the industrialization process, both in the colonial and postcolonial periods, but the South Korean version of what Chalmers Johnson has

10. On the growth of post-1945 big business, see Seok Ki Kim, "Business Concentration and Government Policy: A Study of the Phenomenon of Business Groups in Korea, 1945–1985," Ph.D. diss., Harvard University Graduate School of Business Administration, 1987; and Jeong-Ro Yoon, "The State and Private Capital in Korea: The Political Economy of the Semiconductor Industry, 1965–1987," Ph.D. diss., Harvard University, 1989. See also Jones and Sakong, *Government, Business, and Entrepreneurship,* pp. 269–78.

11. T. A. Bisson, *Japan's War Economy* (New York: International Secretariat, Institute of Pacific Relations, 1945), pp. 3, 100–102.

12. Richard J. Samuels, *The Business of the Japanese State: Energy Markets in Comparative and Historical Perspective* (Ithaca: Cornell University Press, 1987), p. 287.

termed the "capitalist developmental state" has been even more authoritarian than the Japanese.[13] Indeed, one might say without much exaggeration that the whole process of private capital accumulation in Korea since the colonial period has been filtered in one way or another through the state.

In part such financial dependence on the state has been a reflection of the scarcity of available private domestic capital, especially after the Korean War. Another factor, however, has been the desire on the part of the country's various regimes, including the colonial government-general, to maintain control over the allocation and flow of capital and credit for both economic and political reasons. The Rhee government, for example, used its control over U.S. aid funds and projects to create an overlapping and largely corrupt network of interests among big business, the bureaucracy, and the Liberal Party that seemed geared more to keeping Rhee and his associates in power than to developing a viable national economy.[14] Through their ownership or supervision of all the country's banks, their power to set interest rates, and their approval and guarantee of all commercial loans and investments from foreign countries, the more economically oriented regimes of Park Chung Hee and Chun Doo Hwan were able to direct capital toward targeted industries and to ensure corporate cooperation with their various five-year development plans.[15]

Such state control over the financial system has of course also left little practical room for political dissent from the business community. In 1988 Chung Ju Yung (Chŏng Chuyŏng), the founder and current honorary chairman of the Hyundai Group, admitted before a South Korean National Assembly committee investigating the corruption and other "irregularities" in the Fifth Republic that Korean business had donated large sums of money to Chun's personal political vehicle, the Ilhae Foundation, in order

13. Chalmers Johnson, *MITI and the Japanese Miracle: The Growth of Industrial Policy, 1925–1975* (Stanford: Stanford University Press, 1982), pp. viii, 317.

14. On the Rhee regime, see Sungjoo Han, *The Failure of Democracy in South Korea* (Berkeley: University of California Press, 1974). See also Stephan Haggard and Byung-kook Kim, "The Transition to Export-Led Growth in Korea, 1954–1966," paper prepared for the conference on the Role of the State in Economic Development: Republic of Korea, University of California, Los Angeles, August 14–16. For a new South Korean study of this period, see Yi Taegŭn, *Han'guk chŏnjaeng kwa 1950-nyŏndae ui chabon ch'ukchŏk* [The Korean war and capital accumulation in the 1950s] (Seoul: Tosŏ Ch'ulpan Kkach'i, 1987).

15. For a wide-ranging study of the state's control of the financial system in South Korea, see Jung-en Woo, *Race to the Swift: State and Finance in Korean Industrialization* (New York: Columbia University Press, 1991). See also Eckert, *Offspring of Empire,* chap. 3, and Jones and Sakong, *Government, Business, and Entrepreneurship,* chaps. 3 and 4, passim.

to avoid government reprisals against it.[16] And indeed, the refusal of the Chun regime to approve emergency bank loans to cover the Kukje ICC Group's short-term debt in 1985 may well have been due in part to the reluctance of Kukje's founder and chairman to make such political contributions both to Chun and his younger brother, who was then head of the New Village (Saemaŭl) Program. At the very least, the fact of Kukje's sudden demise as a result of the withdrawal of government support underscored the financial power of the state to make or break a company even of chaebŏl rank (Kukje ICC was the seventh largest chaebŏl in turnover at the time).[17]

Two other controls have been particularly effective in keeping South Korean businessmen economically and politically subordinate to the state. One has been the state's allocation of business licenses, which precisely define and limit the scope of a firm's activity; all business owners have been required to obtain such licenses from the appropriate government ministry or department in order to establish, modify, or expand a company. Another important state control over business has existed in the Office of National Tax Administration (ONTA), established in 1966, which subjects firms judged guilty of tax evasion not only to payment of additional taxes and penalties but also to criminal prosecution. ONTA has been an important tool for ensuring that business profits and expenditures flow only into officially approved areas and for punishing businessmen who have violated state economic guidelines and regulations or somehow offended the governing authorities. Indeed, one confidential consulting report recently prepared for an American firm interested in a possible joint-venture in South Korea called ONTA "the ultimate control agency of the government."[18] The use of ONTA for political purposes has also been facilitated by the complexity and ambiguity of the national tax laws, which make it difficult for any company, however scrupulous, to avoid breaking the law at some point, and which also permit the state to exercise considerable discretion in judg-

16. *Han'guk kyŏngje sinmun,* November 10, 1988.

17. Mark Clifford, "Filing for Divorce" and "Playing the Game," *Far Eastern Economic Review,* April 21, 1988, pp. 58–60. See also *Korea Newsreview,* April 9, 1988.

18. On the various types of state control over business, see Jones and Sakong, *Government, Business, and Entrepreneurship,* chap. 4, passim. The consulting company that prepared this confidential report requested that its name and the name of the American company for whom the report was prepared not be publicly disclosed.

ing whether or not—and if so, to what extent—a particular firm has been guilty of a tax violation.

Such state controls notwithstanding, it would be misleading to suggest that coercion has been the only factor at work here. As in Japan, though not to the same degree, there has been an element of reciprocity in the South Korean government-business relationship. Since the colonial period, the state has consistently recognized the importance of private business in promoting economic development. The Park regime in particular chose to cultivate a cooperative relationship with business leaders, gradually bringing them into the decision-making process through both formal and informal channels, showering public praise and honors on them for achieving or exceeding development goals, and selectively allowing them to become rich.[19]

The strong commitment to economic development for political as well as economic reasons by Park and his successors has also curtailed the South Korean state's ability to act in a completely dictatorial or arbitrary fashion toward the capitalist class. Simply put, the chaebŏls have become too important to the economy for the state to ignore their needs and demands. This was already clear in 1972, when many of the major South Korean business groups were facing the possibility of bankruptcy as a result of excessive short-term, high-interest borrowing from the banks and the even more expensive curb (private money-lending) market. In August of that year Park issued a presidential emergency decree (the so-called 8-3 Decree) that replaced all such high-interest loans with long-term bank loans on very favorable terms. Since that time the government has generally continued to provide special emergency loans to chaebŏls threatened by bankruptcy.[20] A notable exception here, of course, was the Kukje case mentioned above, but it is important to remember that in terms of assets, sales, and number of employees, Kukje was clearly a second-tier chaebŏl. One doubts that the government would have allowed a chaebŏl of the size of Samsung, Lucky-Goldstar, Hyundai, or Daewoo to go under so easily. Indeed, in 1989 the Roh Tae Woo government announced that it would in effect save the Daewoo Shipbuilding and Heavy Machinery Company with a generous debt

19. On the colonial period, see Eckert, *Offspring of Empire,* chap. 4. On the post-1945 period, see Jones and Sakong, *Government, Business, and Entrepreneurship,* pp. 58–77, 98, 140.

20. Seok Ki Kim, "Business Concentration," pp. 156–57, 260–61.

rescheduling and loan package because the company's potential bankruptcy threatened the stability of the Daewoo Group as a whole and the jobs of tens of thousands of workers.[21] It is also worth noting in this context that although Kukje as a group ceased to exist, its various corporate parts were sold off to other companies and continued to function.

Another factor that has given the chaebŏl some leverage with the state is the state's own adoption in the 1960s of an outward-oriented development strategy based on the inducement of foreign capital and technology and the promotion of exports. By linking South Korea's economy in a structural sense to the international capitalist economy, such a policy has, first of all, made it difficult for the state to take any action against the private sector that might adversely affect the country's acquisition of foreign capital or the sale of South Korean products in the international export market. As in the recent case of Daewoo, the state has thus found itself repeatedly coming to the rescue of financially troubled chaebŏls, in spite of numerous and often simultaneous attempts to force the chaebŏls to rationalize their corporate and financial structures.[22] The fact is that the financial collapse of a South Korean firm of world stature like Daewoo or Hyundai would not only create domestic problems, but would also in all likelihood damage the international credibility of the company in question and send a signal to potential foreign investors that South Korea is not so secure a credit risk as previously assumed.

Shortly after seizing power in 1980, the Chun regime quickly discovered some of the inherent limits that South Korea's link to the international economy could impose on the government's ability to restructure the private sector. That August the government announced a new plan to reorganize the heavy and chemical industries along lines that would eliminate competition among rival domestic producers and create specialized monopolies for supposedly more efficient export production. In accordance with this new plan, Hyundai and Daewoo, the main competitors in the automobile and power-generation equipment industries, were to cease competition and effect an exchange of properties that would make each firm a virtual monopoly producer in one of these two areas. Chung Ju Yung of Hyundai and Kim Woo Chung (Kim Ujung) of Daewoo were summoned to the

21. *Korea Newsreview,* April 1, 1989.

22. Seok Ki Kim, "Business Concentration," passim, and Jeong-Ro Yoon, "The State and Private Capital," chap. 5.

Ministry of Commerce and Industry and ordered to work out such an arrangement within a week. Both Chung and Kim reluctantly agreed to go along with the new state policy, and a deal was struck wherein Hyundai would take over the automobile industry and leave the production of power plants to Daewoo. The South Korean firms' respective foreign joint-venture partners, however, were not at all pleased with the government's summary actions. General Motors, which had a 50 percent joint-venture agreement with Saehan Motors, the automotive arm of Daewoo, was particularly upset, especially when it discovered that the new joint venture with Hyundai would offer GM only 20 percent equity. GM sent its vice president for Far Eastern operations to Seoul to tell Chun personally, and in no uncertain terms, that the new arrangement was not acceptable, and the government eventually backed down.[23]

A second result of the structural linking of the South Korean economy to the larger capitalist world has been to develop the knowledge and experience of the private sector to a point where it is now as—or more—capable of making sound economic decisions than the state, especially in the context of the growing complexity of both the South Korean and the world economies. Indeed, a recent study of the development of the semiconductor industry in South Korea between 1965 and 1987 demonstrates that it was private capital, not the state, that identified the potential of the industry and then built it into a leading sector of the economy.[24] Even the South Korean state itself has gradually come to recognize the importance of transferring more economic decision-making power to the private sector. An assistant deputy prime minister recently commented in an interview that "Excessive government intervention in the private sector has created, as an unwanted by-product, distortion in the market, and has discouraged private initiative and efficiency of investments which are vital to the growth of a market economy."[25]

Economic "liberalization" *(chayuhwa),* including the encouragement of more private initiative, has in fact become a key government strategy for boosting economic growth in recent years, and one result of the new policy has been to increase the influence of the chaebŏl in the financial sector.

23. Ron Richardson, "The Generals' Vision of Corporate Harmony," *Far Eastern Economic Review,* September 5, 1980, pp. 56–58.

24. See Jeong-Ro Yoon, "The State and Private Capital."

25. Quoted in Seok Ki Kim, "Business Concentration," p. 242.

Since the early 1980s the major chaebŏls have gradually been acquiring ownership of many of the nonbank financial institutions, and between 1981 and 1983 the government auctioned off its shares in the five city banks. As Seok Ki Kim has pointed out, the government tried to keep the banks out of the hands of the biggest capitalists by forbidding the twenty-six largest chaebŏls from participating in the sale and by restricting the maximum single personal or corporate shareholding to 8 percent. The result of the sale, nevertheless, was that the ten largest chaebŏls as a whole managed to acquire anywhere between 12 percent and 52 percent of the various bank shares through their nonbank financial institutions and through family members of the chaebŏl owners.[26]

Although the state still retains basic control of the financial system and monetary policy through the Ministry of Finance, which supervises the Bank of Korea through the Monetary Board, appoints all senior bank officials, and clears major credit allocations, the entry of the chaebŏl into the financial sector in the early 1980s represented a significant institutional change in the government-business relationship that had been forged in 1961. And it may well turn out to be a harbinger of even greater independence, political as well as financial, for South Korea's bourgeoisie in the years to come. Ownership of financial institutions, for example, not only allows the chaebŏl to expand by circumventing certain government regulations, such as on the purchase of real estate, but also facilitates the mobilization of funds for whatever causes or parties the chaebŏl may choose to support.[27] If the political situation in South Korea continues to be liberalized, it would not be at all surprising if the political influence of big business—as the major source of political funding—were to increase proportionately.

Apropos of this, it is important to keep in mind that South Korea's capitalists, though clearly at the mercy of the state in many respects, have been far from passive or unsuccessful in their dealings with it. Both as individuals and as a group through the Federation of Korean Industries (FKI) and other business organizations, they have not hesitated to lobby the government on issues that directly concerned them. The initiative for the 8-3 Decree of 1972, for example, which relieved the chaebŏls of their crushing short-term debt and simultaneously lowered interest rates across

26. Ibid., pp. 283–86.
27. Ibid., p. 285.

the board, originally came from the FKI.[28] Similarly in 1982, in the midst of another serious financial crisis after the second oil shock and the contraction of the world economy, the FKI carried out a successful campaign to persuade the government to lower interest rates. When the rates were officially reduced in June of that year from 17 percent to 10 percent, the chaebŏls were able to cut their interest expenses by over 40 percent—at a substantial cost to the state-controlled banks, including the Bank of Korea, which were lending out money to chaebŏls that had been borrowed from international lenders at much higher rates.[29]

With the liberalization of both the economic and political climate in South Korea after June 1987, South Korea's business leaders began to assert their class interests vis-à-vis the state even more vigorously. The FKI in particular intensified a long-standing campaign for greater corporate autonomy, including the complete independence of the commercial banks. At a joint meeting of Roh's Democratic Justice Party (DJP) and the FKI in October 1988, for example, Chung Ju Yung spoke bluntly about the necessity of guaranteeing a market economy under private leadership and the baneful effects of state interference in company management:

> You [addressing the DJP officials] must guarantee self-regulation in company management based on the principle of a privately led market economy. In the past [we] recognized that it was appropriate for the bureaucratic elite to direct [our] companies. But the passion that entrepreneurs feel in regard to the development of [their] companies is strong, and the era of desktop policy-making by the bureaucracy is over. If bureaucrats interfere in company management by drawing up excessively detailed plans, the result will only be to impede company development.[30]

Yang Chung Mo (Yang Chŏngmo), the founder and former chairman of the disestablished Kukje Group, even filed a lawsuit to regain control of some of his companies, arguing that he was forced by the Chun government to sign over his stock to Hanil Synthetic Fiber at a fraction of its real value. FKI officials openly supported his case, citing it as a classic example of the

28. Ibid., pp. 178–80.
29. Ibid., pp. 263–65.
30. *Han'guk kyŏngje sinmun,* October 27, 1988.

kind of government intervention the business community wants to see come to an end.[31]

In the brief era of parliamentary politics that characterized the first two years of the Roh Tae Woo presidency, the FKI also began to assert its political independence from the government. From their inception chaebŏls had been subject to numerous and substantial unofficial taxes in the form of forced donations to a variety of state-sponsored causes and to ruling party politicians. Such unofficial taxes were particularly onerous during the Fifth Republic, when businessmen were pressured into contributing tens of billions of wŏn to various political, social, and cultural projects and events, including the 1988 Olympics and several organizations in which former president Chun or one of his family members had a personal interest. According to an FKI survey, such unofficial taxes in 1986, even without the inclusion of secret political contributions, were equal to more than 1 percent of total sales and about 7 percent of total labor costs.[32] In 1988, however, the existence of a new government publicly committed to reform and the victory of the opposition parties in the spring parliamentary elections emboldened the FKI to try to establish its own political priorities. Speaking as chairman of the FKI at a press conference after the FKI's joint meeting with the DJP in October 1988, Koo Cha Kyung (Ku Chagyŏng), the head of Lucky-Goldstar, announced that "in the future [we] will collect all political funds openly within the business community, and [we] will distribute [these funds] only to those parties supporting a free-market economy."[33] While the latter half of this statement was clearly aimed more at the opposition parties, and especially at Kim Dae Jung's Party for Peace and Democracy, than at the ruling DJP, it also constituted a warning to the DJP that the FKI intended to use its formidable concentration of wealth politically, through the election process, to push the ruling party into giving more control of the economy to the private sector.

Whether the members of the FKI can actually achieve such economic and political independence, of course, especially given the state's still strong hold over the financial system, remains to be seen. In early 1990 the reemergence of the DJP (now called the Democratic Liberal Party, or DLP) as the majority party in the National Assembly after its merger with two of the

31. Mark Clifford, "Filing for Divorce."
32. Ibid. See also *Korea Newsreview*, November 55, 1988, and April 1, 1989.
33. *Chosŏn ilbo*, October 27, 1988.

three main opposition parties seemed, at least initially, to make the question of business autonomy even more problematic. Nevertheless, the state's various attempts to regulate the growth of the chaebŏls in the 1980s, documented in a new study by Jeong-Ro Yoon, were not particularly successful, in spite of the state's control of the allocation of credit.[34] As Yoon notes, there seems to be an inherent contradiction in the state's policy of promoting economic growth through the concentration of private economic power while at the same time trying to control this process.

Class and Society

Economic and political power do not in themselves constitute or assure the hegemony of any group or class in a given society. Indeed, as Hobsbawm has suggested, the acquisition of such power is only one moment in a continuous process of hegemonic construction.[35] A group or class becomes hegemonic only when it comes to be generally acknowledged and accepted as providing leadership for the society as a whole, and history in fact is richly stocked with forgotten classes, cliques, parties, and other groups who for one reason or another were unable to move beyond the realm of coercion to popular consent. Indeed, one need only look at the recent collapse of the Communist regimes in Eastern Europe for contemporary examples of such failure.

The Korean bourgeoisie is stronger in this respect than the Communist parties of Eastern Europe, but the class continues to be surrounded by an aura of public disapproval and illegitimacy. Within the larger society there is little genuine respect or affection for the chaebŏls, and public criticism of the conglomerates is becoming increasingly vocal and severe. Such criticism has come from the center as well as the Left, and even Chung Ju Yung has admitted that the general public tends to think of the country's big

34. Jeong-Ro Yoon, "The State and Private Capital," p. 207. In the 1992 National Assembly elections Chung's new Unification National Party won a total of 31 seats, which has allowed it to establish a negotiating presence in the assembly. The ruling DLP won 149 out of a total of 299 seats, one seat short of a majority. See *Korea Newsreview,* March 28, 1992, pp. 4–5.

35. Eric J. Hobsbawm, "Gramsci and Marxist Political Theory," in *Approaches to Gramsci,* ed. Anne Showstack Sasson (London: Writers and Readers Publishing Cooperative Society), pp. 28–29.

businessmen as "criminals."[36] Attacks on the chaebŏls by the growing intellectual Left have been especially virulent, as in the following statement by the well-known critical economist and dissident, Pak Hyŏnch'ae:

> These are the people who not only pretend not to see the poverty and ruin of the common people, but who, on the contrary, like "a sterile womb that is never filled," devote themselves entirely to the pursuit of profit. Their minds are fixed only on the interests of a certain favored class or wealthy stratum, with no thought for the welfare of the nation or the wealth of the people, including the prosperity of the nameless masses.[37]

The problem here is really twofold, involving two basic, and often related, aspects of hegemonic leadership in a capitalist society. The first involves the question of material concessions to other classes, and especially to the working class. The second concerns the question of bourgeois moral-philosophical leadership in the society.

Where capitalist hegemony has been relatively strong, as in the West and postwar Japan, it has invariably entailed an agreement by the bourgeoisie to sacrifice certain short-term economic and political advantages for the sake of a more stable capitalist system. To be sure, concessions to workers in the form of higher wages, better working conditions, and the freedom to organize, bargain, and strike have not come easily; in general they have been extracted slowly and in piecemeal fashion from a reluctant business sector in a protracted and often violent historical struggle, and in many cases they have been granted only when the state itself finally took an active role in persuading or forcing the bourgeoisie to concede.[38] In the end, however, the long-term effect has always been to enhance bourgeois hegemony by giving the working class a material interest in the continuance of the capitalist system.

36. Yi Wŏn Su, *Chŏng Chuyŏng: kŭ nŭn nugu in'ga?* [Who is Chung Ju Yung] (Seoul: Chayu Munhak Sa, 1983), p. 133. See also "Korea's Powerhouses under Siege," *Business Week,* November 20, 1989, pp. 52, 55.

37. Pak Hyŏnch'ae, *Han'guk chabonjuui wa minjok undong* [Korean capitalism and the nationalist movement] (Seoul: Han'gilsa, 1984), p. 260.

38. On Japanese labor-management relations, see Andrew Gordon, *The Evolution of Labor Relations in Japan: Heavy Industry 1853–1955* (Cambridge: Council on East Asian Studies, Harvard University, 1985), and Sheldon Garon, *The State and Labor in Modern Japan* (Berkeley: University of California Press, 1987).

In South Korea the bourgeoisie has historically evinced little capacity or willingness to look beyond its own narrowly defined class interests and envision a capitalist system that genuinely embraces and accommodates the working class. One sees a clear demonstration of such myopia in the period of working-class activism precipitated by Roh's declaration of reform in June 1987. To be sure, the new atmosphere of relatively free and aggressive unions threatened to reduce short-term corporate profits, but it also raised the possibility of a transition to a more equal and balanced relationship between capital and labor after more than two decades of labor repression, a change that one might argue was not only politically long overdue but also economically necessary for further development.

The response of the business community to the new atmosphere of relatively free and aggressive unions, however, especially in the beginning, was characterized by fear, anger, and even reaction. In November 1989, for example, South Korea's six major business organizations, the Korean Chamber of Commerce and Industry, the FKI, the Korean Foreign Trade Association, the Korean Federation of Small Businesses, the Korea Employers' Federation, and the Federation of Korean Banks, announced their decision to establish a joint body, the National Federation of Business Organizations, to coordinate the business response to labor problems and to ostracize any company that attempts to follow a separate course of action. Speaking on behalf of the six groups, Yi Tong Ch'an, president of the Korea Employers' Federation, vowed to uphold the principle of "No work, no pay," to oppose "unreasonable wage increases," and to deal forcefully with "violent and subversive acts, as well as unjust demands, such as those that encroach on the areas of management and personnel."[39]

The roots of such intransigience run deep in Korean history. Structural constraints such as a lack of natural resources, a limited source of indigenous capital, and a weak technological base have made it difficult for Korean capitalists to transcend a short-term economic perspective toward the

39. *Han'guk kyŏngje sinmun,* November 17, 1989. See also Asia Watch, *Retreat from Reform: Labor Rights and Freedom of Expression in South Korea* (New York: Asia Watch, November 1990), pp. 27–37, 47–62. According to the Labor Ministry, the number of labor disputes and wildcat strikes has decreased by 28.2 percent and 38 percent, respectively, from the previous year. Ministry officials interpret this decrease as a tendency on the part of workers to resolve disputes through "dialogue and negotiation." See *Korea Newsreview,* December 28, 1991, p. 11. The Asia Watch report, however, suggests that various forms of intimidation and repression (by individual corporations as well as by the government) may also play an important role in accounting for the decrease.

working class. Inexpensive, intelligent labor has, in fact, been Korean capitalism's only real source of comparative advantage throughout the industrialization process, and Korean entrepreneurs since the colonial period have used every means at their disposal, including the use of the police and hired thugs to ensure that labor costs have remained as low as possible. By adopting a policy of export-led growth that oriented all major businesses toward the international market, the Park government also raised the Korean capitalist's interest in low wages to a new height in the 1960s, a concern that continues to preoccupy Korean business even today.

Precisely because of its own interest in export-led growth, the South Korean state, like its colonial predecessor, has taken an active and often violent role in the suppression of labor activities that have threatened to disturb the country's comparative advantage in the international marketplace. Such unequivocal support from the state decade after decade strengthened many Korean businessmen in the belief that they could treat their workers as they chose with virtual impunity. Thus by the mid-1980s, as South Korea's top chaebŏls were moving upward on *Fortune's* list of the world's richest companies, Korean workers were suffering from what many of them regarded as unfairly low pay and from the longest working day in the industrialized world.[40]

Elitist attitudes arising out of Korea's particular capitalist history have also played a part in circumscribing the bourgeois desire or capacity for some form of progressive social compromise with the working class. South Korea, it should be remembered, has never experienced a social revolution. But the peninsula has had a long history of oppressive landlordism that continued into the 1950s, as well as a less well known but statistically significant history of institutionalized slavery that was officially abolished

40. On labor-management and labor-state relations in South Korea, see Jang Jip Choi, "Interest Conflict and Political Control in South Korea: A Study of the Labor Unions in Manufacturing Industries, 1961–1980," Ph.D. diss., University of Chicago, 1983; *Human Rights in Korea, January 1986: An Asia Watch Report* (New York: Asia Watch Committee, 1985), pp. 170–288. See also Edward J. Baker, "'Within the Scope Defined by Law': The Rights of Labor under the Yushin System," paper written for East Asian Legal Studies, Harvard Law School, September 1, 1979; James M. West, "South Korea's Entry into the International Labor Organization: Perspectives on Corporatist Labor Law During a Late Industrial Revolution," *Stanford Journal of International Law* 23 (1987), pp. 477–546. For a comparative study of labor control in East Asia, including South Korea, see Frederic C. Deyo, *Beneath the Miracle: Labor Subordination in the New Asian Industrialism* (Berkeley: University of California Press, 1989). See also Hagen Koo, "From Farm to Factory: Proletarianization in Korea," *American Sociological Review* 55 (October 1990): 669–81.

in 1894 but which seems to have continued to some extent on an informal, private basis in various parts of the country throughout the colonial period and even into the early 1950s. Many of South Korea's capitalists are descended from this traditional land- and slaveowning class and have consciously or unconsciously helped to create an authoritarian corporate culture in which workers have been regarded by managers with varying degrees of paternalism or disdain, but rarely, if ever, as equals or even junior partners in a common enterprise.[41]

Such attitudes are implicit in many of the official company histories, where striking or otherwise disgruntled workers are often depicted as simple, naive, and easily led astray by subversive leftist forces.[42] Even those businessmen who have taken a strong personal interest in their workers' welfare have been loath to acknowledge that the workers have any kind of right to make demands on the company. In July 1987, for example, in the first wave of labor unrest that swept the country in the aftermath of Roh's June 29 proclamation, a highly successful small-medium exporter expressed to this author his moral outrage that his workers had gone on strike even though he had always treated them well, providing them with relatively high wages and bonuses and a superior work environment complete with showers and other facilities. What he could not understand or accept was that the workers themselves might have found his paternalism, however sincere, inadequate to their needs and, more to the point, that they might have felt that they had a legitimate right to voice their grievances. The only explanation he would accept for the strike was that it had been instigated by radical students posing as workers, that is, that the workers had been duped into striking by sophisticated outside agitators.

There might, of course, have been no problem in this particular case had the workers themselves subscribed to the paternalistic view of their company president. But they did not. There has always been a robust egalitarian

41. On traditional Korean landholding and landlordism, see Palais, *Politics and Policy,* pp. 58–85. On Korean slavery, see Ellen Salem, "Slavery in Medieval Korea," Ph.D. diss., Columbia University, 1978; Palais, "Slavery and Slave Society in the Koryŏ Period," *Journal of Korean Studies* 5 (1984), pp. 173–90; Orlando Patterson, *Slavery and Social Death: A Comparative Study* (Cambridge: Harvard University Press, 1982), passim. The question of how long and to what extent private slavery continued on an informal basis in Korean society has never been clearly answered, but even today one can find Koreans of landlord background who speak of having had slaves *(nobi)* in their household as late as the Korean War.

42. See, for example, Pak Inwhan, ed., *Kyŏnbang yuksimnyŏnsa* [Sixty years of Kyŏngbang] (Seoul: CH Kyŏngbang, 1980), pp. 268, 269.

ethic in Korean popular culture that has coexisted with or confronted the hierarchical values of traditional Korean aristocratic society.[43] The absence of a social revolution in South Korea, moreover, has not prevented the influx of liberal, or even radical, ideas into the country, which have interacted with this indigenous egalitarianism. Indeed, the cultural impact of South Korea's close relationship with the United States since 1945 has ensured that such ideas would spread, even if official U.S. policy toward South Korea has often tolerated undemocratic political practices in the country for the sake of an overarching geopolitical concern with Communist containment.

Such ideas have found fertile ground in South Korea's oppressed working class. They have been widely diffused as a result of the rapid spread of universal education since 1945 (The literacy rate in South Korea is over 90 percent). And they have also been vigorously propagated among the working class in the past two decades by dedicated students and Christian church groups such as the Protestant-sponsored Urban Industrial Mission and the Young Catholic Workers, which have also educated workers with respect to their legal rights and taken a prominent role in a wide range of labor issues and activities, including the formation of autonomous labor unions. The result has been a dramatic increase in working-class consciousness and militancy, which first burst forth on a large scale in 1979–80 during the brief hiatus in authoritarian rule that followed the assassination of Park Chung Hee. The subsequent seizure of power and imposition of a harsh antilabor regime by a new military junta led by Chun Doo Hwan was successful in temporarily containing the new labor activism, but it erupted again on an even more massive scale as soon as the government relaxed its grip in 1987. To its own detriment, South Korean business has largely been slow to recognize the historical significance of this new phenomenon or reluctant to come to terms with it.[44]

Hegemony, Gramsci frequently reminds us, is not only a matter of material concessions. It is also a question of moral-philosophical leadership of the entire society by the dominant class or group. Such leadership is of course ideological in the sense that it supports the economic and political

43. This is one of the main themes of the classic work by anthropologist Vincent Brandt, *A Korean Village: Between Farm and Sea* (Cambridge: Harvard University Press, 1971).

44. See Choi, "Interest Conflict," pp. 67–168; Deyo, *Beneath the Miracle*, pp. 135–40; Koo, "From Farm to Factory," pp. 677–78.

interests of the dominant class, but the ideology that gives rise to such leadership should not be understood in a purely negative sense simply as a "false consciousness" imposed on subordinate classes and groups through various forms of control or manipulation. Ideological hegemony in the Gramscian sense is attained only when the dominant class or group succeeds in uniting the people around itself so that its development or expansion comes to be seen as "the motor force of a universal expansion, of a development of all the 'national' energies." The world view of the dominant class thus becomes the "common sense" of the society as a whole, "implicitly manifest in art, in law, in economic activity, and in all manifestations of individual and collective life."[45]

The process by which such hegemony is achieved is complicated and uncertain, contingent on a fortuitous historical convergence between the interests of the dominant class or group and the interests of the rest of the society. Capitalist ideological hegemony in the West, for example, has rested to no small degree on the historical role of the bourgeoisie not only in generating national wealth but also in championing revolutionary values of economic and political freedom that have had great popular appeal. To be sure, such values were not promoted simply for their own sake; they also served fundamental bourgeois interests at the time. In the end, however, this largely accidental conjunction of class interest with popular values and aspirations provided the historical basis for what has so far proved to be an enduring capitalist ideological hegemony.

In South Korea the bourgeoisie's ideological hegemony has been weak to nonexistent. In part this may be explained by the still relatively weak political position of the class relative to the state. Throughout the history of Korean capitalism, it has been the state that has structured and controlled the educational and legal systems and acted as ultimate censor over the bourgeois press and publishing industry. While the interests of the class and the state have often overlapped, the state's basic position toward the bourgeoisie has generally been ambivalent, if not suspicious, an attitude that Park, for example, made quite explicit soon after he seized power in 1961.[46]

45. Gramsci, *Prison Notebooks,* pp. 53, 181–82, 260, 328.

46. See Park Chung Hee, *Our Nation's Path: Ideology of Social Reconstruction* (Seoul: Hollym Corporation, 1965), pp. 217–19. The original work was published in Korean in 1962 as *Uri minjok ŭi nagal kil.*

As already suggested, however, increased political power would not in itself necessarily enhance bourgeois ideological hegemony. The growth of a notably freer private press in the past decade, for example, has resulted in greater, not less, criticism of the capitalist elite. Once again the origins of the problem are deeply rooted in Korean history and culture, especially in the origins and development of Korean capitalism itself. Unlike their counterparts in the West, Korean capitalists have not in general enjoyed a felicitous historical convergence of class interest with popular values and aspirations. Indeed, the two have more often than not been at odds.

One area of conflict has involved what Keynes has called "the essential characteristic of Capitalism, namely the dependence upon an intense appeal to the money-making and money-loving instincts of individuals."[47] Such instincts are no less common to Koreans than to other people, and the existence of private property is a well-established fact of premodern, as well as modern, Korean history. One looks in vain, however, for anything remotely resembling the ideas of Adam Smith or John Locke in either elite or popular Korean culture. The pursuit of personal profit has never been raised to the level of a moral precept in Korea, and even today the right of private property, though guaranteed by law in South Korea, falls far short of being the sancrosanct tenet it has long been in the West.[48]

This is so not only because of Korea's different cultural legacy but also because of the relative lateness of its capitalist development. Capitalism as a conscious strategy of national development antedated its development as a socioeconomic system, and the original formulation of what might be called a Korean capitalist morality came not from a bourgeoisie, which did not exist at the time, or from an intellectual elite who, like Smith and Locke, were themselves enmeshed in an already developing capitalist society, but rather from late Chosŏn reformist scholars like Yu Kilchun (1856–1914). Such men were steeped in a long neo-Confucian tradition that emphasized communitarian values and were interested in capitalism primarily as a way to augment the wealth and power of the country to save it from imperialist domination. Ideas of Confucianism, nationalism, and capitalism thus all fused in the late nineteenth-century Korean intellectual milieu to produce

47. John Maynard Keynes, *The End of Laissez-Faire* (London: Hogarth Press, 1926), p. 50.
48. See Hahm Pyong-Choon, *The Korean Political Tradition and Law: Essays in Korean Law and Legal History* (Seoul: Hollym Corporation, 1971), pp. 78–79, 187–204.

a moral vision of capitalist activity stressing national needs and goals and denigrating the purely private pursuit of wealth.

This vision has continued to inform all discourse on capitalist development in Korea and to provide a moral ideal against which Korean capitalists have been publicly judged. Since there is virtually no allowance for the pursuit of personal profit in the ideal, Korea's capitalists have been forced, in effect, into a more or less permanent state of siege and hypocrisy with respect to their most fundamental activity. Their only form of defense on this issue has been to commission a plethora of justificative publications, including official corporate histories, biographies, and ghost-written autobiographies. As in the following excerpt from a 1979 biography of Kim Yongwan, one of South Korea's business doyens and the original chairman of the FKI, such works invariably stress the unselfish, nationalistic orientation of the businessmen in question. The passion and excess with which Korean capitalists feel compelled to deny the element of personal profit-seeking suggests not only the lady protesting too much but also the extent to which such profit-seeking is considered unseemly or unacceptable by the South Korean public.

> As our economy shifted in the direction of a highly industrialized society in the midst of adverse domestic and international conditions, [Kim Yongwan] . . . as FKI chairman, always kept watch against excessive selfishness on the part of entrepreneurs and devoted all his energies to seeing that business profits were returned to society. . . . Like Kim Sŏngsu and Kim Yŏnsu, who never desired the profits of [their] business for their own personal consumption and enjoyment . . . Kim Yongwan also based his behavior on the principles of frugality and moderation, incorporating these principles into [his] daily life. Thoroughly imbued with [a spirit of] public consciousness, he always put the welfare of the state and nation first and never worked for personal profit or prestige.[49]

Capitalists in other countries with a Confucian legacy, most notably Japan and Taiwan, have experienced a similar problem with respect to

49. Tongŭn Ki'nyŏm Saŏphoe, ed., *Tongŭn Kim Yongwan* [Kim Yongwan] (Seoul: Tongŭn Ki'nyŏm Saŏphoe, 1979), p. 8. Kim Sŏngsu and his younger Kim Yŏnsu were members of the Koch'ang Kim family mentioned earlier. See Eckert, *Offspring of Empire*.

public attitudes toward private profit, and one can find ample evidence of a similar business hagiography at work there as well.[50] In South Korea, however, the problem has been intensified by other factors peculiar to the country's history and mode of capitalist development. The question of nationalism provides a case in point. There would undoubtedly be more tolerance for personal and corporate profit seeking in South Korea if the country's bourgeoisie had impeccable nationalist credentials. In fact, they do not.

The vision of a moral capitalism first articulated by Yu Kilchun and echoed by virtually every writer on the subject thereafter has defined "nation" in essentially two ways: first, in political terms as a nation-state in the midst of other competing, and potentially hostile, nation-states; and secondly, in human-cultural terms as a group of people who identify themselves as Korean. The moral role of the capitalist in this vision is to enhance the strength and integrity of the former and to enrich the life of the latter. As Yu himself wrote over a century ago:

> If within [his own] country the merchant, carrying out his work with skill and in accordance with the proper moral principles, provides comfort and benefit to the common people and prosperity to the state, it may well be said that his merit *(kong)* is comparable to [that of] the general who defends the country and that his virtue *(tŏk)* is the same as [that of] the prime minister who governs it. In terms of its great moral standing and glorious work, one may indeed say that [commerce] is manly statecraft, the occupation of a hero.[51]

The Korean bourgeoisie has compiled a very mixed historical record in

50. On attitudes toward capitalism in late Imperial China, see Benjamin Schwartz, *In Search of Wealth and Power: Yen Fu and the West* (Cambridge: Belknap Press, Harvard University Press, 1964). On Japan, see Albert M. Craig, "Fukuzawa Yukichi: The Philosophical Foundations of Meiji Nationalism," in *Political Development in Modern Japan,* ed. Robert E. Ward (Princeton: Princeton University Press, 1968), pp. 99–148, and Byron K. Marshall, *Capitalism and Nationalism in Prewar Japan: The Ideology of the Business Elite, 1868–1941* (Stanford: Stanford University Press, 1967), pp. 1–12. My information concerning business hagiography in Taiwan comes from Thomas Gold, professor of Sociology at the University of California at Berkeley, during a discussion at the American Academic of Arts and Sciences in Cambridge in May 1989.

51. Yu Kilchun, *Sŏyu kyŏnmun* in *Yu Kilchun chŏnsŏ,* vol. 5 (Seoul: Ilchogak, 1971), p. 390.

both of these areas of enjoined nationalist endeavor. There is little question that South Korea's remarkable economic growth since the 1960s and its concomitant new prestige in the world, evinced most recently by the holding of the 1988 Summer Olympics in Seoul, have made many, perhaps most, South Koreans feel proud, and businessmen like Hyundai's Chung Ju Yung have repeatedly stressed in their public statements the role of the private sector in bringing such changes about. Chung has even used the need to compete successfully in an intensely competitive international economic arena as a justification for the failure of Korean capitalists to "project a sense of morality."[52]

Despite such public pride in the country's new international economic status, however, the fact that the process of private capital accumulation in South Korea has taken place not only through a dependence on the state but also through a dependence on foreign capital, technology, and markets has left a number of South Koreans feeling uncomfortable and exposed the businessmen to charges of "compradorism" from students and the intellectual elite.[53] Chung, for one, has vehemently denied that he has been anything less than a "national capitalist,"[54] but it has been impossible for him to deny that his company's very successful Hyundai Excel car has been to no small extent the product of Japanese technology, purchased at the cost of certain corporate concessions in equity and management to Mitsubishi.[55] For the typical American economist, with his or her eye fixed on South Korea's soaring post-1961 gross national product (GNP), such transnational capitalist interaction may seem not only uncontroversial but also

52. Chŏng Chuyŏng, *I Ach'im edo sŏlleim ŭl an'go* [Feeling the thrill again this morning] (Seoul: Samsŏng Ch'ulpansa, 1986), p. 353. Chung said: "There are no businessmen whose behavior is based solely on morality like religious men. If a businessman acts like a religious man, how can he undertake his responsibilities in the overseas market, where the competition is intense? How can he win out over the advanced countries? If all businessmen were to project a sense of morality in [everything] they said and did like moralists and religious men, not a single one would be victorious in international competition."

53. See Carter J. Eckert, Ki-baik Lee, Young Ick Lew, Michael Robinson, and Edward W. Wagner, *Korea Old and New: A History* (Cambridge: Korea Institute, Harvard University, 1990), chap. 20.

54. Chŏng Chuyŏng, *I Ach'im edo*, p. 360.

55. According to the original joint-venture agreement between Hyundai and Mitsubishi, the latter acquired a 10 percent equity share in Hyundai Motor Company and the right to appoint two part-time directors. See Yi Yangsŏp, *Hyŏndae chadongch'a ishimnyŏnsa 1967–1987* [Twenty years of Hyundai, 1967–1987] (Seoul: Hyŏndae Chadongch'a Chusik Hoesa, 1987), pp. 439–45. See also *Business Week*, December 23, 1985.

good economic strategy. For South Koreans, however, the historical experience of imperialism and colonialism has made such interaction a matter of nationalist concern as well as a sensitive political issue. During the decades of colonial rule, for example, the Korean bourgeoisie was willing to trade its national identity for economic growth, and public suspicions of capitalist priorities continue to run deep, fed both by historical memory and by an increasingly open press and publishing industry, through which a variety of critical perspectives and reassessments of Korean history are now being publicly aired.

The bourgeois record on providing "comfort and benefit to the common people" has also been a source of public criticism. A key issue here has been the question of equity in the distribution of wealth, an area in which the material and ideological aspects of the problem of capitalist hegemony in the Korean context clearly overlap. By contrast, Western capitalists since the Industrial Revolution have been relatively cushioned from personal accountability on this score by Smithian and Darwinian logic. Such logic has allowed them to argue that inequity is an inevitable consequence of some men pursuing their self-interest with more passion and skill than others, a system of distribution by natural selection that Keynes compared to giraffes with the longest necks getting nearest to the trees "by dint of starving out the others."[56] In 1892, for example, at the height of early American capitalism, the authors of a book on the "marvelous career" of financier and railroad speculator Jay Gould wrote that

> the equitable distribution of wealth, the riches that arise from the soil, the climate, the intelligence, the toil, the skill, the thrift of the country at large is a most difficult problem, and has thus far been an impossible task. If there is a mass of value in the possession of one man equal to $100,000,000, can we be quite sure that in the long run and in the largest way, it would be better to parcel it out into a hundred fortunes of a million each, or that any further subdivision would more completely answer the highest social requirements.[57]

No South Korean businessmen would dare take such a public stand on

56. Keynes, *The End of Laissez-Faire*, pp. 29–30.
57. Murat Halstead and J. Frank Beale, Jr., *Life of Jay Gould: How He Made His Millions* (Clare, Mich.: Edgewood Publishing Co., 1989), p. 7.

the question of distribution. While it has probably been more honored in the breach than in practice throughout Korean history, the moral principle of equity in the distribution of wealth is as old, perhaps, as Korean society itself and deeply embedded in traditional philosophy and statecraft.[58] Through Yu Kilchun and others it has also become a cardinal precept of the moral capitalist vision. Yu wrote, for example, that although a merchant is entitled to a certain profit *(nogo)* for his efforts, there are limits to what constitute "reasonable" accumulation. Most important, such accumulation must not interfere with the merchant's responsibility to provide for the people. Indeed, according to Yu, the state has an absolute, unequivocal right and responsibility to prevent anyone from "monopolizing the profits of the common people."[59]

What, then, is the bourgeois record on this crucial issue? A few basic facts will serve to identify the problem. In 1985 the top ten chaebŏls alone had aggregate net sales that amounted to about 80 percent of South Korea's GNP, or about 16 percent in terms of value added. In both cases this represented a continuous expansion over time: in 1974, for example, the figures were, respectively, about 15 percent and 5 percent.[60] The concentration of wealth has also been augmented by intermarriage among the leading chaebŏl families.[61]

Such concentration of wealth may be statistically lower in South Korea than in other countries, as many economists have pointed out.[62] But in South Korea, it has been steadily increasing and the moral basis for such inequity has never existed. Furthermore, as noted above, until 1987 the continuous enrichment and expansion of the private sector has taken place in conjunction with, and to no small extent because of, the economic and political suppression of organized labor. Since 1970 there has, in fact, been a perceptible trend toward income inequality (as measured by the Gini coefficient).[63]

It is hardly surprising, therefore, that public criticism of the chaebŏl has

58. See Hahm, *The Korean Political Tradition and Law,* pp. 78–79; see also Brandt, *A Korean Village,* p. 77.

59. Yu Kilchun, *Sŏyu kyŏnmun,* pp. 382–83.

60. See Seok Ki Kim, "Business Concentration," pp. 2–3.

61. See Pak Yongjŏng, "Chaebŏl: ise wa inmaektŭl" [Chaebŏl: The second generation and personal connections], *Wŏlgan Chosŏn* (September 1980): 270–86.

62. Jones and Sakong, *Government, Business, and Entrepreneurship,* pp. 266–67.

63. See Hagen Koo, "The Political Economy of Income Distribution in South Korea: The Impact of the State's Industrialization Policies," *World Development* 12 (1984): 1029 – 37.

also been steadily growing. Indeed, the popular term chaebŏl itself carries the negative connotation of "business clique," much as the equivalent Japanese term *zaibatsu* did in prewar Japan, and it is never used by the businessmen themselves (who prefer the term "group" or "big company"). Although more sympathetic critics have called the chaebŏl a "necessary evil,"[64] it has become increasingly common for the chaebŏl to be called "octopus tentacles" *(mun'ŏbal),* in reference to their concentrated and expanding power over the South Korean economy.[65] A particular source of public anger has been the constant speculation of the chaebŏl in real estate, which has diverted capital from productive resources and sent the price of land in certain areas of Seoul and other cities to astronomical levels.[66] In a recent study of South Korean business concentration, for example, Seok Ki Kim concluded that between 1960 and 1972 "the *chaebols*—especially the largest ones—possessed (and have continuously possessed) large amounts of real estate, of which a considerable portion was non-business related, idle properties. In many cases, the *chaebols'* decision to build factories was more influenced by the prospective land price hike than by efforts to organize the production."[67] According to Kim, since 1972 such speculation by chaebŏls has continued, despite attempts by the government to control it.[68]

Given the above facts, it has been very difficult for South Korea's capitalists to mount a successful defense against public criticism. Perhaps the strongest argument they have been able to muster is that they have tried to return some of their profits to society by using portions of their corporate shareholdings to set up tax-free private social welfare foundations, which, in turn, have used the money to build hospitals and support needy students and scholars.[69] Such private foundations, however, are still relatively new to South Korea (most were established after 1970), and their combined donations still total less than 2 percent of the official government budget for

64. See, for example, Chosŏn Ilbo Kyŏngjebu, *Chaebŏl ishiboshi* [Chaebŏl: The twenty-fifth hour] (Seoul: Tonggwang Ch'ulpansa, 1982), p. 11.

65. Chŏng Chuyŏng, *I Ach'im edo,* p. 351. Another popular phrase is "chaebŏl republic" *(chaebŏl konghwaguk)* in reference to South Korea. Ibid.

66. Ibid.

67. Seok Ki Kim, "Business Concentration," p. 130.

68. Ibid., pp. 287–88.

69. Chŏng Chuyŏng, *I Ach'im edo,* p. 358. A series of articles on some of the major foundations appeared in the *Maeil kyŏngje sinmun* beginning on June 2, 1989.

social welfare.[70] Some critics have charged, moreover, that the foundations permit "legalized tax evasion" by the chaebŏls and that so long as they remain under chaebŏl influence, they can be used by the chaebŏl owner and his family to retain control over companies that might otherwise be forced by the government or popular pressure to go public.[71] The South Korean public thus remains skeptical of the motives behind the establishment of the foundations in spite of their documented contribution to worthy causes. As Chung Ju Yung has lamented: "I continue to think that using a social welfare foundation to return the profits of [our parent company] Hyundai Construction to poor people who truly need help is the best course of action. But the public is not able to understand my true feeling [about this]. That's because the people have no trust [in me]."[72]

Chung has tried other, even less successful arguments to counter criticism on the equity issue. In a confrontation with students at Pusan National University in 1984, he suggested that the distribution of wealth is a problem for the government (through the tax system) rather than for business, a view that can hardly be expected to find favor in a society that insists that its capitalists be moral men and take responsibility for the results of their actions.[73] He went on to propose still another argument, based on the assumption that there were many different kinds of "haves" and "have-nots" in the world and that monied "haves" were not necessarily better off than educated or talented "haves" without money. Indeed, he suggested that although he himself might be a monied "have," he was also very much a "have not" in terms of education. The implication of Chung's remarks, of course, was that economic inequity was not really a social problem because everything balanced out in the end: although some people lacked money, they nevertheless had other things that even people with money did not:

70. Ku-Hyun Jung, "Corporate Philanthropy in Korea," paper presented at the International Symposium on Organized Private Philanthropy in East and Southeast Asia, Bangkok, August 7–9, 1989, pp. 21–22. I am grateful to Matthew R. Auer of the Fletcher School of Law and Diplomacy for bringing this paper to my attention.

71. See *Maeil kyŏngje sinmun,* June 2, 1989, p. 18. The first major government effort to induce the firms to go public was in May 1974, but it was not very successful: see Seok Ki Kim, "Business Concentration," pp. 161–62. See also Chŏng, *I Ach'im edo,* p. 351, for a popular critique of the chaebŏls for refusing to go public; Chung Ju Yung's response is on pp. 357–58.

72. Chŏng Chuyŏng, *I Ach'im edo,* p. 358.

73. Ibid., p. 361.

> People talk today about the haves and the have-nots. As for me, when it comes to talking about the haves and the have-nots, I don't consider only people with money as haves. There are many [kinds of] haves in addition to those [people]. I think that among these [other haves], people with a learned background have the best [possession]. If my parents, as they were passing from the scene, had asked [me] to choose between [a legacy of] property and [a legacy of] learning, I would have chosen knowledge. So I think that it's a mistake for our society today to judge someone a have or a have-not on the basis of whether or not [he] has a lot of money. Of course a person with money is clearly a have, but a person with education is also no less a have [than a person with money]. A poor person with musical talent is also a have. If [a person] has [some kind of] skill, he is also a have. When [a person] has something that another person does not have, that person has to be considered a have. Money is not the one and only measure of inequality.[74]

Given Korean sensibilities on this issue, Chung's attempt simply to dismiss the problem of economic inequity with Panglossian optimism must surely rank as the most unconvincing of all such statements in defense of the chaebŏls' concentration of wealth, especially coming, as it did, from a man who at the time was personally at the top of the tax rolls in the country and who was presiding over one of the largest conglomerates in the world.[75] But it reflects, at the same time, the paucity of moral arguments available to the chaebŏl in trying to counter public criticism against them. For in spite of their great wealth and growing political power, South Korea's capitalist elites have been forced to live and operate in an ethical world that is not of their own making.

Perhaps the greatest stumbling block to capitalist ideological hegemony has been the bourgeoisie's long and special relationship with the Korean state. Here again there are two aspects to the problem. The first concerns the means by which Korean businessmen have acquired their wealth. Since Yu Kilchun all Korean exponents of the moral capitalist vision have insisted not only that businessmen be unselfish and patriotic but also that they earn their money on the basis of their own character and abilities, developed

74. Ibid.
75. See *Business Week,* December 23, 1985.

through study and experience, rather than on the basis of any special favors or privileges from the authorities. South Korean intellectuals, for example, both conservative and radical, have often held up the spiritually oriented, self-made "Calvinist type" entrepreneur celebrated in the work of Max Weber, especially his famous *Protestant Ethic and the Spirit of Capitalism,* as concrete historical models of exemplary businessmen.[76]

On the basis of such standards, much of the great private wealth in South Korea has come to be publicly regarded as "illicit accumulation." Although there is no question that South Korea's capitalist elites have exhibited personal diligence and intelligence in developing their companies, especially in the post-1961 period, it is also clear from numerous studies that they have historically been the recipients of a cornucopia of special privileges and favors from the state. As noted above, the whole process of capital accumulation in South Korea since the colonial period has taken place in one way or another under state auspices or through state-controlled organizations like the special and commercial banks—to such an extent, in fact, that one might well speak of Korean capitalists as state-made men. Merely the fact that most of the capital used for investment has come from state-controlled domestic banks or from foreign lenders supplied with ROK guarantees (debt-equity ratios of 8:1, for example, have not been unusual) and that South Korean businessmen have been able to count on state assistance and bailouts in times of trouble has in itself considerably reduced the element of personal risk-taking in the South Korean entrepreneurial environment.[77]

Such special treatment of the capitalist elite by the state has been one of the main foci of public attacks on big business, and on at least one occasion, in the highly charged political environment of 1960–61 that followed the ouster of Syngman Rhee, such attacks came close to dismantling the existing capitalist structure. As when confronted with other kinds of criticism, South Korea's businessmen have found themselves without a strong defense. Threatened with major confiscations in 1961 for "profiteering" under the Rhee regime, for example, the business community had little recourse with

76. See Pak Hyŏnch'ae, *Han'guk chabonchuŭi wa minjok undong,* p. 259.

77. See Seok Ki Kim, "Business Concentration," passim; Jeong-Ro Yoon, "The State and Private Capital," pp. 148–203, passim. See also Kyong-Dong Kim, "Political Factors in the Formation of the Entrepreneurial Elite in South Korea," *Asian Survey* 16 (January–June 1976): 465–77, and Lawrence Minard, "The Fragile Miracle on the Han," *Forbes,* February 11, 1985, pp. 38–41. See also Hagen Koo and Eun Mee Kim, "The Developmental State and Capital Accumulation in South Korea."

respect to changing public opinion but to play on South Korean fears of "communization" and a North Korean takeover.[78] More recently Chung Ju Yung has tried to argue that special government treatment for the capitalists is now a thing of the past, a phenomenon of the 1950s that had involved only "one or two" companies. The facts, as we have seen, do not support such a view. And even Chung himself, while insisting that what critics have called "collusion with the government" has been nothing more than "cooperation" for the sake of national economic development, has been forced to acknowledge that government and big business have shared an "indivisible" relationship because the business sector "has existed as part of the state."[79]

There is another aspect to the government-business relationship that has tarnished the business elite's moral standing in South Korean society: the support for authoritarian politics that has been an integral part of that relationship. When capitalism first began to develop in Korea, there was considerable expectation among its intellectual supporters that the Korean bourgeoisie would follow in the steps of its Western counterpart and become a revolutionary social force for democratic political development. In 1921, for example, an editorial in *Tonga ilbo* proclaimed that "it is no exaggeration to say that the gradual rise of a commercial and industrial class is providing the motive force for the democratization of politics."[80]

Subsequent history, however, proved this statement to be not so much an exaggeration as a misreading of the conditions under which capitalism was developing on the peninsula. The various Western bourgeoisies emerged for the most part in conflict with politically restrictive or authoritarian state structures that sought to block capitalist development, and they had a natural interest in overturning or reforming these structures along more democratic lines. In Korea, however, from its earliest burst of growth in the 1920s to its recent position of economic preeminence, the bourgeoisie has coexisted more or less comfortably with a variety of authoritarian governments, none of which has ever deliberately sought to hinder capitalist growth, and most of which have positively supported it. As a result, the Korean bourgeoisie has never had a compelling material incentive to promote democratic politics. On the contrary, the structural commitment to

78. See Sungjoo Han, *The Failure of Democracy,* pp. 165–70, esp. p. 169.
79. Chŏng Chuyŏng, *I Ach'im edo,* pp. 352–53.
80. *Tonga ilbo,* May 11, 1921.

low labor costs discussed above has given the class a certain vested interest in the perpetuation of authoritarian rule. It is worth noting, for example, that the impetus for significant political change in South Korea, with the exception, perhaps, of Chung Ju Yung's disastrous attempt to enter politics in 1992, has never come from the business elite; it has come instead from activist students, workers, and members of a politically frustrated middle class, all of whom, in various ways and to differing degrees, have been critical of the government-chaebŏl political and economic nexus.[81]

South Korea's capitalists have in fact paid a high price in terms of public esteem for their historical accommodation to authoritarianism, especially in a postcolonial world of proliferating democratic values. In South Korea nearly every government since 1948 has suffered from a legitimacy problem that has been connected in one way or another with a perceived violation of democratic principles, a problem that has helped shape a largely negative public attitude toward big business. Few Koreans today would argue that the country's capitalist elite has played an historically progressive role in the country's political development.[82] Indeed, the generally reactionary role of the bourgeoisie in this regard has helped provide the more radical side of the South Korean political spectrum with a rationale for advocating the restructuring or even abolition of the existing capitalist system.[83]

Conclusion

Joseph Schumpeter has emphasized that capitalism is not a stationary system but an evolutionary process of continuous "creative destruction," a point worth noting as we try to assess the stability of the capitalist structure in South Korea.[84] In the West, capitalism has exhibited two great

81. See Eckert, *Offspring of Empire,* part 3; "Authoritarianism and Protest, 1948–1988," in Eckert et al., *Korea Old and New: A History,* chap. 19; *Human Rights in Korea,* pp. 1–89. See also Hagen Koo, "Middle Classes, Democratization, and Class Formation: The Case of South Korea," in *Theory and Society* 20 (1991): 485–509.

82. See, for example, a discussion on this subject by several well-known scholars, published in the mainstream monthly magazine *Sindonga:* "Han'guk ŭi chabonjuŭi wa chayujuŭi [Capitalism and liberalism in Korea], *Sindonga* (August 1986): 27–95.

83. For a comprehensive view of current trends and debates in radical South Korean politics and see Pak Hyŏnch'ae and Cho Hŭiyŏn, eds., *Han'guk sahoe kusŏngch'e nonjaeng* [Debates on Korean social formations], 2 vols. (Seoul: Tosŏ Ch'ulp'an, 1989).

84. Joseph A. Schumpeter, *Capitalism, Socialism, and Democracy* (New York: Harper Colophon Books, 1942), pp. 82–84.

strengths throughout its long history. One, of course, has been an undeniable propensity to stimulate economic production and growth, the material results of which have awed even the greatest critics of capitalism, including Karl Marx. The other has been a remarkable resilience and flexibility, which time and time again have confounded the prophets of doom. To some extent one can see these same strengths at work in South Korea today. Certainly the productive forces unleashed by the country's particular form of capitalism have been prodigious, capturing the attention not only of the Koreans themselves but of the whole world. And in spite of a certain structural rigidity discussed above, the capitalist system in South Korea has also been undergoing a process of change, especially in the last decade, and does not in any case seem to be on the verge of collapse.

One might go even further. It might well be argued that political and economic change since 1987 has created an opportunity for the South Korean bourgeoisie to strengthen its hegemony as never before. The opening up of the political system, for example, has allowed private Korean capital, now impressive by any standard, to assert itself in the electoral process with more confidence and independence than at any time in the past. Further democratization is also likely to enhance bourgeois political power, as it has historically in the Western capitalist democracies and Japan. The growing complexity and competitiveness of a new global market, moreover, especially since the demise of the Soviet Union and the end of the Cold War, may also lead to a greater role for the business elite in the national management of the economy, especially if that economy seems to be faltering under the direction of professional politicians and bureaucrats.

Nevertheless, it must be said in the final analysis that the evolution of Korean capitalism still has a good way to go before the *chaebŏl* achieve the kind of hegemonic position in South Korea that the bourgeoisie has long enjoyed in the West. The South Korean state is still, for the moment, the master of capital, especially through its control of the financial system. Even more important in the long run, perhaps, is the problem that Korean capitalists face in winning the hearts and minds of the people. As this chapter tried to show, a highly critical, even negative, attitude toward the chaebŏl runs deep in South Korean society and cuts across class and occupational lines. Among the most critical voices are those of the country's intelligentsia, the very group that, as Gramsci notes, is most instrumental in the articulation of a particular society's hegemonic philosophy or world view.[85] If and when bourgeois hegemony is ever attained, it will involve not merely a political triumph of class over state but also an ideological victory, a signification that South Korea's capitalists have finally succeeded in identifying themselves more closely with the aspirations and values of a wide spectrum of classes and groups in the society.

85. Gramsci, *Prison Notebooks,* pp. 5–23.

4
The State, *Minjung*, and the Working Class in South Korea

Hagen Koo

One of the most remarkable phenomena to occur in South Korea in recent decades was its swift transition from a relatively simple agrarian society to a fully class divided industrial society. In the 1950s or even in the 1960s, one rarely heard people talking about social classes in Korea. To be sure, there was much concern over widespread poverty and unemployment, but the language of classes was largely absent. To the extent that it did exist, it was a language referring to the rich and the poor, or to broad social strata, such terms as *sangryuch'ŭng* (upper strata), *chungryuch'ŭng* (middle strata), *sŭhminch'ŭng* (the underprivileged), or *haryuch'ŭng* (lower strata). But none of these terminologies conjures up an image of conflictual class relations or a relationship involving domination and subordination.

In the 1970s, however, the word *minjung* (people or the masses) emerged as a powerful term for political struggle and social movement. *Minjung* implies a broad alliance of "alienated classes," people alienated from power and from the distribution of the fruits of economic growth.[1] It became a

1. Wang-Sang Han, *Minjung sahoehak* [*Minjung* sociology] (Seoul: Chongro Sŏchŭk, 1984).

powerful opposition ideology and a political symbol, and provided a new social identity for all who participated in political, social, and cultural movements in opposition to the authoritarian system. Simultaneously, more specific terms for class, such as *kŭnro kyech'ŭng* (workers' stratum), *nodongja kyeg'ŭp* (working class), *chungsanch'ŭng* (middle strata), and *chungan kyeg'ŭp* (middle class), have also come into frequent use. The term *chaebŏl* (conglomerate capital), though not a new word, assumed a more specific class meaning as its members and its boundary have become more clearly defined.

But it is during the 1980s that class became an unmistakable reality in South Korea. Gradually, the working class emerged as the most visible class force, asserting its independence from a broad *minjung* alliance. Despite harsh repression, the labor movement has grown and workers acquired a relatively high level of class identity and political consciousness. The middle class, too, has emerged as an important political force, exerting pressure for political and economic liberalization on the authoritarian regime.

Political liberalization since 1987 has opened a large arena for the development of class politics. The violent labor unrest that erupted during the summer of 1987 and spring of 1988 and the state's temporary inability to deal with it effectively demonstrated the working class's potential power, which had been growing steadily during the previous two decades. Alongside blue-collar workers, many white-collar workers also organized unions to demand improvement of working conditions and autonomy from state control. Partly in response to working-class activism, the mainstream middle classes gradually turned conservative, supporting the reactionary government of Roh Tae Woo. South Korea has indeed become a class society in which the social dynamics emanating from class relations influence the direction and form of social and political change.

The purpose of this chapter is to explore the formation of the working class in South Korea in the course of rapid export-led industrialization during the past three decades. As is well understood among scholars, class formation is not an all-or-nothing phenomenon but a continuous process within which class consciousness and organization develop or regress along a continuum.[2] One critical question to be investigated is to what extent, in what form, and by what mechanisms the individuals who occupy a common

2. See Ira Katznelson, "Working-Class Formation: Constructing Cases and Comparisons," in *Working-Class Formation: Nineteenth-Century Patterns in Western Europe and the United States*, ed. Katznelson and Aristide Zolberg (Princeton: Princeton University Press, 1986).

class position developed a collective consciousness and organizations to act on their common interests. In this analysis, special attention is paid to the role of the state in shaping the dominant pattern of capital accumulation and the labor regime in Korean industries, thereby affecting the nature of working-class struggles. The major thesis of this study is that the formation of the working class in Korea has occurred at a remarkable pace, partly because of the sheer rapidity and intensity of industrialization itself and partly because of the state's intervention in the economy and in labor relations. This analysis, therefore, highlights the important role played by the state in the process of class formation.

The history of Korean working-class activism is not continuous, but involves two historical periods, separated by a relatively long period of political turmoil and internal war. The first period, 1920s–1948, begins with Japanese colonialism and extends to the postwar years. This was a time of active labor mobilization and political struggle. The second period covers the early 1960s, when South Korea embarked on its new program of export-oriented industrialization, to the present. The interim period witnessed the formation of the fiercely anti-Communist government of Syngman Rhee, the outbreak of the Korean War, and the postwar political and economic repercussions. The labor movement all but disappeared during this interregrum. The working-class movement was reborn with the initiation of export-oriented industrialization in the early 1960s, and with a different generation of workers. Although this chapter focuses on the second period, an examination of the legacy of the first period and of the intervening years provides the historical context necessary to comprehend the subsequent class formation.

Legacies of the Early Labor Movement (1920s–1950s)

The modern Korean labor movement began with the rapid industrialization of the colonial period. As Carter Eckert describes in Chapter 3, industrial growth during the latter period of Japanese colonialism was quite impressive, especially in mining, chemical industries, railroad construction, and hydroelectric plants. This industrial development triggered rapid growth of Korean factory workers from 49,000 in 1921 to 80,000 in 1925, and then to 102,000 in 1930.[3] The majority of them were hired by Japanese

3. Yun-Hwan Kim, "The Formation Process of Modern Wage Labor," in *Han'guk nodong munjeŭi kujo* [The structure of Korean labor issues], ed. Yun-Hwan Kim et al. (Seoul: Kwang-

employers, because large industries were owned mostly by Japanese capitalists.

The labor movement began to emerge in the early 1920s with a fairly large number of labor conflicts directed against the Japanese employers and managers.[4] The number of labor disputes occurring in the 1930s surpassed even what we saw in the 1960s and the 1970s. In 1920, for example, there were 81 cases of labor disputes involving 4,559 participants. The number increased to 160 cases in 1930, involving 18,972 workers. The climax of the labor conflicts during this period was the Wonsan general strike of 1929, a three-month-long bitter struggle waged by some 2,000 workers. But the labor movement during this colonial period was primarily a series of political struggles against Japanese colonial rule rather than purely economic actions. Workers were mobilized not so much as a class but as a nation against Japanese colonial rule. After the 1930s, under harsh repression by the colonial government, the labor movement became an underground movement with closer ties to the communist movement.

After Korea's liberation from colonial rule in 1945, the labor movement surfaced with stronger organization and leadership than before. Within three months of the liberation, strong leftist unions were created under the umbrella organization of the National Council of Korean Trade Unions (Chŏnp'yŏng). Even before the formation of this national organization, Korean workers had become active at the plant level, taking over and managing many factories that were left behind by Japanese owners. With the formation of Chŏnp'yŏng, a more active labor movement emerged, clashing violently with police and the U.S. military occupation forces. Between August 1945 and March 1947, there were 2,388 labor demonstrations involving 600,000 participants. This was the most violent period in the history of the Korean labor movement, until the late 1980s.

But this strong labor movement did not last long. In order to counteract the leftist labor movement, right-wing groups, backed by the American

---

minsa, 1978), p. 67. See also Jin-Sung Chung, "The Living Conditions and Low Wages among Korean Workers in Chosun under Japanese Rule," in *Han'guk chabonjuŭiwa imkŭmnodong* [Korean capitalism and wage labor], ed. Hwada editors (Seoul: Hwada, 1984).

4. For studies on the labor movement during the colonial period, see Yun-Hwan Kim and Nak-Jung Kim, *Han'guk nodong undongsa* [History of the Korean labor movement] (Seoul: Ilchogak, 1970); Yun-Hwan Kim et al., eds., *Han'guk nodong munjeŭi kujo;* Hwada editors, ed., *Han'guk chabonjuŭiwa imkŭmnodong;* Keum-Soo Kim and Hyŏnch'ae Pak, ed., *Han'guk nodong undongron I* [Study of the Korean labor movement, vol. 1] (Seoul: Miraesa, 1985).

military force, created a new labor organization, the Federation of Korean Trade Unions (FKTU or *Noch'ong*) in March 1946. The FKTU had no grass-roots base and had no real interest in promoting workers' welfare. Its main objective was simply to destroy the leftist labor unions, which it succeeded in doing. Numerous violent clashes occurred between the leftist and rightist unions. Gradually, the leftist unions were destroyed by the combined forces of police, rightist unions, and the U.S. military government. The fatal blow to the leftist labor movement came during a railroad strike at Chungryangri in Seoul, in January 1947. Bloody confrontation occurred between leftist and rightist labor groups, ending with the decimation of the leftist labor leaders; hundreds of them were killed or executed, and thousands were imprisoned. In March 1947, the U.S. military government outlawed the Korean Communist Party, which put an end to the already weakened communist labor organizations. And this was the end of the first period of active working-class movement in Korea.

The following years (from 1948 to 1960) were a dark period for the Korean labor movement. During this period, organized labor was crushed and mutilated by the Rhee regime. Labor unions degenerated as Rhee's political tool, while workers' protests at the workshop level were stifled by poor economic conditions and the hysterical anti-communist atmosphere that prevailed in the postwar period.

With the fall of the Rhee regime in April 1960, the first wave of labor demonstrations appeared, with an unprecedented number of labor disputes (227 cases). In 1960, workers were able to obtain wage increases from 15 to 50 percent, and they created 315 new unions. Perhaps the most noteworthy development during this period was the formation of white-collar unions among teachers, journalists, bank employees, and other clerical workers. Especially significant were the teachers' unions, because they were left-leaning and challenged the state's ideological control of school curricula.

But this new wave of labor mobilization lasted only a year, wiped out by the military coup of May 1961. The junta arrested labor activists, dissolved the existing top union organization, installed a new union structure with a leadership handpicked by the security agency, and laid down new labor laws that strictly prohibited unions' political activities while expanding the scope of state intervention in labor relations. A new labor regime thus emerged to facilitate the outward-looking industrialization strategy that would soon radically change the working lives of millions of Koreans. The contemporary Korean working-class movement had to start anew under this new repressive regime and in the context of the new world market-oriented industrialization.

The legacy of history, however, matters even where the chain of events is fractured and discontinuous—in Korea's case, largely in a negative way. The past working-class struggles left behind mostly bad memories, fear, and justification for the government's persecution of labor activists. "The tradition of the dead generations," as Marx once wrote about the France of the 1850s, "weighs like a nightmare on the minds of the living."[5] In South Korea, this nightmare is the memory of communist agitation and the persecution of communist sympathizers. Those in power are always wary of possible communist penetration into organized labor, whereas ordinary workers are always fearful of being labeled communist sympathizers. The union movement is generally treated as a security problem, and anti-communist ideology is used by the government as a pervasive means of labor control.

Culture also matters, because it provides interpretive schemes through which individuals make sense of what they experience. In England and other European countries, the traditional artisan culture provided the early proletarian generation with its ideology, language, and organizational resources. "From this culture of the craftsman," Thompson writes, "there came scores of inventors, organizers, journalists and political theorists of impressive quality."[6] And these artisans constituted "the actual nucleus from which the labor movement derived ideas, organization, and leadership."[7] Korean traditional culture, however, provided few such resources to the first generation of the industrial proletariat. Korea lacked the strong artisan culture or craft organizations found in Europe. Few in number, Korean craftsmen were mostly dependent workers hired by the government to make specialized products for the court and the nobility, and they occupied a very low position in the Confucian hierarchy of social status. The Confucian cultural tradition has negatively affected the labor movement in many ways: it discourages horizontal interest-group formation, while emphasizing solidarity based on primordial relationships; it accords low esteem to manual work and encourages individual mobility based on educa-

5. Karl Marx, "The Eighteenth Brumaire of Louis Bonaparte," in *Surveys from Exile,* trans. David Fernbach (New York: Vintage Books, 1974), p. 146.

6. E. P. Thompson, *The Making of the English Working Class* (New York: Vintage Books, 1963), p. 831.

7. Ibid., p. 193.

tion; and it encourages patriarchal and paternal relationships between employer and workers. In short, unlike their early European counterparts, Korean factory workers had to create their working-class history under very unfavorable historical and cultural conditions.

Reemergence of Working-Class Struggles (1960s–1970s)

Coming from this tradition, Korean workers were slow to develop any strong collective response to their experiences of proletarianization.[8] The export-oriented industrialization strategy was firmly in place by the mid-1960s, bringing many new workers from rural areas to booming export industries. It is estimated that between 1957 and 1980 approximately eleven million Koreans migrated from rural to urban areas. As a consequence, the agricultural labor force declined precipitously; in the late 1950s, four out of five working people in South Korea were farmers, whereas in the mid-1980s only one out of four remained on the farm.[9] The majority of the young labor force released from agriculture was absorbed directly into the manufacturing sector. The number of nonfarm wage workers increased from 2.1 million in 1966 to 4.1 million in 1975, and to 7.7 million in 1985.[10] Clearly the pace of Korean industrialization has been extraordinary; the change that took a whole century in the West took only two decades in South Korea.

Given such a drastic industrial transformation, favorable demographic and structural conditions existed for an active labor movement, but the majority of new industrial workers in the 1960s were too absorbed in adapting themselves to factory work to react collectively to their new working conditions. The high level of unemployment and underemployment in both rural and urban areas allowed workers little bargaining power. Conditions and wages in small industries were poor, but workers tried to

8. For studies on the labor movement in the 1960s and 1970s, see books cited in note 3. For English language materials, see Young-Ki Park, *Labor and Industrial Relations in Korea: System and Practice* (Seoul: Sogang University Press, 1979); Jang Jip Choi, Labor and the Authoritarian State: Labor Unions in South Korean Manufacturing Industries, 1961–1980 (Seoul: Korea University Press, 1989); George Ogle, *South Korea: Dissent within the Economic Miracle* (London: Zed Books, 1990).

9. Economic Planning Board, *Annual Report on the Economically Active Population* (Seoul: Economic Planning Board, annual).

10. Kwan-Mo Suh, *Han'guk sahoe kyegŭp kusŏngŭi yŏnku* [A study of class structure in Korean society], Ph.D. diss., Seoul National University, 1987, p. 118.

cope at an individual level. Unions did organize in the public sector, but few could be found in private enterprises. Although the frequency of labor disputes (an average of a hundred cases yearly) and the percentage of unionized workers throughout the 1960s (11.2 percent in 1965 and 12.4 percent in 1970) were not necessarily low compared to the 1970s, the nature of the labor movement in this early period did not yet fully reflect the contradictions of capital accumulation in the process of export-oriented industrialization. It was too early for sufficient collective experience and collective responses to emerge.

The end of the 1960s, however, began to witness rapid changes. The first crisis of export-oriented industrialization occurred at this time, caused by serious balance of payments problems and widespread business failures in foreign-invested firms. Massive layoffs, a wage freeze, and delayed payments caused many labor protests in the export sector. The center of labor volatility clearly shifted from the public sector to the private export sector, where the crudest exploitation of labor prevailed. Labor demonstrations in the late 1960s and the early 1970s were largely unorganized and individualistic protests against wretched working conditions in the many small sweatshops of the garment and textile industries. Organized spontaneously in protest against intolerable working conditions in peripheral industries, these demonstrations had little impact on developing a new labor movement, at least not until 1970, when a shocking event galvanized the Korean labor movement.

On November 13, 1970, a young worker named Chun Tai Il immolated himself in a desperate attempt to publicize the inhumane conditions in garment factories. He was a tailor working in a small garment factory at the Pyungwha Market in the eastern section of Seoul, where many small garment shops were located. These garment shops were archetypal sweatshops of the kind portrayed in Charles Dickens's novels. The majority of workers in this area were teenage women from the countryside; they worked thirteen to fifteen hours a day with only two days off per month. Physical conditions were extremely bleak, with little ventilation, no sunshine in the daylight hours, and little space to move around or even to stand upright because the ceilings were too low. Most of these young workers suffered from chronic stomach problems and other job-related illnesses. In protest against such inhumane conditions, Chun wrote many letters to the Bureau of Labor Affairs and other organizations requesting their intervention, but no one in a position of power responded to Chun's pleas, forcing him to act out the most dramatic and tragic form of protest. During a demonstration organized with a few fellow workers at the market, Chun poured gasoline over his body and set himself on fire. As his body was engulfed in flame, he gripped a booklet describing the Labor Standard Laws in his hand, as a reminder of the blatant violations of these laws by the employers. People heard him shouting from the flames, "We are not machines!" "Let us rest on Sunday!" "Abide by the Labor Standard Laws!" He died in a hospital emergency room, where he uttered his last words to his mother and fellow workers, "Please do not waste my life."[11]

Chun's self-immolation became a powerful symbol for the working-class movement. His death was a dramatic announcement that factory workers had become a potentially powerful political force in a rapidly industrializing society; his heroic act portended the arrival of a new era in the Korean labor movement.

One important consequence of Chun's suicide was its impact on intellectuals, students, and church leaders. It awakened them and made them realize where society's most serious problems lay and how strategic the labor movement could be for their democratization struggle. Student-labor linkages began to develop during this period, as did the labor involvement of activist church groups. Thus economics and politics became closely entwined to shape the character of the working-class activism to come.

Partly as a reaction to this development, and partly as an effort to attack economic problems arising from the export-oriented-industrialization strategy, the regime of Park Chung Hee tightened control over labor and closed up all the legitimate space for organizing labor. With the installation of the Yushin (revitalization) system in 1972, a Korean version of the bureaucratic-authoritarian regime, union organizing was severely curtailed and workers were deprived indefinitely of the right to participate in collective actions. Simultaneously, the Park regime moved toward heavy chemical industrialization, channeling the bulk of national resources to chaebŏl-dominated heavy industries. While this strategy permitted an impressive rate of economic growth, the workers in small- and medium-scale industries continued to suffer from low wages, poor working conditions, and despotic labor relations in the workplace.

Workers' consciousness slowly began to change in the second half of the

11. Chun Tae Il, *Nae chukŭmŭl hŏttoei malla* [Don't waste my life: A collection of Chun's writings] (Seoul: Tolpege, 1988).

1970s, in close association with the continuing process of proletarianization.[12] The number of factory workers grew rapidly during this time, and they became concentrated in only a few geographic areas, creating working-class communities. And by the end of the decade the new urban working class began to reproduce itself in cities, even though a large proportion of these workers still had their origins in farm families. As a consequence of such structural changes, South Korean workers began to acquire a common identity with other workers and a feeling of class solidarity, as they realized the importance of collective struggles in improving their work conditions.

Thus from the mid-1970s onward, despite harsh government repression workers in the labor-intensive export sectors began to mobilize as part of the union movement. The major objective of their struggles was to create independent grass-roots unions in opposition to the official unions, which acted as an arm of the government and fostered management's control of labor-organizing activities. Women workers employed in textiles, food processing, and other light manufacturing industries played a leading role in this "democratic union movement." The most significant demonstration of their effectiveness during this period was the Dong-Il Textile labor conflict, which lasted for three years.

In the absence of any help from existing unions or their local communities, workers turned to church organizations and to students for help. Beginning in the early 1970s, several church groups had been actively involved in the labor arena. Of particular importance was the role of Catholic youth groups (JOC) and the Urban Industrial Mission (UIM).[13] These religious organizations exploited their own international networks and relatively secure standing in relation to the state to provide shelter for female workers' labor-organizing activities. Church leaders waged public campaigns against co-opted union leadership and the government's repressive labor policies while providing educational programs to workers. The UIM was especially active in helping female workers create independent, grass-roots unions in the textile and electronics industries. About 20 percent of the

12. The relationship between the Korean proletarianization pattern and the labor movement is examined in Hagen Koo, "From Farm to Factory: Proletarianization in Korea," *American Sociological Review* 55 (1990): 669–81.

13. For more information, see Seung-Hyuk Cho, *Han'guk kongŭphwa wa nodong undong* [Korean industrialization and the labor movement] (Seoul: Pulbitt, 1984); Choi, *Labor and the Authoritarian State;* Ogle, *South Korea.*

newly organized independent unions of the 1970s are estimated to have been assisted by the UIM.[14]

Students also played an important role in raising workers' collective consciousness during the 1970s. Especially important in this regard were the night schools they set up near factory towns. Workers' night schools began to appear in the early 1970s just after Chun Tai Il's self-immolation, initially in response to young workers' perceived aspirations for higher education. Gradually, however, the emphasis shifted from routine curricula to consciousness-raising programs tailored to the audience of workers. These night-school classes provided an important arena where workers learned to articulate their daily work experiences using a new political language, and where they could develop close links with the intellectual communities that were involved in the democratization movement.

Then toward the end of the 1970s, the South Korean economy encountered serious problems arising from several coinciding events: the second oil shock and subsequent world recession, overinvestment in heavy chemical industries, the adverse balance of payments, runaway inflation, competition from low-wage Third World countries in export markets, and so on. Plant closings and layoffs occurred frequently, causing labor volatility in many sectors. It was within this context that the "YH incident" occurred in 1979. In August of that year, several hundred female workers who were employed at a wig factory known as the YH Company staged a demonstration against the plant's closure. Predictably, police and company-hired thugs moved in and used violence to break up their demonstration. Driven out of their factory, the protesters then took over the headquarters of the opposition political party (the New Democratic Party) to continue their fight. Thus party politics became accidentally involved in labor activism. The government reacted with repression, which in turn triggered nationwide protests against the Park regime. As the political crisis escalated, the ruling group became split internally, which eventually resulted in the assassination of President Park by his own chief of the Korean Central Intelligence Agency.

Several months of political liberalization and uncertainty followed Park's death. The spring of 1980 was a time of political activism and democratic hopefulness after a two-decade-long winter of authoritarian rule. The military was lurking, seeking the right moment and the right excuse to step in, but the people enjoyed a new sense of power and freedom to speak out

14. Seung-Hyuk Cho, *Han'guk kongŭphwa.*

without immediate fear of police repression. Civil society was suddenly resurrected.

Workers did not fail to take advantage of this political opening to press for their pent-up demands. A wave of labor unrest erupted during the spring wage-negotiation period of 1980. The number of reported labor disputes increased from 105 in 1979 to 407 in 1980. A majority of these disputes concerned economic issues: 287 of the 407 cases reported for 1980 were concerned with delayed payments and 38 with wage increases, while the rest dealt with plant closings, layoffs, and the like. But the labor struggles during this liberalization period were not simply a reaction to current economic problems. They were also a response to the ways in which the state and management had controlled workers. A major objective of these labor struggles was to dismantle the company-controlled unions *(ŏyong chohap)* and organize independent unions, a natural extension of the "democratic union movement" that had appeared in the 1970s. Workers' resentment toward the co-opted union leadership was very strong, and the most violent labor conflicts erupted where official unions had acted as the tool of management's control.

The political activism that emerged in the spring of 1980 came to an abrupt end, however, when the military finally moved in on May 17, 1980. Chun Doo Hwan came to power after a bloody massacre of hundreds of rebels in Kwangju, an accident that would have a lasting effect on the trajectory of the political movement in South Korea.

The *Minjung* Movement

Before proceeding to describe the development of the working class in the 1980s, it is important to consider the development of an important social movement that occurred outside the industrial arena but with tremendous influence on the working-class struggles—the *minjung* movement, which began in the mid-1970s and became a major social, political, and cultural movement in the 1980s.[15] *Minjung* literally means the people or the masses; as a movement, it resembles populist movements in Latin America. Like early populism in Latin America, the Korean *minjung* is an

15. See the Commission on Theological Concerns of the Christian Conference of Asia, ed., *Minjung Theology: People as the Subjects of History* (New York: Orbis Books, 1983); Jae-Chun Yoo, ed., *Minjung* (Seoul: Munhakwa Jisung, 1984).

alliance of popular sectors—including workers, peasants, and segments of the middle class—that oppose the undemocratic, authoritarian state. The term conveys a strong nationalist desire for economic and political independence. Both forms of populism are broad movements, aimed not only at political change but also at social and cultural change.

Despite these similarities, the Korean *minjung* is not identical to its Latin American counterpart. Populism in Latin America occurred in the early decades of this century, when the economies of Latin American countries were dominated by landed oligarchic interests tied to the metropolitan capital. This populist movement was, therefore, formed by an alliance between the national bourgeoisie and the popular sectors against the oligarchic structure.[16] Leadership of the movement was in the hands of the national bourgeoisie and other middle-class elements, and the success of the movement put them in power. The Korean *minjung* movement, however, took shape in a rapidly industrializing society as a reaction to the consequences of capital accumulation led by monopoly capital. From the beginning, therefore, the bourgeois element was missing from this populist class alliance, so *minjung* as a concept is more directly opposed to monopoly capital, precisely because monopoly capital represents the dominant mode of production in South Korea today. Consequently, the Korean *minjung* is a relatively more homogeneous category in terms of class character than the Latin American populist alliance of the 1930s, and bears a closer relationship to working-class formation.

The *minjung* movement in Korea is not simply an economic struggle. Rather, it is a primarily political struggle, and as such it reflects some unique political and social conditions of contemporary Korea. Although the word *minjung* already existed in the Korean vocabulary, it came into frequent use as a new political term after the early 1970s. With the installation of the Yushin regime in 1972, the term quickly became a symbol and a slogan among diverse groups—students, writers, journalists, church leaders, and opposition party leaders—united by their common opposition to the Park regime. Led by students and progressive intellectuals, the *minjung* movement sought to reach and mobilize workers and farmers in struggles for political and economic democratization.

16. Guillermo O'Donnell, *Modernization and Bureaucratic-Authoritarianism* (Berkeley: Institute of International Studies, University of California, 1973); Fernando H. Cardoso and Enzo Faletto, *Dependency and Development in Latin America* (Berkeley: University of Califor-

As South Korea marched into heavy chemical industrialization accompanied by enormous capital concentration, and as political repression increased under the Yushin regime, the dissident movement was not stifled but rather became hardened, producing a core of radicalized dissident leaders. Simultaneously, the concept of *minjung* was sharpened into an ideology and a political strategy. In the early 1980s, after the bloody massacre in Kwangju, *minjung* became firmly established as the dominant antihegemonic ideology. It is a broad ideology, touching on economic, political, and social realities in society. Economically, it rejects dependent capitalist development and advocates a radical restructuring of the economy in order to achieve distributive justice; politically, it elevates national unification to the position of ultimate goal, and to this end it seeks to repel the anti-communist security ideology and to end U.S. intervention in Korean affairs; socially and culturally, it promotes concepts of national identity and independence. And as a political strategy *minjung* activists seek to forge a close alliance among students, industrial workers, and small farmers. Since the late 1970s, many student activists have penetrated the factories as students-turned-factory-workers with the mission of raising workers' consciousness and developing ties between the student and workers' movements.

The *minjung* movement has had an enormous cultural and intellectual impact, resulting in "*minjung* sociology," "*minjung* literature," "*minjung* theology," "*minjung* art," and so forth.,[17] The dominant theme in these diverse cultural movements is to put the *minjung* above other privileged groups and to search for a national identity and a national ethos in the world of ordinary people. There is a strong nationalistic and nativistic sentiment in all these efforts. Interestingly, in this quest for national identity, intellectuals turned to Korean shamanism as a spiritual source of nationalist ideology and to shamanistic rituals as a means of raising criticial consciousness and comradeship among the participants of the social movement. In this way, history has been reappropriated, and shamanism is now used to mobilize the spirit of the opppressed.[18]

---

nia Press, 1979); David Collier, Introduction to *The New Authoritarianism in Latin America,* ed. Collier (Princeton: Princeton University Press, 1979).

17. Jae-Chun Yoo, *Minjung.*

18. Chungmoo Choi, "Shamanism and the Making of the Revolutionary Ideology in Contemporary Korea," paper presented at a conference on Communities in Question: Religion and Authority in East and Southeast Asia, Bangkok, Thailand, 1989.

What then is the specific meaning of *minjung* and how is it related to class politics in South Korea? Although all kinds of social protests have been waged in the name of the *minjung,* the protagonists are rarely specific about its definition. In an early attempt to define this category, sociologist Wan-Sang Han equates *minjung* with a category of the "alienated," those who are alienated from power, from economic distribution, and from cultural life as well.[19] But among radical intellectuals, *minjung* is used as a class category. A well-known Marxist scholar, Pak Hyŏnch'ae, thus states: "Minjung is composed of the working class as its core element and of small farmers, small independent producers, the urban poor, and a segment of progressive intellectuals."[20] But there are many others who oppose his narrow Marxist conceptualization. Sang-Jin Han, for example, argues that *minjung* must be understood primarily as a political rather than an economic category, and as such it includes not only workers and peasants but also large segments of the middle class, because the latter are as opposed to the authoritarian rule as the former.[21]

In my view, the most useful way of understanding the *minjung* movement is to regard it as a *class-based political movement.* It is class-based in the sense that widening income gaps and sharpening class relations have provided the "raw materials" for its development. Korean economic development has engendered an acute sense of distributive injustice, not only among the lower class but also among much of the middle class. Yet the *minjung* movement does not simply represent an economic protest stemming directly from class inequality. Rather, it represents a *political articulation,* and, as such, the processes occurring at the political level play a critical role in determining the form and the content of this broad-based political movement. At the political level, the nature of the state is a critical variable. In fact, the *minjung* phenomenon can be understood as a manifestation of the particular relationships existing between the state and social classes in contemporary South Korea.

19. Wan-Sang Han, *Minjung sahoehak.*

20. Pak Hyŏnch'ae, "Defining the Class Nature of *Minjung,*" in *Han'guk sahoeŭi kyegŭp yŏngu, I* [Study of social classes in Korean society, vol. 1], ed. Jin-Kyun Kim (Seoul: Hanul, 1985), p. 49.

21. Sang-Jin Han, "The Logical Structure and Issues of *Minjung* Sociology," *Sahoe kwahak kwa chŏngchaek yŏnku* [Social science and policy study] 8 (1986).

That the structure of the state shapes the form and content of political struggle is now a well accepted idea.[22] Important questions to be examined, however, are what aspects of the state influence political struggles and class formation, and in what manner. In South Korea, we can isolate four aspects of the state that have influenced the rise of the *minjung* movement. The first is the character of the regime, that is, the bureaucratic-authoritarian nature of the Park and Chun regimes and their lack of political legitimacy. The second is the state's role in economic development, especially its economic policies facilitating enormous capital concentration and economic disparities. The third is the dominant ideology of the state, namely the anti-communist, security-oriented ideology. And the fourth is the dependent character of the South Korean state.

As Han correctly argues, the rise of the bureaucratic-authoritarian regime in the early 1970s and its harsh repression of civil society provided the main impetus for the emergence of the *minjung* movement.[23] The lack of political legitimacy of the successive regimes in South Korea made their authoritarianism even more repugnant. Both Park and Chun sought to claim their legitimacy through economic performance, but the development strategy they adopted generated a new source of resentment despite the impressive economic growth fostered.

The role of the "developmental state" in South Korea is well documented in Chapter 2 by Haggard and Moon and requires no further discussion here. One fact that needs to be stressed here is that the South Korean developmental state has sacrificed the public sense of distributive justice in its blind pursuit of accelerated economic growth. The entire development strategy has been based on intimate collusion between the state and conglomerate capital in close collaboration with international capital.[24] In pursuit of this strategy, enormous economic disparities were allowed to grow

22. An excellent review of this literature is found in Theda Skocpol, "Bringing the State Back In: Strategies of Analysis in Current Research," in *Bringing the State Back In,* ed. Peter Evans, Dietrich Rueschemeyer, and Theda Skocpol (New York: Cambridge University Press, 1985); see also John A. Hall, "Introduction," in *States in History,* ed. Hall (Oxford: Basil Blackwell, 1986).

23. Sang-Jin Han, "The Logical Structure."

24. Hagen Koo and Eun Mee Kim, "Developmental State and Capital Accumulation in South Korea," in *States and Development in the Asian Pacific Rim,* ed. Richard Appelbaum and Jeffrey Henderson (Beverly Hills, Cal.: Sage, 1992).

between those who participated in the benefits of economic growth and those who were excluded from those benefits. A strong sense of relative deprivation was felt not only among poor workers and farmers, but also among the middle class. It is this sense of relative deprivation, both an objective and subjective condition, that provided the social base for a cross-class alliance within the *minjung* movement.

Anti-communist ideology, which has been used by successive South Korean regimes to maintain control over civil society and to bolster their own legitimacy, is also a critical component of the *minjung* ideology. The authoritarian regimes in South Korea have been focused on security, allowing no legitimate space for leftist expression. In such an ideological context, intellectuals and political activists found it safer to use the term *minjung* than to popularize Marxist terminology. The nationalistic sentiment expressed by the language of *minjung* is certainly in line with another important state ideology of nationalism. In this way, the state has provided a repertoire of vocabularies for social movements.

Finally, nationalist sentiment has inspired popular reaction against the state's dependence on foreign power and against the national division created and perpetuated by foreign intervention. Increasingly, as Choi argues in Chapter 1, Korean intellectuals pointed to national division as the root cause of all political, social, and cultural problems in the country. Reunification involves two opposing interests, they argue, between the ruling class and the masses, and between the United States and the Korean *minjung*. Consequently, the *minjung* has a mission and a moral responsibility to push for reunification.

In sum, the *minjung* movement is a social, political, and cultural movement, the form and content of which have been shaped by the particular nature of the state in South Korea. But its material base was provided by the contradictions generated by South Korean industrialization. A new structure of class inequality and class conflict gave *minjung* political expression in the unique context of South Korea. But the movement is not coterminus with the process of class formation. That is, the working-class movement developed in close relations with the *minjung* movement, but had its own dynamics and its own momentum. While drawing on the *minjung* movement for organizational and ideological support, the working-class movement developed according to its own logic and contradictions, as we can see more clearly in the 1980s.

Deepening Working-Class Struggles (1980–1987)

The 1980s was the critical period for the formation of the South Korean working class.[25] If the 1970s saw the awakening of class awareness, the 1980s witnessed the growth of class identity and class solidarity among industrial workers. Interestingly, each decade was ushered in by an extraordinary event that would determine the tone and character of political struggles to follow in the coming decade: Chun Tai Il's self-immolation in 1970 and the Kwangju massacre in 1980. If Chun's death fired the imagination of thousands of workers and stirred the consciences of students and intellectuals, the Kwangju tragedy thoroughly exposed the regime's brutality and further politicized and radicalized the opposition. Because of their political struggles, workers' class consciousness and class identity grew rapidly in the 1980s.

Coming to power without a shred of legitimacy, Chun Doo Hwan took exceptionally repressive measures to restore the mobilized civil society to its formerly dormant condition. Thousands of political activists were rounded up and, along with hoodlums and racketeers, were sent to jails or "purification camps." The regime cracked down especially hard on labor, abolishing the newly created independent unions one by one and expelling labor activists from union leadership. Chun's regime was determined to destroy the democratic union movement and wipe out "impure elements" from the industrial arena. Employers took advantage of this antilabor atmosphere and fired hundreds of workers who had actively participated in the democratic union movement. These fired workers were then blacklisted by the security agency and barred from gainful employment. This attack on the democratic union movement continued until 1983.

As a consequence of all these antilabor policies, the number of unions dropped dramatically, from 6,011 before May 1980 to 2,618 by the end of the year; the number of union members also decreased from 1,120,000

25. A number of Ph.D. dissertations have been written recently in the United States on the South Korean labor movement in this period: Eun-Jin Lee, "Changing Strategies of Labor Control in the Semiconductor Industry in a Peripheral Country, S. Korea: A World-System Perspective," Ph.D. diss., University of California at Los Angeles, 1989; Jeong Tak Lee, "Economic Development and Industrial Order in South Korea: Interactions between the State and Labor in the Process of Export-Oriented Industrialization," Ph.D. diss., University of Hawaii at Honolulu, 1987; Ho-Keun Song, "State and the Working-Class Labor Market in South Korea, 1961–1987," Ph.D. diss., Harvard University, 1989.

to 950,000 during the same period (see Table 4.1). Over the next three years, organized labor found no legitimate space in which to operate, and the labor movement was forced into a state of apparent quiescence.

Table 4.1. Number of Labor Disputes, Labor Unions, Union Members, and Unionization Rates, 1963–91

Year	Disputes	No. of Unions	Union Members (in thousands)	Org. Rate[a] (%) A	B
1975	133	3,585	750	23.0	15.8
1976	110	3,854	846	23.3	16.5
1977	96	4,042	955	24.3	16.7
1978	102	4,301	1,055	24.0	16.9
1979	105	4,394	1,088	23.6	16.8
1980	407	2,618	948	20.1	14.7
1981	186	2,141	967	19.6	14.6
1982	88	2,194	984	19.1	14.4
1983	98	2,238	1,010	18.1	14.1
1984	113	2,365	1,011	16.8	13.2
1985	265	2,534	1,004	15.7	12.4
1986	276	2,658	1,036	15.5	12.3
1987	3,749	4,086	1,267	17.3	13.8
1988	1,873	6,142	1,707	22.0	17.8
1989	1,616	7,883	1,932	23.4	18.7
1990	322	7,698	1,887	21.7	17.4
1991	234	7,656	1,803	19.8	16.0

Source: Punkt Pyŏl Nodong Tonghyang Punsǫk [Quarterly labor review] (Seoul: Korea Labor Institute, 1991, 1992).

[a]Organization rate: A = union members as proportion of total number of nonagricultural, regularly employed workers; B = union members as proportion of total number of employed workers.

Ironically, however, the Korean working-class movement grew stronger and more mature during the first years of the Chun regime. Below a surface of political passivity, students, workers, and other dissident groups reflected on their defeats in 1980, on the meaning of the Kewangju massacre, and on their future strategy. This was a period of much important theorizing as to the nature of South Korea's "social formation," the historic mission of the *minjung* movement, and the extent of U.S. involvement in the country's destiny.[26] Marxist discourse strongly influenced the intellectuals, and a radical political culture predominated the *minjung* movement. In this period, church influence on the labor movement declined considerably, as labor activists gradually became disenchanted with church leaders' mild approach to labor struggles. They realized that in the face of the determined efforts of the Chun regime to pulverize the democratic union movement, church organizations were of little help and church leaders' humanitarian concerns looked too meek and passive to represent workers' recent experiences with the repressive regime. As church influence on labor organizations waned, activist students' influence increased proportionately. In the first half of the 1980s, hundreds of radical students, who were either expelled from school because of political activities or who had dropped out, entered the industrial arena as factory workers to help raise workers' consciousness and broaden the linkages between workers' grass-roots organizations and the larger political movement outside the industrial arena. The number of college students who became factory workers was estimated to have reached three thousand or more in the mid-1980s.[27] Efforts to achieve a worker-student alliance (no-hak yŏndae) thus permeated the labor movement of the decade. The government defined these students-turned-workers as "disguised workers" and sought, with little success, to eradicate such "impure elements" by outlawing "third-party intervention" in labor affairs.

After its brutal repression of political activists and organized labor during its first years in power, the Chun regime began to seek a broader basis for its legitimacy. In 1984 the government released a number of political prisoners, allowed dissident professors and students to return to school, and relaxed its iron-fisted control over labor-organizing activities. This partial political relaxation encouraged an upsurge of militant union activity. When the labor movement resurfaced in 1984, it demonstrated greater organizational strength and a higher level of political consciousness among workers than ever before. Workers swiftly organized numerous independent unions (about 200 independent unions were formed in 1984) and fought to revive those unions previously dissolved by the government. Of particular significance was the effort to revive the Chunggye districtwide labor union, which

26. Pak Hyŏnch'ae and Hee-Yon Cho, ed., *Han'guk sahoe kusŏngche nonchaeng, 1* [Debates on social formation of Korea, vol. 1] (Seoul: Chuksan, 1989).

27. Ogle, *South Korea,* p. 99.

had symbolized the whole democratic union movement during the 1970s. An alliance of workers, students, and other political activists staged public rallies and activated the union in defiance of the government ban. Labor disputes increased in frequency from 98 cases in 1983 to 113 cases in 1984, and to 265 cases in 1985.

The character of such labor conflicts had changed noticeably by the mid 1980s. Increasingly, the focus of workers' struggles was no longer on isolated economic issues but on organizing new independent unions, and their new tactics centered on promoting solidarity struggles among workers across several factories located within the same industrial area. The heavy concentration of factories in a very few industrial parks and close personal networks developed among labor activists over the years made this strategy feasible. The labor strike that most clearly demonstrated this changed character of the labor movement was the solidarity strike that occurred in Kuro Industrial Park in June 1985. Sparked initially as a protest against the arrest of three union leaders at Daewoo Apparel, the strike escalated into a solidarity strike involving five different firms and drawing wide support from students and dissident groups, who staged sympathetic demonstrations outside the factory gates almost every day during the ten-day-long solidarity strike. The strike ended in a brutal police attack with severe casualties to strikers. Some two thousand workers were fired or forced to resign from their jobs, adding to the list of resentful, hard-core labor activists. The Chun regime subsequently ended its reconciliatory overtures and resumed its policy of harsh repression against labor. Yet the new labor volatility continued with greater intensity and organizational strength.

Working-Class Identity and Consciousness

Out of these struggles, workers developed a stronger sense of class awareness and identity. The change in class awareness is most clearly reflected in the rise of "working-class literature." Indeed, one of the most remarkable features of the contemporary, South Korean working-class movement is the development of a distinct literature produced by factory workers. Unlike its early European and American counterparts, the new South Korean proletariat is a highly literate population with strong educational aspirations. After long hours of hard work and fatigue, many workers sacrificed sleep in order to write about their hardships, anguish, broken dreams, and relationships with fellow workers and superiors. Workers' night schools played an instrumental role in encouraging workers to write essays, poems, and diaries, and small publication houses run by activist students made these writings available to a wider audience, further encouraging workers' literary writing efforts.

The common concerns expressed in workers' essays were, naturally, physical hardship, abusive treatment by superiors, longing for their rural homes, poor health conditions caused by poor work environments, and so forth. But probably the most cogent theme running through their essays is their concern over status and their perception of the society's contemptuous attitude toward factory workers. In the 1960s through 1970s, factory workers were often called *kongsuni* (factory girl) or *kongdoli* (factory boy), insinuating an image of a housemaid or a servant, only working in a factory environment. The label *kongsuni,* in particular, has been hurtful to young female workers, many of whom left their rural homes with high aspirations for upward social mobility. Their stories are replete with despair at the negative social image held toward factory workers.

> Women working in factories are *kongsuni;* men working in factories are *knogdoli. Kongsuni* and *kongdoli* are contemptible guys, nothing worth counting, just loose folks. They call us this way as a whole group. We have to be *kongsuni* even if we hate it, simply because we are working in factories. If someone asks us where we are working, we simply say, "I work at a small company." But *kongsuni* cannot really hide their identity. They show it however hard they try to do makeup and dress up nicely. They pay more attention to clothes, hairdo, and makeup in order to hide it. People fault us for spending money on appearance without making enough money, but our reason is to take off the label of *kongsuni* they put on us.[28]

Workers' typical reactions to this situation were to try to get out of the factory and to achieve upward mobility through education. Their eager responses to workers' night schools, established by church organizations and students, sprang from their strong desire to leave factory work for clerical work or independent business. But experience soon told them that the extra hours they endured to obtain a high school certificate by examina-

28. Dolbege editors, *Kŭrŏna urinŭn ŏcheŭi uriga anida* [But we are not yesterday's ourselves: Collection of Workers' essays] (Seoul: Dolbege, 1986), p. 111.

tion did not get them anywhere and that their aspiration for (middle-class) cultural refinement was nothing more than vanity and fanciful dreams. Gradually workers began to accept factory work as their destiny and developed a positive identity as factory workers. By 1980 factory workers numbered about 2 million, about one-fourth of the total labor force; thus factory workers were not novel and could not continue to be treated as objects of social disdain. Pejorative words like *kongsuni* and *kongdoli*, by and large, disappeared from the vocabulary, and general terms like *kŭnroja* (working people) gave way to a more specific term, *nodongja* (worker), as a standard designation of factory workers. Workers' writings in the mid-1980s were more likely to express a positive sense of being a factory worker and a growing sense of collective identity and group solidarity:

> I am a worker. I am not ashamed of the word "*kongsuni.*" My line would be in great trouble if I were absent. And, if everybody in our line were absent, the company wouldn't be able to operate. However pompously the office workers behave in front of us, they will starve without us. So I have pride. We have power. Although we are weak as individuals, if we are united we can overcome anything. Yes, I am a *kongsuni.*[29]

Many factors contributed to this growing working-class identity and group solidarity: a rapid increase of factory workers, a growing proportion of high-school educated and urban-grown workers, a geographical concentration of factories in a few industrial centers and a concomitant development of working-class communities, and increasing opportunities to participate in social activities with workers from other firms. But more important were the experiences gained from participation in unionization struggles and in educational and cultural activities outside their workplaces. A significant difference is evident between those who participated in collective struggles and those who did not. In general, the former tend to demonstrate a stronger sense of working-class identity and "class opposition" (in Mann's terms).[30] Participation in night schools and small discussion circles organized by students had a similar effect.

29. Ibid., p. 114.

30. In Mann's definition, "class opposition" refers to "the perception that the capitalist and his agents constitute an enduring opponent to oneself." See Michael Mann, *Consciousness and Action among the Western Working Class* (London: Macmillan, 1973), p. 13.

In the latter half of the 1980s, workers' writings grew in number and maturity, and sought to grow out of a subordinate status within the larger *minjung* literature, still dominated by intellectuals and professional writers. Naturally, working-class writers were able to describe their daily experiences—their despair, anger, and aspirations—more realistically and authentically. In time these writers found the category of *minjung* too broad and vague to express and interpret their own life experiences as factory workers and their relationships with the capitalists. The growth of working-class literature as an autonomous genre stimulated intellectuals to look more critically at the *minjung* literature. In this self-critique, early leaders of the *minjung* movement were now accused of revealing a "petty citizen" (or petty bourgeois) mentality—vague humanitarianism, sentimentalism, and fatalism, and of lacking a firm, positive vision of the future. (Chapter 5 by Uchang Kim describes this interesting development in more detail.) By mid-decade there had appeared several working-class poets, of whom Pak No Hae is the best known.[31] His poems, published as *Dawn of Labor* (1984), express workers' alienation and exploitation with great simplicity and cogency, and had a considerable impact in literary circles.

Maybe

Maybe I'm a machine
Absorbed in soldering subassemblies
Swarming down the conveyor,
Like a robot repeating,
The same motions forever,
Maybe I've become a machine.

Maybe we're chickens in a coop.
Neatly lined up on our roosts,
Hand speed synchronized in dim light,
The faster the music,
The more eggs we lay,
Maybe we've become chickens in a coop.
. . . .

31. His real name is Pak Ki Pyŏng. He was arrested in October 1990 on a charge of organizing a revolutionary communist labor organization.

They . . .
They who extract and devour
Our pith and our marrow,
Maybe they are barefaced robbers,
Turning humans into machines,
Into consumables,
Into things buyable and sellable.
Maybe they are dignified
And law-abiding barefaced robbers.

Those gentle smiles,
That refined beauty and culture,
That rich and dazzling opulence,
Maybe all of that is ours.
(translated by Kyung-ja Chun)

Expressed in his poems is far more than working-class identity or class opposition; there is a firm structural understanding of the inequities and injustices of class society and a hint of an alternative society. To what extent his view was shared among other workers is difficult to determine. Most likely, he belongs to a small minority of politically conscious workers. But by the mid-1980s a significant proportion of workers seems to have developed more than a rudimentary form of class consciousness with strong working-class identity and class opposition. Naturally, a higher level of class consciousness existed among those who participated in extra-firm networks of social and cultural activities and/or in the unionization movement. But even among the rank-and-file workers, a considerable amount of change in consciousness was observed by the latter half of the decade.[32]

Post-1987 Developments

This changing level of class solidarity and consciousness was demonstrated most clearly in the summer of 1987 when a sudden political opening

32. Two excellent analyses of Korean female workers' essays are available in Korean: Hyun-Paek Chung, "Women Workers' Consciousness and World of Work: Centering on the Analysis of Workers' Essays," *Yŏsŏng* [Women] 1 (1985): 116–62; Ki-Nam Park, "A Study of Change in Women Workers' Consciousness: From the 1970s to the mid-1980s," M.A. thesis, Yonsei University, 1988. A more systematic survey data analysis is available in Korean Social Studies

appeared, an event well described in Chapter 1 by Jang Jip Choi. As the regime's ability to exercise its repressive power diminished momentarily, a violent wave of labor conflicts erupted and spread swiftly across the country, halting production at almost all major industrial plants. Between July and September 1987 about 3,500 labor conflicts occurred, more than the total number of labor disputes during the entire Park and Chun regimes. In August more than a hundred new labor disputes arose daily, which was about the annual average occurrence of disputes in the past (see Table 4.1).

Labor conflicts during this period differed from previous ones in several ways. First, the center of labor conflicts during this period shifted from light manufacturing to heavy chemical industries (such as metal, shipbuilding, automobile, and chemical industries), from small-to-medium-scale enterprises to large *chaebŏls*. Giant conglomerates like Hyundai, Daewoo, and Samsung, which represent the muscle of Korean economic power and which had been boasting their union-free operations, endured the most intense labor conflicts and the largest financial losses. This shift in locale of labor conflicts also meant a shift in the main actors of the labor movement. Whereas the labor movement in the 1970s was led by female workers in light manufacturing, the new labor movement was dominated by male workers employed in core industries of the South Korean economy. Two-thirds of them had received a high school education.

Second, the main issue of labor conflicts during this period was the organization of independent unions and dismantling company unions *(ŏyong chohap)*. Workers' resentment of the co-opted union leadership was deep and strong, and their past struggles convinced them that what they needed most were unions that could genuinely represent their interests. Between July and September, they organized more than 1,060 new unions, which they proudly called "democratic unions." These new unions amounted to 39 percent of the unions before July 1987. In one year (from the end of 1986 to the end of 1987), union membership increased from 1,036,000 (12.3 percent of total wage workers) to 1,267,000 (13.8 percent); by 1989 the number increased to 1,932,000 (18.7 percent).

Third, labor protests in 1987 and afterward demonstrated a high level of class solidarity and organizational skills. Interfirm solidarity strikes, only a trickle during the first half of the 1980s, became widespread in 1987.

Institute, *Han'guk sahoe nodongja yŏngu 1* [A study of Korean workers, vol. 1] (Seoul: Paeksan Sŏdang, 1989).

Solidarity strikes were made possible by the geographic concentration of industry and the close social networks developed among labor activists, and were thus most visible in such industrial cities as Ulsan, Changwon, Masan, Okpo, and Guro.

Fourth, the union movement was not confined to blue-collar workers but found strong resonance among white-collar workers as well. A white-collar union movement occurred first among the employees of banks and other financial institutions. It was immediately followed by more aggressive unionization efforts among workers employed in intellectual occupations—journalists, printers, school teachers, and researchers employed in government-sponsored research institutions. Unlike blue-collar industrial workers, the white-collar union movement was not primarily occupied with the economic improvement of workers but with broader political and social issues. Intellectual workers in particular were mainly concerned with the state's political and ideological control over their work—journalists reaffirmed the noble mission of a free press, teachers proclaimed their resolve to serve no longer as a tool of the government's ideological indoctrination of students, and researchers employed in government-sponsored institutions refused to act in the interest of political power and pledged to restructure their institutions to serve the public's true interests.

The main efforts of the "democratic labor movement" in the following years concentrated on establishing national-level organizations and on amending labor laws that continued to repress labor activities. Efforts to establish a national labor organization started in December 1987 with the creation a regional labor association in twin cities of Masan and Changwon, the most highly developed industrial region, with many aggressive local unions led by militant labor activists. Other regions followed suit. By July 1989, 17 regional labor associations were established, incorporating 628 local unions and 246,000 union members. In addition, workers employed in *chaebŏls* formed separate associations consisting of local enterprise unions belonging to the same *chaebŏl* group. White-collar workers in the service sector also formed 11 loosely organized occupational associations, to which 925 unions and 144,200 members belonged. These labor associations played important roles in labor strikes and collective bargaining in 1988 and 1989.

The culmination of this organizational movement was the creation of the National Council of Korean Trade Unions (NCKTU). Denied legal status by the government, NCKTU nevertheless emerged as a powerful challenger to the official union structure, the Federation of Korean Trade Unions (FKTU). In 1990, NCKTU included 574 unions and some 190,000 members (which amounted to 8 percent of unions and 10 percent of union members claimed by the FKTU). Fifteen regional associations and two occupational associations belonged to NCKTU, but unions belonging to *chaebŏl* groups and white-collar unions did not join. Thus at present the NCKTU membership consists largely of workers employed in small- and medium-scale industries.

After such notable growth in labor's organizational strength during the first two years of political liberalization, however, the tide began to turn as the state and capital rebounded with a counterattack on the independent labor movement from the early 1989. Starting during the 1989 spring wage bargaining period, the Roh Tae Woo goverment ended its hands-off posture toward labor and began to be actively involved in labor disputes by sending in riot troops to break up strikes and arresting hundreds of labor activists. The security agencies were reactivated to run down labor activists and detect "impure elements" in the labor arena. After the NCKTU was formed, virtually all its key leaders were either detained or in hiding, creating a serious vacuum in the national leadership of the democratic labor movement.

Capital also made a concerted effort to deal with the growing labor power. In 1989 large capitalists formed the National Association of Managers (NAM) to devise and enforce synchronized measures toward labor. As a sister organization of the Federation of Korean Industries (FKI), the peak organization of big business, the NAM coordinated the capitalist strategy of wage negotiations in close consultation with the government, while orchestrating media campaigns against the "violent, leftist" labor movement. As a first organizational project, the NAM established the "no work, no pay" rule and enforced it across all industries against violent, yet futile, resistances from labor, and with full endorsement of the state. Here we see the workings of a capitalist state in stark simplicity. For, as Poulantzas argues, the most important function of the capitalist state is to help organize capital as a class and to keep labor disorganized.[33]

As the 1990s began, the gains made by the worker struggles of 1987 and 1988 began to slip away. The number of unions and unionized workers peaked in 1989, and so did the number of labor conflicts (see Table 4.1). Under focused repression and intimidation, the NCKTU was unable to

33. Nicos Poulantzas, *Political Power and Social Classes* (London: New Left Books, 1974).

reproduce its leadership and has been unable to expand its organization base beyond small-scale, labor-intensive industries. Internal divisions within the democratic labor movement became more visible, as workers employed in large *chaebŏl* firms became reluctant to act together with the more radical NCKTU leadership. Recent studies indicate that white-collar unions and the unions representing blue-collar workers employed in large firms are considerably more trade union–oriented, while the NCKTU leadership is more political union oriented.[34] The democratic labor movement's weakness was evident in its inability to have repressive labor laws amended. After some modest revisions in 1987 and 1988, the ruling party steadfastly stalled the more substantial revision of labor laws demanded by labor organizations. The labor law of 1992 thus retained all the important restrictive clauses, including prohibition of a "third party" involvement in labor activities (to prevent students and political activists from penetrating into the labor arena), representation by only one union (to prevent the formation of independent unions in opposition to company unions), prohibition of union political activities, denial of rights of organization among teachers and civil servants, and so forth.

The resumption of state repression of labor is closely related to a changing political orientation among the middle classes. A traditional ally of labor, the new middle class became increasingly conservative and somewhat hostile to the aggressive labor movement in the 1990s.[35] A slowdown of economic growth and narrowing wage gaps between blue-collar and white-collar workers must have played an important role in their changing attitude. Losing support from the middle classes and unrepresented by any political party, the blue-collar unionists have had to carry out lone battles against the intensifying state-capital offensives in the 1990s.

Despite all these signs of retreat in the labor movement, working-class formation itself has grown steadily with broadening networks among working-class organizations and collective efforts to develop working-class culture and institutions. This development can be seen most clearly in the mushrooming of working-class institutions, such as workers' newspapers, magazines, schools, dance and play groups, writing contests, and a variety

34. Ho Keun Song, "The State and Organized Labor in Transition to Democracy in South Korea," *Working Paper Series #2*, Institute for Social Research, Hallym University, 1992; Jang Jip Choi, "Why Is the Korean Labor Movement Failing to Organize Itself into a Class? An Analysis of the Post-1987 Labor Movement" (in Korean), a paper presented at the annual meeting of the Association of Korean Political Science, Seoul, 1992.

35. Ibid.

of other activities. In the late 1980s, most labor organizations published their own newspapers, more important of which include *Minju nodong* (Democratic labor), published by the Association for Labor Welfare, *Nodongja sinmun* (Workers' daily) published by the Industrial Mission located in Yŏngdŭngpo, and *Chungye nojo sinmun,* a union newspaper published by Chungye-district garment unions. In addition, several monthly magazines appeared, targeted exclusively at the working-class audience. Working-class cultural activities also blossomed: Every labor union sponsored cultural activities, such as mask dances, plays, and performances of *pungmul* (peasant music), all of which helped enhance workers' solidarity and collective consciousness and foster working-class culture.

A major outgrowth of these cultural activities at a local level was the formation of the National Council of Workers' Cultural Movement Organizations in the winter of 1988. Its inaugural statement indicates that the working-class movement in South Korea today has indeed matured: it is no longer just an economic struggle but a cultural and political movement toward a new vision of democratic society, and the industrial workers have gained a clearer sense of being a historic agent for bringing about a new society.

> Now, workers have arrived at a historical point where their struggles must move beyond the boundaries of individual enterprises and make a qualitative leap with a national-level solidarity, move beyond struggles for livelihoods and leap into national liberation and human liberation that will determine who are the true masters of this land. . . . We will try to detect and disclose the culture of external forces and military dictatorship that has penetrated deep into every corner of our life, we will try to promote cultural struggles in our daily lives by cultivating a collective, oppositional culture, and ultimately we will seek to establish a culture (philosophy), arts, and a social movement that recognize the people as the master [of this nation].[36]

Conclusion

What we have seen above is the remarkable development of the Korean working class. The class formation that took more than a century in Europe

36. National Council of Workers' Cultural Movement Organizations, *Inaugural Statement* [in Korean], in *Nodongja munhwa* [Workers' culture] 1 (1989): 110.

and America took not more than three decades in Korea. In Europe, working-class formation has been an outcome of long struggles among artisans, journeymen, and outworkers as well as political struggles against ancient regimes. It was artisans, rather than factory workers, who led struggles against the encroachment of mass factory production, and they had fought against capitalist production several centuries before factory workers emerged as the main actors in class struggle. But in South Korea it was factory workers who came forward most quickly to assume their historical role, without much assistance from their forebears. The rapid formation of the South Korean working class is especially notable because the Korean cultural and political climate has been, at best, inimical to the development of class consciousness and class organization. What, then, accounts for this rapid development?

This rapid evolution can be mostly explained by the nature of recent South Korean industrialization itself. In Europe, industrialization developed slowly through several centuries of continuous change that transformed rural industries and urban craft production, ultimately ushering in mass factory production. Contrary to a popular conception of the Industrial Revolution, the industrialization that occurred in Europe was a continuous, incremental, and gradual process.[37] South Korean industrialization, however, has been more abrupt and discontinuous. Korean workers' intense reactions to the process of proletarianization are largely attributable to the density and abruptness of change they have experienced. Enmeshed in this swift process of industrialization, Korean workers have been subjected to a high level of exploitation without much cultural or ideological preconditioning. Capitalists, for their part, have pursued maximum labor exploitation under the protection of an authoritarian capitalist state. By any measure, the exploitation of labor in Korean industry has been extraordinarily high, and labor relations have been despotic and patriarchal.

These objective conditions of proletarianization are primarily responsible for the relatively high degree of class formation witnessed today in South Korea. But I do not believe these conditions suffice. In Taiwan, Hong Kong, and Singapore, for example, a similar pattern of industrialization has not produced the same kind of working-class formation. There exist, of course, some differences between South Korea and these countries in terms of the

37. Charles Tilly, *As Sociology Meets History* (New York: Academic, 1981); John Walton, "Theory and Research on Industrialization," *Annual Review of Sociology* 13 (1987): 89–108.

pattern of proletarianization and the degree of labor exploitation, but these differences are not sufficient to account for the much higher level of labor conflict in Korea over the past two decades. In order to explain what is unique about the South Korean class formation process, we must recognize the importance of political struggles outside the industrial arena and their effects on the consciousness and the organizational strength of labor.

The efficacy of political and ideological struggle for class formation in South Korea has been most clearly demonstrated by the role of the *minjung* movement in influencing the course of the working-class movement, for that movement provided workers, in their early stages of struggle, with leadership, a new language, and organizational shelter, thereby broadening their scope and the objectives. Through their close affiliation with *minjung* circles, workers became more highly politicized and assumed a clearer sense of class identity and consciousness. It is quite possible that without the *minjung* movement, and without the active participation of students and church groups in the labor arena, working-class formation in South Korea might have been much slower.

This is not to suggest that the development of the South Korean working class can be understood only as a consequence of the *minjung* political movement. On the contrary, the *minjung* movement can be regarded as one consequence of the contradictions inherent to export-oriented industrialization and as a reflection of workers' grass-roots struggles in the industrial arena. Without the workers' desperate struggles in the 1970s and 1980s and broad social sympathy for their plight, the *minjung* movement would not have developed into such a potent political and social force. If the *minjung* movement was a facilitator of the working-class movement, it was the workers' everyday struggles that have provided the *minjung* movement with its material base, its inspiration, and its vitality.

This close articulation of the political and economic levels of struggles explains the unusually rapid process of Korean working-class formation over the past two decades. And in order to understand this interconnectedness between the two forms of struggle, it is essential to consider the state's role in economic and political development, for the interventionist state provides a common object and arena of struggle for both the working-class and the *minjung* movements. Thus in the final analysis, the character of the state and its role in the process of industrial transformation are to be regarded as the key variables in accounting for the pattern of class formation in contemporary South Korea.

5

The Agony of Cultural Construction: Politics and Culture in Modern Korea

Uchang Kim

State, Society, and Culture

Though debate about the precise nature of its relationship never ceases, a close relationship unquestionably exists between politics and culture—if only to infer from the notice taken throughout the ages by the state, the supreme product of political activities, of the potential use of arts and literature for political purposes—through patronage, subvention, or coercion. The view taken by the modern totalitarian state that culture is a branch of politics, warranting the state to take a direct hand in cultural affairs and employ cultural workers as engineers of the soul to mold the people for the revolutionary task set by it, is only an extreme view of this close and yet ambiguous relationship. The Korean tradition strongly subscribes to the idea that culture should constitute the mainstay of the state. The cultural revolution of the twentieth century evolves from this tradition, but with important departures from it because of new complications arising from modern conditions.

The Confucian orthodoxy in culture was in a way opposed to the totalitarian state's view of culture, for it placed culture above politics, and not the reverse. It was founded, at least in theory, on rejection of *xing (hyŏng),* the ultimate coercive instrument of the state, in favor of gentler ways of influencing the conduct of the subjects of the state, such as rites *(li, ye),* virtue *(de, dŭk),* letters *(wen, mun)* or even music *(yue, ak).* The ruler was to rule not by force, but by example of his virtue, including the practice, promotion, and regulation of rites, letters, and music. As *The Book of Rites* puts it, "When the prince makes ritual and music both achieve their proper roles, he is called a virtuous prince."[1]

In the East Asian tradition, culture was considered not an object of state policy, but rather the determinant of that policy. The major preface to *The Book of Poetry* says that poetry and other cultural media could be used by the ruler to influence the ruled, just as it could be used by the ruled to admonish the ruler: "The one above uses *feng* (airs/moral influence) to transform those below, and those below use *feng* (airs/admonition) to criticize the one above."[2] The Confucian view of the use of poetry and the arts more often emphasized the fact that the rulers have more things to learn from poetry and the arts than the other way around. If so, communication from below can be effective only if it remains free and unsponsored. Even if poetry and other cultural activities remained within the purview of politics, culture would work for the state through society, not through direct political intervention.

All this seems to imply that the traditional state in Korea allowed culture considerable freedom, but there are ways of limiting human freedom other than through political power. As has been articulated by liberal political thinkers, starting with John Stuart Mill, constraints imposed by the intangible demands of society can be no less limiting, especially when freedom concerns ideas and sentiments held within the inner realm. The opposition set up in modern political thinking between the state and society points to two different forms of human collectivity, differentiated on the basis of how much coercive power each form of collectivity can bring to bear on its constituents. This differentiation leads to a society as a collectivity arising spontaneously and freely, and a state as a collectivity finding its ultimate form in an organization with coercive instruments. If we divide up all human activities springing from either society or the state, culture would

1. James Legge, *The Li Ki,* vol. 2, p. 131.

2. Quoted in James J. Y. Liu, *Chinese Theories of Literature* (Chicago: University of Chicago Press, 1975), p. 115.

fall into the domain of the former rather than that of the latter. The Confucian view of culture recognizes both the political relevance of culture and its rather loosely regulated existence in society. In other words, it did not subordinate culture to politics, but at the same time, it confined culture to what is socially useful—mostly as didacticism serving morality. In the spontaneity of the artistic processes, however, an artist or cultural worker is likely to claim total freedom for cultural creation—not only from any political pressure but also from any socially imposed purposes.

The cultural dynamics in twentieth-century Korea can be seen not so much in terms of a conflictual relationship between state and society as in terms of a tripartite opposition and conjunction between state, society, and culture, or more broadly in terms of the tension between politics and culture, with state, society, and culture variously ranged along this main axis of tension. Culture is not necessarily on the side of society. Just as culture can be sustained or repressed by the state, so can it be nurtured or constrained by society. The deeper impulses lying behind cultural work transcend any form of collectivity, whether state or society, and pose complicated problems for them. In other words, the aesthetic aspect of human nature is always problematic with regard to man's social mobilization or political organization, for the aesthetic is what relates to the senses, and the natural inclinations and sensuous diversities of individuals are difficult to discipline for a social or political purpose. The nonsocial or antisocial elements of human nature have a natural affinity for imaginative writing and arts, causing collectively minded orientations to the apprehension of the subversive nature of all artistic activities; the arts are representative of the discontents of civlization, always dangerous but especially potent when the basic civilizational order is in crisis.

Acknowledging its potential dangers, apologists for art, both Eastern and Western, have spoken of its civilizing function. Art begins with the senses and impulses lying deep within humanity, but it culminates in tangible products of art, which help make human sensibility harmonious and more amenable to public life. German idealism called the process *Bildung* out of which Schiller developed the idea of aesthetic education *(aesthetische Erziehung)*, which would do justice both to the sensuous individual, public morality, and the requirements of the state. In the Sino-Korean tradition, *wenhua* or *munwha* (culture) means civilizing change resulting from the discovery of patterns in sensuous human life, and that change is ultimately to be the foundation of the state and society. In any case, one might posit an ideal order of human existence embracing all aspects of individual, social, and political existence and to conceive of this ideal order as gradually maturing, as it were, from internal to external forms, that is, from aesthetic culture to society to the state.

But the ideal order of events aesthetic and cultural apologists would like to see happen has been completely reversed in the actual historical unfolding of events in modern Korea. First, the state came into being, and society was set against it, because it was felt external to it, and then culture was often opposed to attempts at social mobilization, even though it often got swept up in social and political struggles. In fact, throughout Korean modern history one can detect a continuous struggle by the aesthetic claims of Koreans to find a place in Korean society but often in dishonorable collusion with illegitimate political power.

The postliberation cultural history of South Korea, excluding a brief political interlude before the inauguration of the Republic of Korea, begins with a rejection of politics and also a moral and social compulsion from the collectivity. It soon becomes clear, however, that culture as an autonomous activity is impossible in a disordered polity; culture requires the premise of a stable moral and political order from which other elements of the collectivity can be developed. In the absence of this premise, cultural activities come paradoxically, to take upon themselves the task of providing it, with the result that the task of culture is narrowed down to what is demanded by moral duties and political objectives, losing the fuller human dimension of the aesthetic. Aesthetics become politics. Yet aesthetics becoming politics may return to itself in the end: politics may become a nurturing ground for aesthetics.

The following uses literature, as the most representative and articulate example, to adumbrate the fate of culture in postliberation Korea through the processes of politicization, depoliticization, and repoliticization.

Revolution and Literature

That liberation from colonial rule should let loose the political passions of the entire nation, and that literature and the arts should become instantly political, if not in achieved products, at least in the discursive rhetoric of the times, is more than understandable. The need to participate in building the new nation was obligatorily recognized by people of all political persuasions. It was, however, Marxists who proclaimed most clearly the primacy of political objectives in any cultural practice. As Kim Tongsŏk put it, "the honor of a writer will be kept only when he is dedicated to the cause of national liberation even if it means sacrificing literature, and life as well."[3] Even the writers on the Right could not refute the call made by the Left. Kim Tongri and Cho Jihun, the representative nationalist theoreticians, went so far as to subscribe to the idea of a "national social revolution" as the theme of all writing—to the idea that writing should work "for national and class liberation";[4] they agreed that the writer must write to "rectify the contradictions and shortcomings of capitalist society."[5]

But in the case of the rightists, their hearts were not in the chorus they joined. They were firm in rejecting the violent revolution and subordination of art to revolutionary politics. Whatever they conceded in their public rhetoric in terms of recognizing the need to work for social change, they were reluctant in practice to go beyond the belief in the importance of nationalistic and humanistic values they wanted to uphold in their work. It was the position of the nationalists and humanists that eventually triumphed, and literature returned to what they thought to be its proper domain, turning away from politics, until the tide began to turn again in the 1970s. The nonpolitical theory and practice of literature and the arts triumphed largely because of the forced removal of the Left from the political scene of South Korea, either by repression or voluntary emigration to the North. But apart from the accidental spillover from the contemporary political situation, there was perhaps an irrepressible impulse in modern Korean history that made the humanistic or belletristic position more acceptable to many writers—an impulse representing the return of the aesthetic. To see this, the brief period of political literature immediately after the liberation must be located within the longer rhythm of Korean cultural history—and the repeated attempts of the aesthetic to return must be regarded as having achieved some results but also ending in political and moral dishonor.

Confucianism, as noted, prescribed that political rule must be stabilized

3. Quoted in Hong Chongson, *Yŏksachŏk sarm kwa bip'yŏng* [Historical life and criticism] (Seoul: Munhak kwa chisŭng sa, 1986), p. 127.

4. Cho Jihun, "Minjok munhwaŭi tangmyŏn kwaje" [The present task of national culture], in Shin Hyŏngki, ed., *Haebang samnyŏnŭi bip'yŏng munhak* (Literary criticism in the three-year period after the liberation) (Seoul: Segye, 1988), p. 372.

5. Kim Tongri, "Sunsu munhak kwa chesam segyekwan" [Pure literature and the third world outlook], in Shin Hyŏngki, *Haebang samnyŏnui bi p'yŏng*, p. 347.

through virtue and culture, which meant, if not subordination of culture to politics, at least confinement of artistic freedom to what is acceptable in a well-ordered polity. Especially in the neo-Confucian orthodoxy of the Chosŏn dynasty, the politico-moral imperative of society over culture was supreme. There was a clear recognition that the arts and literature could tread a dangerous path of their own when detached from the state, the ultimate source of political and moral authority. The pursuit of literary art per se, for instance, separate from the study of the classics in moral and political philosophy, was regarded as a dangerous and decadent heresy to be guarded against.

This was in line with the general nature of the social order during the Chosŏn dynasty, which was puritanical and repressive toward various expressions of the natural man. Modern writers and artists experimenting with new modes of artistic expressions inspired by Western models felt a sense of liberation at the passing of the moralism of the old era. It was as if the repressed were just waiting to return regardless of the consequences. There was excitement, they felt, in the new discovery of the individual, sexuality, and the senses, liberated from the watchful eyes of the ethical state. This excitement was in large part behind the cultural awakening of the early twentieth century represented by Ch'oe Namsŏn, Yi Kwangsu, Kim Tongin, Yi Sang, and others.

But this enthusiasm was to have tragic political consequences, for the liberation from the old regime meant a new enslavement to the Japanese colonial authorities and their culture. The new liberation was in fact brought about by the forces of the new slavery. The contradiction was represented by what is sometimes called "culturalism" *(munhwachuŭi),* an advocacy of modern culture that blithely ignored the political situation of the country and through its apolitical individualism helped destroy the old collectivities, thereby sapping the moral and political will of the people. The secret collusion between culture and colonialism was soon to be graphically illustrated by the flirtation and collaboration of many of the early modernizers with Japanese imperialism. In the early 1920s and then the 1930s, the "culturalist" attitude clashed sharply with the strong political awareness of writers who organized themselves into the Korean Proletarian Artists' Federation (KAPF) in 1925. Their program condemned bourgeois, nonpolitical literary endeavors, advocating instead "spontaneous literary production on the subject of the poor and the oppressed" and eventually "objective-conscious literature" *(mokchŏk ŭisikchŏk munhak)*; "objective" meaning the elevation of individual resistance to colonialism based on proletarian class consciousness.[6]

However, because the colonial authorities tried to stamp out the movement for proletarian arts and literature, a more individualistic kind of literature, expressing lyrical emotions and dealing with nonpolitical life, came to constitute the mainstream of Korean writing until it too had to come to an end as writers and artists were mobilized for collaborative ventures in support of the war efforts of Japanese imperialism through their writing, speech-making, or visiting the troops on the front lines. And then in 1942 the use of the Korean language as an official medium was prohibited.

With the liberation, politics could return, but once again, as noted, the contradictory dynamic of politics and culture was set in motion, with political and moral legitimacy on one side and evasive political irresponsibility and the upholding of aesthetic values on the other.

Vestiges of Agrarian Visions

With the inauguration of the Republic of Korea in 1948 and the Korean War, the brief political phase of the postliberation period comes to an end. It was largely forces extraneous to culture—repression and war—that disjoined politics and culture. It is clear, however, that in the elimination of the political theory and practice of literature in the antebellum years there was more than a simple political conflict between the Left and the Right. In the position of nonpolitical writing, what is often called "pure literature" *(sunsu munhak),* there was to be sure, conservative or reactionary recalcitrance. This is evident even in the obvious artificiality with which conservative writers work up nativist or primitive sentiments—the inexplicable sadness of life, transience, trials of endurance, resignation, compassion, and soon, for example, in the stories of Kim Tongri, collected in *The Records of Yellow Earth (Hwangt'ogi)* (1949), offering them as alternative themes of universal significance over against politics. Yet the fear that the "pure literature" writers entertained over their creative freedom was real enough, and so was their sense of the subtlety and complexity of life beyond the reductive formulation of political ideology. The age was, to use a phrase

6. Pak Yonghi, "Munye undongŭi mokchŏk ŭisikron" [Objective-consciousness in literary agitation], *Chosŏnchikwang* (July 1927): 1–6, reprinted in Sin Hyŏngki, *Haebang Samnyŏnui bi p'yŏng,* pp. 125–26.

Sartre used in his critical homage of Merleau-Ponty, that of the butcher who left no room for a man of subtlety; a man of subtlety could survive only in evasion, subterfuge—and even collusion.

The same dilemma is perceivable again in the stories written in the 1950s from a liberal or conservative point of view. By the early 1950s ideological struggles in South Korea had been determined one-sidedly—in large part by repression, which left a permanent legacy of bad conscience for any defense for liberal culture in South Korea. Yet once again a degree of genuineness must be admitted in some writers' rejection of the political imperative of the Left.

Hwang Sunwŏn's *The Children of Cain (K'ainŭi huye)* (1945), perhaps the only novel-length account of land reform in North Korea, is the best example of the antithesis between the rough justice of a revolutionary process and a subtler understanding of humanity, which Hwang sets out to defend, though he is not without a sympathetic understanding of the former. Thematically, the central conflict in the novel turns on the discrepancy between an ideologically conceived political program and what is felt to be the natural working of interpersonal relations in a traditional agricultural community. These relations were, of course, determined by the exploitative hierarchy of landlord and tenant, but over time, through a person's life or the history of the system, they had modulated into crisscrossing networks of feelings and attitudes hard to conceptualize or classify in objective categories. The process of land reform and the revolution demand that everyone learn these objective categories. But learning to reject their relevance as applied to people's concrete relations constitutes the central experience of the hero of the novel.

An ideological preconception's intrusion on the reality of life in the village is best illustrated in the scene in which a Communist cadre comes with a group of farmers to expropriate land and confronts the protagonist, the landlord. After a short give-and-take between them, a woman, who has been serving the landlord, tries to intercede with the revolutionaries on behalf of her master. She has unchallengeable credentials as one of the downtrodden, being a daughter of one of the hero's tenants and a servant in the household of the landlord. But her servitude is entirely voluntary; she offered to work for him, in spite of his hesitation and reluctance, because after the rough vicissitudes of life involving an unhappy marriage with a brutish man, she had found in his household a center of moral consideration and humane concern. However, to the Communist organizer, her basic situation can be defined only in terms of economic and sexual exploitation existing between lord and peasant. "He [the landlord] must have taken advantage of his position as landlord and violated our comrade, daughter of a tenant and another man's wife."[7] Ojaknyo, the tenant's daughter, declares, as a stratagem of defense for her master and property, that everything now belongs to her, but for the organizer there is no way of suspecting her real motive.

> I understand, comrade [he says sympathetically]. You have slaved so long for this man and for this house. I will report it to the proper authorities. They will take care of the matter. . . . Have you kept an account of the work you have done so that you may receive due compensation?[8]

The organizer's sympathetic attitude serves to highlight the distance between the ideological version of her life as explained for her by the official and realities of her life history—discord with her father, an unhappy marriage to a rough drunkard (whose raw manliness is admiringly depicted by the author), her succumbing to a cholera epidemic from which she was nursed back to life by the hero, and so on. As Hwang Sunwŏn sees it, there are many evil consequences to the revolutionary changes in North Korea—hypocrisy, bad blood, servile opportunism, undeserved suffering—but the main point of the novel remains that the ideological scheme of things does not do justice to the multifaceted reality of interest, loyalty, love, hate, and work found in the natural community of a traditional society.

Yi Bŏmsŏn's short story, "The People of the Village of Cranes" *(Hakmaŭl saramdŭl)* (1957), though a clumsier and more simplistic allegory, makes a similar point in a more straightforward way: an ideologically planned revolution is unnatural and artificial; in an agrarian village, the revolution is an imposition, while people's folkways are almost second nature and so must be respected.

In the story, a communist cadre arrives in a village and tries to rouse the villagers to revolutionary fervor and violence. But the revolution does not make sense to them: the slogans "liberation," "exploitation," "reactionar-

7. Hwang Sunwŏn, *K'ainŭi huye* [The children of Cain] (1954), in *Hwang Sunwŏn chŏnjip,* [Collected works of Hwang Sunwŏn, vol. 8] (Seoul: Munhak kwa chisŏng sa, 1981), p. 345.
8. Ibid., pp. 346–47.

ies," "revolution," and "heroism" are all abstract words beyond their comprehension. On the whole, the political order being intiated by the hastily organized people's committee with its meetings and speech-making is alien to them, compared with the natural order maintained by ancient customs centering on respect for the village elders.

The artificiality of the new order is symbolically represented by an incident involving the cranes that annually nest in the tree at the center of the village. When they do well and give birth to a large number of young, it is taken to be an auspicious sign for the village; if they fail to do so, the villagers fear that evil events may befall them. In the year of the revolution, the birds come, but newborn birds are found dead, having dropped to the ground, surely a bad omen for the village and for the Communist order being established there. The villagers' superstitious belief about the cranes enrages the young cadre, who regards it as a plot by the reactionaries to sabotage the revolution. To root out the source of the reactionary rumor, he shoots down the mother crane from the tree. The cranes have been worshipped by the villagers; they have been objects of reverence and affection, a symbol of the benevolent regularity of natural order. Now they are gone forever.

Sŏnu Hwi's "The Flower of Fire" *(Bulkkot)* (1957) is a story with a clear ideological purpose, but it is worth looking at, for it illustrates in a more complex situation a similar defense of natural order against attempts at political mobilization. The hero of the story is an intellectual who would prefer to lead a retiring life outside the public arena but who is, repeatedly drawn into political conflicts in spite of himself. His complex fate is foreshadowed from his birth—he was the posthumous son of a martyred patriot. As a student he is drafted into the Japanese army in its war against China, from which he runs away to join Mao Zedong's army in Yanan, though he leaves it too as soon as an opportunity presents itself. Other occasions, even after the liberation, force him into various schemes of political activism, but he is always only a reluctant participant, and his natural impulse is to evade these schemes as much as possible. However, he is not without a sense of justice; instances of injustice he observes constantly impel him into small and yet courageous acts of rebellion against authorities. His last rebellion is against the Communists as he tries to rescue, almost against his will, an innocent victim branded as a reactionary in the people's court. The last scene of the story shows him hiding in a cave waiting for a showdown with the pursuing Communists. In the meantime, he realizes the necessity of joining a general fight against the Communists, for the right to remain free of forced political mobilization.

In the hero's mind, this coerced mobilization is contrasted with a life lived at the level of the immediate and concrete. Throughout the story, the sensory appeal of nature and the life lived in nature is elevated to an order of existence above ideologies, as in the following passage:

> There comes from the kitchen the smell of fish being broiled over the fire as he stretches his legs heavy with fatigue from the day's work. He feels his stomach rumbling. His mother scolds him for the impatience with which he succumbs to his appetite; she says he is like a child. The flower-bed is bright with colors, over which comes the sound of cicadas and birds. This is life—a life for man. This is the small right man is entitled to enjoy—by the mere fact of his being born into life.[9]

These details of the sensory experience of an ordinary life are cited to offset the waste of ideological battles being waged in society. Sŏnu Hwi's appeal is thus to nature that is supposed to be above mundane politics.

But it is also possible to say that nature is what has become habitual, that it too is an outcome of cultural elaboration of man's social life. To affirm the priority of nature over artificial politics is, in both the East and the West, a favorite conservative strategy for justifying the status quo. Sŏnu Hwi's conservative ideology is obvious. There is a naïveté and a lack of understanding of the revolutionary processes in Yi Bŏmsŏn's "The People of the Village of Cranes," and Hwang Sunwŏn's criticism may be said to apply more to the clumsiness than the substance of the persuasive techniques of the revolution. However, the kind of realism existing in the perception of these writers leads us to suspect that the revolutionary ideology born in the industrial city is probably not relevant to the traditional rural village. Also, there is an undeniable perennial appeal, it must be admitted, in the idea of a social order that has become second nature and therefore is felt to be self-perpetuating.

However, whether the vision of a natural order subsisting on its own against any attempt to effect change was a condition of naïvete or not, it

9. Sŏnu Hwi, "Bulkkot" [The flowers of fire], in Kown Yŏngmin, ed., *Haebang sasipnyŏnŭi munhak, 1* [Forty years of literature after the liberation, vol. 1] (Seoul: Minŭmsa, 1965), p. 236.

was ineluctably destined to be shattered by the political turmoil sweeping through the country as a whole and by the encroaching modern world, which rendered it a naive dream open to corruption from political manipulations.

Existentialism of War and Poverty

An order of harmonious natural relations among men, as an ideal and reality, would soon vanish in Korean society, as the Korean War, the hardships and moral degradation it brought, and subsequent industrialization transformed traditional life in Korea. As a matter of fact, when Hwang Sunwŏn, Yi Bŏmsŏn, and Sŏnu Hwi were writing their stories of the life of natural acceptance, the life they were accepting in reality was one of humiliating misery and alienation. Japanese colonial rule, the dislocation and unrest of the interregnum after the liberation, and the destruction of the war wreaked havoc with people's lives.

Closer to the reality was existentialism, with its vision of nihilistic angst, which became the dominant current in the intellectual life of the 1950s. Although Hwang Sunwŏn generally preferred to write about elemental humanity beyond social relations, as noted by many critics, and tried to maintain an optimistic view of the human condition, he produced many works during the 1950s about the degradation of contemporary life lived in moral and material squalor. "The Tightrope-Walker" *(Gogyesa)* (1952), an autobiographical short story, depicts his plight in refugee-crowded wartime Pusan, without an adequate job or housing (his family lived scattered in several houses of relatives and came together for meals). There is in it a self-commiserating sense of the precariousness of existence as implied in the title of the story and a large dose of bitterness about the society that produced this precariousness. But his anxiety about his personal situation becomes social criticism in his other works—depiction of the corruption and despair of a life in an orphanage in *The Graft of Humanity (Ingan jŏpmok)* (1955) and later the existential agony of youth caught in the chaos of war in *Trees on the Stiff Hill (Namudŭl bit'ale sŏda)* (1960).

Yi Bŏmsŏn, in spite of the theme of an agrarian idyll in "The People of the Village of Cranes," is better known as the writer of gloom and despair throughout the 1950s and the 1960s. His short story, "The Stray Bullet" *(Obalt'an)* (1959), is perhaps the best known of his stories, and also the darkest. The hero of the story is a low-ranking white-collar worker who cannot afford lunch or dental care (and so must endure his toothache); his sister is driven to prostitution with American soldiers; his brother is in prison for robbery; his mother lies ill, mentally deranged with an obsession to return to North Korea from where they had fled a short time earlier. Other writers also chronicled the years from the Korean War through the early 1960s and all reported the desperate conditions of life. The titles of some representative stories alone would convey an idea of the prevailing mood of the times: "The Victim," "Sketches of the Human Zoo," "The Superfluous Man" (by Son Ch'angsŏp); "The Skeletal Remains," "Exiled" (by Song Byŏngsu); "The Sound of Sinking," "Flight from Home," "Hunger, Thirst, and Echo," "Another Man's Land" (by Yi Hoch'ŏl); "The Victim," "The Dog That Had to Kill Itself" (by Yi Bŏmsŏn).

What is remarkable, however, is the fact that the desperate conditions of life are accepted rather passively. It is as if there occurred a paralysis of the will that made it impossible to see beyond the immediate given of suffering and hardship, even though there was no lack of embittered understanding of the political situation that had brought them on. Typical passivity, though expressed with a smoldering sense of resentment, can be seen in such a story as Ha Kŭnch'an's "Two Generations of Victims" *(Sunan idae),* which tells of a father and a son who became victims of wars they did not cause or understand. The father, who lost one of his arms in a Japanese forced labor camp during World War II, goes to meet his son who is returning from the Korean War and finds that the son had had a leg amputated because of a shrapnel wound. The father accepts the misfortune with resignation and tells his son that they could help each other because they may be able to combine his legs and his son's arms, which he demonstrates by carrying his son on his back across a stream on their way home.

In the years from the Korean War to 1960, various forces combined to produce the general political passivity: the immensity of the devastation of the war, the ubiquity of poverty and suffering, which made the equality of hardship the prevailing condition of life with the few exceptions of "profiteers" *(moribe),* the deferential culture of a traditional Korea, and the repressive state organs. Moreover, with the elimination of the Left through the Korean War there existed no alternative politics. This elimination was in the last phase voluntary to a great extent for the writers who went North, but it also made those who chose to stay in the South accept the community of hardship as the price of their voluntary sojourn. In "The Stray Bullet," the hero, against his mother's insistence that they return to

North Korea, puts forward the argument that they fled it for freedom and therefore they must pay for that freedom with hardship. He asks his mother, "Aren't we free in the South, mother?"[10] There are evils in society, to be sure, but they would be regarded as part of whatever freedom there exists. The narrator in Yi Hoch'ŏl's short story, "P'anmunjŏm" (1960) defends the South against a reporter from the North who condemns it as a decadent and corrupt society, saying, "The best thing in life is to be free and to be able to do wicked things a little now and then. That's the way man is."[11]

Industrialism and Wages of Greed

It was not the general condition of dislocation and poverty but the economic recovery and development of the 1960s and the 1970s that awakened political consciousness. Economic development in particular, stirs up dormant negative feelings inevitable in a society torn by ideologies, wholesale dislocation, and strife. The use of state power for the social mobilization required for economic development was bound to meet with popular resistance if such power lacks a popular social base, as was the case with the regimes of Park Chung Hee and Chun Doo Hwan. However, the mobilization had to elicit cooperation from all segments of society, and the power of the state had to justify itself as representing the entire collectivity constituting the state. This accounts for the emphasis in the rhetoric of the 1960s on "the strength of the state" *(kungyŏk)* or "the regeneration of the nation" *(minjok junghŭng)*.

But capitalist development inevitably leads to differential increases of power and wealth. Besides, the motivation at work was individual desire for an improved material life. Consequently, what was unleashed was not the elation of a great collective endeavor but a mad scramble for a greater share of power and wealth, an intensification of competitive struggle for survival—the struggle perhaps more intense because it was not exactly for survival but for material and social advantages since the improving economy made affluence, not survival, the focus of competition. Old social relations became more strenuous and strained; antagonisms of people and

10. Yi Bŏmsŏn, "Obal'tan" [The stray bullet], in Hyŏndae han'guk munhak chŏnjip, 6 [Collected modern Korean literature, vol. 6] (Seoul: Singu munhwasa, 1965), p. 361.

11. Yi Hoch'ŏl, "P'anmunjŏm," in *Yi Hoch'ŏl chŏnjip, 1* [Collectd works of Yi Hoch'ŏl, vol. 1] (Seoul: Ch'ŏnggye yŏnguso, 1988), p. 71.

classes surfaced in all relations; moral and cultural values were emptied of their substance.

Instead of celebrating the economic progress of the nation, Korean writers as a whole criticized its negative effects, both from a cultural point of view, since they were concerned with the deteriorating moral quality of life, and from a political point of view, since they were drawn into sympathy with various movements fighting against a hardening system of repression and exploitation. Typical of the criticism of the deteriorating moral quality of life in a developing society are the observations of Pak Wansŏ in her stories and novels. According to her autobiographical story, "The Ramparts of Mother" *(Ŭmmaŭi malttuk)* (1980), the house in which she began her life as a child of refugees from the North was a rickety old house without running water. Water had to be carried uphill laboriously in buckets on a pole by a water peddler; rainwater had to be carefully saved by all means. In the course of the story, by the 1970s she is living in a modern apartment, with all the modern conveniences—to the point that she is largely free of household chores, "as if the apartment is built to be left entirely unattended."[12] At one point the writer-heroine enjoys a quiet evening in a country house that belongs to a friend, a house that is well heated and enlivened by a fireplace, and which opens onto a snow-covered orchard. If she is far from happy in this story, it is not because of the problematic present but because of the memories of the past, of which the horrors of the war and the brutal political conflict that went along with it form a major part. But what she generally records in her stories is hypocrisy, frustration, fatigue—dehumanization of people caught in the mad pursuit of material and social gains in a society imploding in the overheated economy of development.

Her novel *The Unsteady Afternoon (Hwich'ŏnggŏrinŭn ohu)* (1976) attempts to depict an age permeated with material values, in the form of a history of the three marriages of a middle-class family. The mood of the times is indicated by the first daughter of the family, who declares to her father, "Daddy, I want you to know that there is something I love more than you: the happiness that could only be in a rich man's life, that I must

12. Pak Wansŏ, "Ŭmmaŭi malttuk" [The ramparts of mother], vol. 2, in *Kŭ kaŭlŭi sahŭldongan: Pak Wansŏ munhaksŏn* [Three days of that autumn: Representative works of Pak Wansŏ] (Seoul: Nanam, 1985), pp. 183–84.

have by all means."[13] She marries a rich widower but ends up in a mental asylum. The second daughter of the family marries a poor young man for love, only to be trapped in the slavery of daily housework; the third works out a compromise that would give her money, love, and culture, but she has to pursue her fate in another land, by emigrating to the United States. The complex calculations of modern love in *The Unsteady Afternoon* contrast with the story of a love unadulterated by manipulative interests, suffered and affirmed in the poverty-stricken and difficult circumstances of the Korean War, as told in *The Bare Tree (Namok)* (1970), the author's first novel.

A more direct social criticism of the years of economic development, though mainly in the countryside, can be found in various stories by Yi Mungu. As he describes life in a typical rural community, for example, in *Our Village (Uri dongnae)* (1981), what conditions life in a farming village is the spread of the culture of consumption which transforms values, social relations, and material life. The village becomes an ugly jungle of interpersonal conflict for gain and advantage, with antagonism and manipulative intrigue determining relations among the neighbors, between husband and wife, and between parents and children. Appliances such as refrigerators, television sets, and rice-cookers fill neighbors' minds with envy, helping to sour relations among people. Plastic ware is preferred to traditional utensils. Hamburgers and hot dogs take the place of traditional snacks. Wasteful purchases of consumer goods, gambling parties, pleasure trips, plastic surgery (in the book, genital surgery supposed to enhance sexual pleasure)—all become causes of contention in the family. What feeds this seething cauldron of possessive mania is the Park government's policy for rural development, which probably has honest intentions but which easily becomes an obtrusive administrative invasion into every corner of personal life and soon deteriorates into instruments of manipulation for gain through influence and bribery in the hands of grasping manipulators. Consequently, the villagers lose the autonomy, dignity, and depth of culture that were possible in the settled way of life characterizing the village in premodern times—at least so Yi Mungu seems to think, looking back with nostalgia to the rural life before the inroads of modernization in his stories in *Kwanchon Essays (Kwanchon sup'il)* (1977).

13. Pak Wansŏ, *Hwich'ŏnggŏrinŭn ohu, 1* [The unsteady afternoon, vol. 1] (Seoul: Ch'angjak kwa bip'yŏngsa, 1977), p. 70.

However, Yi Mungu is not entirely pessimistic in his judgment of the new rural developments. He hopes that a humane order of life will eventually be reinstituted after this period of confused struggle for modern advantages, as he suggests in the last episode of *Our Village,* where the villagers, whose sense of injustice has been smoldering, openly rebel against the corrupt village officials. But the rebellion, after bitter accusations and explanations, resolves itself into a ceremony of reconciliation, ending with a feast in which the entire community participates, reaffirming its communality. A character pronounces its basic contract: "We who live by our faith in earth and in heaven do not forget that there are in life decency, neighborliness, friendship, and judgment."[14]

Yi Mungu has been one of the more prominent activist writers who opposed the two military regimes in the 1970s and 1980s with his share of police harassment, but he is not only optimistic about the eventual outcome of the present social and political restructuring but also has a more sympathetic understanding of the present situation than other militant dissidents. A character in *Our Village* offers a putative explanation for the entire process:

> When you build a new house, after demolishing an old one, the work is likely to make your body ache all over as from a fit of ague. Money takes away your land. But where does this taste for money come from? From poverty as it begins to let up a bit after twenty or thirty years of work. Your limbs feel loose as if coming apart, pulled this way and that way. But you shouldn't take it too hard. Wisdom is to know this: how to keep small cuts from developing into big wounds. There is a clever and moderate way of teaching your wives to be patient and modest, to know what is possible and what is not.[15]

This explanation or counsel of patience is spoken by a man who became rich by his real estate speculation. It must be assumed therefore that the author is keeping his distance from it. Yet avoiding a possible charge of being an apologist for the social and moral chaos that is the modernizing

14. Yi Mungu, *Uri dongnae* [Our village] (Seoul: Minŭmsa, 1981), p. 317.
15. Ibid., p. 246.

countryside, Yi Mungu is here trying out a scheme of understanding which is plausible and at least partly his own.

Toward Revolutionary Romanticism

Pak Wansŏ, Yi Mungu, Ch'oe Ilnam, So Chŏngin, Yun Hŭnggil, and others attempted to render a sense of life in the modernizing decades, looking at it, as it were, from inside, from the midst of life as it is lived in its quotidian diversity. Other writers were more political in their depictions; their approach was more external, working toward the lived reality of society from outside, from a political perspective, which came to be characterized as *minjungchuŭi,* or Korean populism. Throughout the 1970s and 1980s populist literature increasingly came to occupy the center of the literary scene as its voice became more militant and attracted sympathetic listeners in a widening circle under the repressive Park and Chun regimes. But at the same time it alienated many readers, by giving up the complex aesthetic maneuvers for engaging the concrete reality of human existence in more than political simplifications.

The rise of populist literature marked a turning point, a choice, on the one hand, and an inevitable historical development, on the other. If a basic impulse behind cultural endeavors, including literature, is toward a life lived in, to borrow Schiller's phrase, "the serene spontaneity of . . . [its] activity,"[16] it is extremely averse to anything from outside that disrupts this spontaneity. Hence at least in part the affirmative character of culture: acceptance of things as they are. Of course, no story or cultural enactment of life would be satisfactory if life were presented only in stasis, with no movement beyond what is given. But this necessary transcendence we would like to see as something working its way out from the interior of life given, as if it were a gift from the spontaneity of life in its own activity. There are times, however, when life contains so much activity, with all its intensification and simplification, that it goes beyond itself, more decisively than in the condition of serene spontaneity, into a definitely perceivable movement. Then the movement takes over and obliterates the manifold moves of life lived quietly. Of course, this movement is not always a simple overflow of an exuberant life; it could be a reactive movement against

16. Friedrich Schiller, "Naive and Sentimental Poetry," in *Naive and Sentimental Poetry and On the Sublime* (New York: Frederick Ungar, 1966), p. 85.

constraints trying to contain it. At least this was the case in the modernizing decades, from the 1960s through the 1980s, in South Korea.

Many writers remained within the felt texture of everyday life, but this so easily bumped against the constraints of life now being shaped economically and politically, making the effort to stay with the felt reality of life a laborious exercise in circumlocution. For instance, as Sŏ Chŏngin does in his short story "The Valley" *(Goltchagi)* (1986), if a writer renders as faithfully as possible the vicissitudes of an old man being dumped at an old folks' home, his rendition becomes redundant or at least tedious in face of the obvious sociological explanation of the breakdown of the extended family, which leaves no room for unproductive old men in the selfish makeup of a new nuclear family. It was then inevitable that a type of literature that grasps life from the external constraints of society would come into being: the literature imbued with what may be called sociologism or, more strongly, political ideology. Thus the dream of an order built up from inside from the civilizing work of morality and aesthetics become more and more irrelevant.

The genealogy of political literature goes back a long way, as noted earlier. It began to make its comeback in the 1960s, in an ascending curve and in an ever-narrowing political focus. In the mid-1960s, when the debate about the commitment of the writer began to attract attention, it was understood as an activity of "the humanist defending the humanity of man and appealing to fellow men in a fight against any incidence of dehumanization."[17] These enraged writers have been influenced by such French writers as André Malraux, André Gide, Albert Camus, and Antoine de Saint-Exupéry.[18] But Yŏm Muung, who, along with Paek Nakch'ong, came to be considered one of the prime theoreticians of committed literature, began to speak of the need to "place literature at the center of the people's practice";[19] Paek spoke of the strategic inevitability, even within a broad humanist concern, of "forming [out of various progressive elements of the population] an exclusive bond of solidarity and a battleline dividing friends

17. Yu Jongho, *Munhak kwa hyŏnsil* [Literature and reality] (Seoul: Minŭmsa, 1975), p. 65.

18. Kim Bunggu, "Jakka wa sahoe ch'amyŏ [The writer and engagement] and "Ch'amyŏ wa ch'amyŏ munhakŭi che yuhyŏng" [Engagement and types of engagement literature] in *Chaka wa sahoe* [The writer and society] (Seoul: Ilchogak, 1973).

19. Yŏm Muung, "Hyŏnsil akŭi chugu" [The pursuit of evil in reality], quoted in Hong Chongsŏn, Yŏksachŏk, p. 19.

from foes,"[20] an obvious call for a kind of proletarian literature, though Paek has never been clear about what segments of the population he thinks the progressive political literature he advocates should work for.

In the field of creative writing, Sin Donghyŏp was the first significant writer and precursor in the literature of populistic politics. His first published poem, "Lands and Rivers of Azalea" *(Chindalle sanch'on)* (1959), on the surface a lyrical recollection of the Korean War, already carries the hidden message that, contrary to the official line, the war was a tragically defeated people's revolutionary war. Sin conveys this message symbolically: soldiers mowed down by a passing American plane rot among the newly blooming azaleas, while hungry men take to the mountains and the rice harvests rot in the fields. (The azalea is dear to all Koreans and is also the national flower of North Korea.) Sin's major work is, however, the narrative poem *The Kŭm River (kŭmkang)* (1967), on the subject of the Tonghak (Eastern Learning) uprising of 1894. It is the first postwar imaginative work committed to a populistic reading of modern Korean history. It tells the story of the nineteenth-century peasants rising up against the landed class and royal power and being defeated by government troops backed by the Japanese army. The poet intends partly to refresh the memory of this popular rebellion but partly also to show the parallels between the past and the present—the present, as he sees it, is determined by corrupt bureaucrats and comprador capitalists taking orders from Americans. He recommends as a remedy another uprising to overthrow the regime of exploitation now reigning in Korea. In the society to be established there would be:

> no landlords
> no officials, no owners of banks,
> no class privilege;
>
> only equal work, equal sharing
> throughout the entire peninsula;
>
> work according to ability,
> distribution according to need;
> crowning it all, ever-expanding
> festivities of the people.[21]

20. Paek Nakch'ong, *Minjok munhak kwa segye munhak* [National literature and world literature] (Seoul: Ch'angjak kwa bip'yŏngsa, 1978), p. 96.

21. Sin Dongyŏp, *Kŭmkang* [The Kŭm river] in *Sin Dongyŏp chŏnjip* [Collected works of Sin Dongyŏp] (Seoul: Ch'angjak kwa bip'yŏngsa, 1975), p. 137.

These verses may be the first explicit reference to socialist principles since the Korean War. But what is remarkable is that Sin's political convictions do not appear as abstract and schematic in the poem as they might have, largely thanks to Sin's poetic talent, which sustains the narrative with speed and fills it with high lyrical moments. The more important reason for our consideration, however, is that his vision of a good society draws heavily on the native tradition of collective cooperation, good will, and festive enjoyment of life he believes to exist among the farmers. For him, the Tonghak rebellion was interesting not only as a model of resistance but also as a more violent manifestation of the agrarian collectivism of Korean peasantry. He found his vision of agrarian collectivism reaffirmed in Marxism and the struggles of peasant societies in Algeria, Palestine, Iran, China, and sub-Saharan Africa.

It may be noted in this connection that Sin Donghyŏp's agrarian nostalgia is shared by the conservative rejection of communism as we have seen in Yi Bŏmsŏm and other writers. The angst in Korea in the modernizing decades has much to do with life's uncertainties in its change from an agrarian to an industrial way of life. But the distance growing between the nostalgia and the changing reality of the society makes an agrarian vision an ineffectual way of engaging contemporary reality. What was obviously needed was a scheme of understanding more directly applicable to the industrialism now replacing the agrarian order. For the active modernizers, it comes from theories of capitalist development; for those who suffer from modernization, it comes from various versions of Marxism. But the task is more difficult for an imaginative comprehension of life under modernization, because it has to deal with the fullness of feelings and lived reality that could develop only in a soil enriched by tradition. Now this abundance was no longer available, and creative writing came to suffer from abstraction and ideology.

Among various early attempts to come to grips with the new reality of industrialism, Cho Sehi's *The Ball Shot Up by the Dwarf (Nanjang'iga ssoaolin chagŭn gong)* (1975–78) was one of the more successful in capturing the contours of the emerging new society. Many lives are woven together in the novel to reveal the fabric of industrialization, as the lower classes of society transformed themselves from rural farmers to desultory wage earners in the city and to an incipient industrial proletariat. Workers also developed a consciousness of their new identity. But Cho Sehi's workers are not yet at the point of becoming a revolutionary or militant working class with its own social programs. There is still too much of the humane and deferential culture of the agrarian past remaining for them to become a class in opposition to the bourgeoisie. It is significant that the central myth supplying a point of moral reference for the novel is a village of peaceful dwarfs supposed to exist somewhere in Germany where there is no terror from the people of normal stature—a village run completely by the dwarfs for the benefit of the dwarfs. The myth gives the whole novel a lyrical quality, making it more accessible to the book-reading public, but it also deprives the situation of the working class of whatever potential for militancy and revolutionary violence there was in it: the time has not yet come when the workers are seen as giants changing society, not dwarfs withdrawing from it.

Hwang Sŏgyŏng's treatment of the new industrial reality is tougher, though it often falls behind Cho Sehi in the density of realized human quality. "The Alien Land" *(kaekchi)* (1974) is widely considered a landmark in contemporary Korean literature in bringing the problem of the workers clearly to literary consciousness. The story, which concerns construction workers in a remote place where the port facilities are being built, focuses on a strike started by the workers to protest their low wages and a work organization that allows workers to be milked by the superfluous supervisors. Admirable as Hwang's intention is, the strike depicted fails to convey a persuasive inevitability. This is partly because the writer has failed to construct the story well in dramatic terms; but it is also because of the kind of situation being described. The situation being treated is not one that would support the confrontational development described in the story. Artistic failure is often a failure of the reality being examined, artistic maturity being covariable with the maturation of the potential in a given reality.

First of all, Hwang Sŏgyŏng has only thinly drawn the characters and circumstances of the workers involved, a reflection of the temporary nature of the community of workers at the construction site. The workers of the story are transient migratory laborers, recently uprooted from their farms and not yet established as a real community with an organic sense of collectivity. The strike, the central incident, is itself somewhat artificial. It is not a natural response of the workers, but something engineered by an outside agitator, an intellectual-turned-worker with a secret design of his own, which he tries to impose on the workers independent of the strike's actual rhythm. His strategy includes allowing a worker to be beaten almost to death, with the idea that this will incite the workers to violence. "One has got to use stratagems to make more people take part," he rationalizes. "What if somebody gets beaten to death? One's head gets cracked, and one can't help it."[22] We can question the moral dubiousness or the naïveté of the protagonist's game of revolutionary cunning, which is shared to a large extent by the writer himself. But the main point for our purposes concerns the distance between this kind of strategic or rational grasp of social processes and the workers' readiness to comprehend and follow the strategy.

True, the story shows a militant class consciousness developing, but that consciousness hovers outside—it does not grow out of the workers' actual lives. There is, however, a reality in the workers' rage against prevailing working conditions. Their visceral sense of injustice develops into a projection of the totality of life, as it is and as it might be, but still in the form of unelaborated emotions and intuitions. This perception easily attaches itself to abstract ideological exaggerations. In this sense, their projection of life, motivated by elemental rage, on the one hand, and easily diverted to ideological schemes, on the other, remains romantic, containing exaggerations in its perception of life's lacks and possibilities.

Repossessing History

The romantic conception of life developed as the writers attempted to see the situation of the emerging working class according to their vision of a coming revolution to be carried by this class. A similar kind of romanticism is represented on a vaster scale by multivolume historical novels that have become prominent in the 1970s and the 1980s. Of these, Pak Kyŏngri's *Land (T'oji)* in twelve volumes (1969–88), Hwang Sŏgyŏng's *Chang Gilsan* in ten volumes (1974–83), Kim Chuyŏng's *The Middlemen (Kaekchu)* in nine volumes (1979–84), and Cho Chŏngrae's *The Taebaek Mountains (T'aebaeksan)* in ten volumes (1986–89) are the most notable examples. These multivolume novels attempt to re-create history, especially recent history, so that human reality can be seen as having a significance beyond what is immediately given. They form part of the cultural movement for meaningful appropriation of the reality of Korean society. Since writers see the present reality as explainable in terms of history, they go

22. Hwang Sŏgyŏng, *Kaekchi* [The alien land] (Seoul: Ch'angjakkwa bip'yong, 1974), p. 54.

back in time in search of historical causes, antecedents, or at least parallels. They naturally call themselves realists because their aim was to see human lives enmeshed in the webs of the social and political forces of the times. ("Realism," as opposed to other modes of literary expression condemned as amoral, escapist, or false, has become a bully word used by the theoreticians of engaged literature to whip the writers into a battleline.) Nevertheless, these novels are more like historical romances, for the movement of history in these stories is more romantically imposed than realistically reconstructed, and so are the details of the history. Above all, a romantic fascination with the depth and height of emotional experience possible in the life of the long-suffering people furnishes a basic impetus for the unfolding of the historical imagination. (Fascination with sheer scope is itself romantic.)

The typical romantic of the 1970s and the 1980s is Hwang Sŏgyŏng. The impulse that finally culminates in the grand romance of history, *Chang Gilsan,* is a desire for affirmation of the vitality of folkish life breaking through the taboos of the established society. His short story "Illegal Slaughtering" (Milsal) (1972) best illustrates how a principle of life undaunted by any hesitation or inhibition is established in a heightened affective state. The story depicts the rite of passage undergone by a young man as he is forced to participate in the slaughter of an ox stolen from a farmer. The slaughterers know well what is involved: they are not only stealing and slaughtering, in violation of the law, but they are also causing considerable damage to the poor owner of the ox, one of the downtrodden. In the bare existence the farmer is eking out, the ox is, as the slaughterers call it themselves, "the pillar of a farm"; they know "they should not do anything like this even if they die of hunger." But they proceed with the theft and the slaughter anyway. "What else can we do?"[23] Thus asking, they justify themselves by invoking the inevitable necessity of life. The lesson of the illegal slaughter is precisely that of accepting the inevitable and going beyond the taboos of ordinary life. The scene of the slaughter graphically illustrates the lesson in brutality.

> The ox thrown to the ground continued to struggle, with his last strength. The blood spurted up, soaking the slaughterers. The assist-

23. Hwang Sŏgyŏng, "Milsal" [Illegal slaughtering], in *Toeji kkum* [The pig dream] (Seoul: Minŭmsa, 1980), p. 131.

> ant, holding tight to the poles of the temporary shack they had built, pushed his feet hard upon the neck of the ox from whom strength was now rapidly ebbing. The principal butcher struck in the iron pick in the skull of the ox and twisted it about to addle up the brains.[24]

The brains flow out. The butcher, scooping them up and tasting them, exclaims, "Delicious!" The rest of the slaughterers rush to the feast of raw brains, blood, and meat in an orgiastic enjoyment.

They are not without a sense of guilt and of the brutishness of the feast, but "life is hard, one has to eat in order to live, life is like that," as one of them says. "It's life that is in question . . . life is as cheap as flies; if you die, you can't eat," another says.[25] The lesson of the rite of passage is summed up: "If one is to live, there is nothing that one cannot do."[26] What is affirmed is the primacy of life, which, often expressed in violence, overrides normal considerations of legality and human sentiment. This affirmation can easily be extended to the situation of the underclasses in general and become a rationale for revolutionary violence. (One can think of Frantz Fanon's psychological insight into the purgative effect of violence for the individual in a revolutionary situation.)

Hwang Sŏgyŏng's major work, *Chang Gilsan,* is an extension of the same psychological dynamic to the situation of a whole society, though this society is not yet modern and the psychological insight has not yet become a realistic perception of a society in revolutionary process. The novel succeeds in conveying the feeling of life among the underclasses in the late Chosŏn dynasty, but less through a credible picture of life than through the same psychological drama of heroic violence as in "Illegal Slaughtering." Consequently, what dominates the intention of realistic re-creation of a past society is still the romantic notion of life, especially as it is refracted through the heroic figures of popular imagination. This is already announced in the title of the novel. The eponymous hero, a legendary bandit, who was born of a slave woman and brought up among outcast entertainers and actors, becomes an actor and a rebel leader. He is a passionate leader and the center of an underclass community characterized by spontaneous goodness, camaraderie, passion, and daring, possible, in the author's

24. Ibid., p. 134.
25. Ibid., pp. 135–36.
26. Ibid., p. 138.

vision, among people who have been cast out of the constraints of respectability and the structure of everyday life. The emphasis in the story is on his personal qualities and others' as well, rather than on actions by people in structurally and socially determined settings. The author evinces a high degree of social awareness, expressed here as sweeping generalizations and a general sentiment of righteousness, not as a result of painstaking attention to the details of the social forces at work in the society he wants to depict.

> Wars, rebellions; beatings and questionings at the hands of the authorities; famines occurring every other year; epidemics sweeping through the country every season—these are what the people had. They naturally wished that some heaven-sent catastrophe would end this rotten world and initiate a new world where men could live with men in warm neighborliness.[27]

As Hwang sees it, everything in society is in a dark flux: the masses have been reduced to subjection to the buffeting of chaotic forces, natural and political, out of which only heroic actions of superhuman dimension could rescue them. Violence, ruthless decisiveness, and even brutality are the natural marks of such heroic actions.

We also observe a dark romanticism in Kim Chuyŏng's *The Middlemen (Kaekchu),* another novel of popular life set in the Chosŏn Dynasty. Because it has less to do with martial matters, is set in a more recent past, namely, the late nineteenth century, and is about a class of people more solidly embedded in the traditional social structure, that is, the itinerant merchants, one might expect it to give the reader a sense of a more ordered world. But the world it reveals is again dark and violent. The vicissitudes of personal fortunes in this world are full of violent ups and downs. The dramas of conspiracy and revenge, particularly of a brutal variety, form the basic material of the novel. As a critic commented, "Brutal and lawless revenge drowns in blood the world depicted in the novel."[28] The blood spilled results from popular justice. The novel has the didactic purpose of promoting populist politics by recapturing history for the people. The author declared as much in his "Afterword": "In the past, succession to the throne,

27. Hwang Sŏgyŏng, *Chang Gilsan,* vol. 9 (Seoul: Hyŏnamsa, 1984), p. 361.
28. Kim Ch'isu, *Munhak kwa bip'yŏngŭi kujo* [Literature and the structure of criticism] (Seoul: Munhak kwa chisŏngsa, 1964), p. 128.

struggle over it, court intrigues, rivalries of powerful families, other concerns of the high and the mighty made up the stuff of history, while stories of the people were like the lighting in the background or they were set aside to the wineshop gossips, leading their life as wild folk stories there."[29] The writer of *The Middlemen* was to set this wrong approach to history right and speak for the people.

As we have noted, such novels as *Chang Gilsan* and *The Middlemen* are only two of many long historical novels that have recently appeared. Koreans obviously have a great need to see their social reality as a whole, and history is, in the current popular Weltanschauung and for our writers, the ultimate envelope covering this reality or the master narrative running through all human practices. Besides, history provides a convenient imaginary distance for an exercise in appropriating social reality. The two novels we have touched on are set in a period at a considerable remove from the present, but the general tendency now is to approach the present. This may be partly because of the natural progress in the collective experiment in the historical imagination and partly because of the gradual relaxation of censorship in the latter part of the Chun Doo Hwan era and after, which has made it easier to deal with sensitive modern or contemporary events. As the times to be reconstructed become more recent, taking advantage of the imaginary distance and therefore maintaining the romanticism of heroic actions became more difficult. More attention to everyday life and the social constraints determining it is an inevitable necessity. Hence, more realism is in order. This realism, though artistically necessary, may also represent progress toward a mature self-understanding of society itself.

The most famous example of a novelistic attempt to come to terms with more recent history is Pak Kyŏngri's *Land*. It is intended to be a saga of the Korean people from the late nineteenth century through the Japanese occupation. The typical segment of Korean life chosen for the purpose is a farming village in Hadong in southern Korea. The novel traces the fortunes of the inhabitants of this village within that locality and outside it as characters are displaced and seek to resettle in Manchuria. In the course of the story, the villagers' lives intersect with the larger currents of national history: the late Yi Dynasty reforms, the Japanese occupation, the mass migration to Manchuria, the armed struggle for independence. Although

29. Kim Chuyŏng, *Kaekchu* [The Middlemen], vol. 9, (Seoul: Ch'angjak kwa bip'yŏngsa, 1984), p. 299, quoted in Kim Ch'isu, p. 126.

Pak Kyŏngri is more concerned with the fortunes of individuals caught up in larger political and historical change than with the change as such, thematically the novel registers the replacement of the agrarian Confucian community by a more diversified social order of mixed economy along with the accompanying new learning and new mentality. With the coming of the modern age, the tale notes the decline of the Confucian moral order, which, while enmeshed in the contradictions of a class society, ensured some humanity in social relations, but Pak's politics unquestionably favors the common people, and her saga attempts to record the outrage of their undeserved suffering in time of social and moral disintegration.

In twentieth-century Korean history two periods that are hard to treat with objectivity and fairness stand out: the period of Japanese imperialism and that of struggle between the Right and the Left, mainly in the postliberation years. Memories of these periods cannot be recalled calmly or be laid to rest, for they involve not only suffering but also shame and guilt, and these memories have become troubled dreams filled with trauma and repression. The question of collaboration with the Japanese, for instance, has never been faced squarely, but it may be in the process of being forgotten, not only because of the passage of time but also because of its diminishing relevance to the present. But the postliberation political conflict carries a deeper trauma. Not only does the brutality involved in the suppression of communism remain vivid in memory, but there are still ex-communists, their relatives, and their families, who suffered and still suffer from the injuries of the suppression. Also, communism or at least some variety of it has long represented an alternative historical route that could again be chosen. It has been therefore regarded as a threat to the existing scheme of things and, from a psychological point of view, a source of discomfort to the conscience that has found accommodation in this scheme. Hence the ambivalence and complexity of the problem of memory regarding communism. But the repressed returns in the realm of politics and history as much as it does in the realm of psychoanalysis. If since the late 1980s we have seen a tremendous upsurge of interest in various aspects of the Korean Communist movement from the revolutionary poetry of the postliberation period to the thought of Kim Il Sung, we have simply been witnessing the return of the repressed. This return has been in preparation for quite a while, as the national psyche labored to repossess the whole of modern history down to the most painful recent past.

The South Korean literature of Communist experience that emerged in the 1970s and 1980s varies, including that which repudiates, that which tries to achieve a fair-minded understanding of, and that which advocates communism as a present source of revolutionary inspiration.

Yi Munyŏl's *The Heroic Age (Yŏngung sidae)* (1984) is a critique. Here the author attempts to test revolutionary politics and socialist ideas in terms of the life of the people who actually lived them, principally through the fate of a Communist from his early initiation in his student days in Tokyo, to his death while trying to escape the impending purge in the party. The end result of the hero's long service for the revolution and the party is weariness and disillusionment, which can be explained by the discrepancies he sees and experiences between the ideal and the real. At the same time, the story of the hero's family is told to reveal the sheer waste and the amount of misery suffered by the general populace in the struggle over an abstract ideology.

In contrast, Kim Wonil's *Twilight (Noŭl)* (1978) is a more effective attempt to deal with the Communist experience, being entirely free of ideological contamination, either leftist or rightist. It deals with the activities of the Communists in a southwestern mountain village who eventually became partisan fighters in the Chiri Mountain area. But the novel is not an attempt to present a frontal picture of these Communist activists in their own terms. They are only sketchily reconstructed through the personal reiminscences of a man who witnessed them as a child and who, taught to see them, including his own father, in the grotesque distortions of the anticommunist propaganda of the government, arrives at a humane understanding of his father and his colleagues, and their all-too-human motives and circumstances. In this respect, *Twilight* is as much a personal novel as a historical novel; maybe more the former than the latter.

This can be seen clearly if we compare it with Cho Chŏngrae's *The Taebaek Mountains,* which covers the same kind of historical material, though with greater size and scope. Nevertheless, the central drama in *The Taebaek Mountains* concerns the guerrillas in the same Chiri Mountains. The novel gives their activities a more objective historical context, describing in detail the configuration of social forces that led to the Communists' insurgency and retreat to the mountains to continue their struggle as partisans; the aftermath stretches to the Korean War and beyond. The author presents a consistently positive assessment of the political activities undertaken by the Communist guerrillas, though he tries to avoid a simplistic ascription of good and evil on the basis of ideological alignment alone.

The Taebaek Mountains was more in line than, say, *Twilight,* with the political-literary trend of the times which demanded a definite political analysis and a committed political position even from literary works of art. It was also in line with the rising interest in the history of guerrilla struggles as evinced in reminiscences, interviews, and accounts of the partisan activities in the postliberation era, the most notable among them being Yi T'ae's *The Southern Army (Nambugun)* (1988). The latter is a highly readable memoir of a surviving partisan, which caused such a stir among the general public that it had been made into a movie. But the popular success of *The Taebaek Mountains* and similar writings is not entirely attributable to a passing intellectual fashion or a prurient interest in what has been suppressed or repressed. The psychological dynamics of Korean society and culture is at that point where everything must be seen in political terms, though this phase may be passing with the post-1987 political transition. As if following the natural momentum of historical dynamics, the examination of more recent history and then contemporary political and social reality has continued, especially toward the end of the Chun regime, as younger writers turned to the narrative re-creation of the Kwangju uprising, prison experience, abuses of power within the armed forces, underground political activities, and labor strifes.

Concluding Remarks

Lévi-Strauss, traveling in foreign parts, once observed how men become unhappy creatures "when history comes too close to them."[30] It is, one may suppose, because the external constraints within which people's lives are lived become too obvious; people feel their imprisoned condition and want to maneuver out of it. In any case, history and politics make humans creatures of externals: physical limits, social constraints, and moral duties. Culture, including literature, is an unceasing attempt to transform or reconstruct these externals so that they appear as if they were part of human interiority. At least, cultural processes make them more acceptable. In an interview with young critics, Cho Chŏngrae explained what kind of historical function a literary work such as his own might perform:

30. Claude Lévi-Strauss, *Tristes tropiques,* trans. by John Russell (New York: Atheneum, 1961), p. 32.

> Looking at history, there seems to be validity in saying that the injuries and conflicts of history cannot be resolved unless they go through the filtering processes of stories and novels. Take the Nazis and the Israelis. There had to be innumerable novels, movies and plays before there could be forgiveness, before there could be acceptance. Only after all the tragic facts were brought to light and emotions and feelings were filtered to a equilibrium, there was acceptance. . . . What we ought to do is to restore tragedies that have been made emotionally uniform and ideologically fixed, for political purposes, and reflect upon them anew. This must be done through literature, not by political slogans or political movements alone.[31]

In spite of the author's intention as stated in the above, *The Taebaek Mountains* seems too political and too external, and does not seem to have quite arrived at the interior of our emotions and feelings where they could be filtered and purified so that they could flow out naturally to the outside world forgiving and accepting, and maybe transforming it to a world forgiven and accepted. The novel does not quite achieve that suppleness of sensibility and understanding that is the gift of a true aesthetic education, though one should not expect this to be provided by only one author. Of course, the novel is not taken up in its entirety with politics—it presents a great many concrete details of life, delights and pains of emotions and senses. Nevertheless, there are rigidities of feelings and ideas, so the story is not easily lifted to a realm beyond that shaped by stereotypical categories of conventional (or revolutionary) politics and morality.

In this respect, Kim Wonil's *Twilight* makes subtler use of language and history to achieve a more credible intimacy with the experience being narrated, an easier task here since the novel is basically about the personal experience of the protagonist who remembers—his experience of the recovery of human meaning in his relationship with his father and with the villagers of his childhood; therefore, there is an exploratory move back to a particular situation, which has a historical dimension but also, unavoidably, a personal complication that must be worked out without reliance on ready-made formulas. Consequently what is achieved in the novel as a whole is a high degree of sensitivity and faithfulness that could take in

31. "Cho Chŏngrae: sangch'ŏbadŭn sidae, ku han kwa bulkkotŭi munhak" [Cho Chŏngrae: The literature of resentment and flame], *Munhak Chŏngsin* (December 1989): 52.

unresolved material of history for transformative forgiveness and acceptance. It is an achievement that could constitute a valuable step to the recovery of historical memory, though these steps would be only minutely incremental. But for some readers, Kim Wonil is too subjective in his approach to history and therefore suspiciously nonpolitical. The experience in question is essentially a private inner event, ultimately weakening whatever political message it might have carried, that is, for those who believe that everything must have such a message. Thus Paek Nakch'ong, the theoretician of populist literature, argues, "The process [in *Twilight*] by which the protagonist arrives at reconciliation with history contains the danger of compromise, of not helping to overcome the division of the country but accepting it."[32]

Such, however, is the temper of this political age. The scandal of the mid-1980s in Korean literature was the attack repeatedly mounted by younger critics against Paek Nakch'ong and other older theoreticians and practitioners of committed literature for being not sufficiently political, for being petty-bourgeois intellectuals, for walking a tightrope between the autonomy of art and the political imperative. In their minds, literature and art should be part of the strategy of political change; the relation of the writer to his readers is that of the political agitator to the masses.[33] At the same time there emerged toward the end of the 1980s young writers who programmatically research topics of class conflict as raw material for their fiction.

This means that cultural development, if we conceive it as a promise of harmonious existence of individuals in a community on the basis of aesthetic education, has come to a stop and yielded all to political struggle. But this arrest is also part of the dynamics of culture. As analyzed here, culture may generate an ideal of humanity and community in opposition to politics and morality, but it cannot do so in the final analysis without the support of politics; the cultural ideal can come only as a crowning

32. Paek Nakch'ong, *Minjok munhak kwa segye munhak* [National literature and world literature], vol. 2 (Seoul: Ch'angjakkwa bip'yŏngsa, 1985), p. 95.

33. For a brief account of the debate, see Yi Songuk, "Sosiminchŏk munhakronŭi t'allak kwa minjok munhakronŭi punhwa" [The fall of the petty-bouregois theory of literature and division in the nationalist theory of literature], and Kim Chaeyŏng, 'Nodongja kyekŭpŭi dangp'asŏngŭl ŭttŏk'e kuhyŏn halkŭtsinga?" [How can the writer realize the party-consciousness of the working class?], in P'alsip nyŏndae sahoe undong nonjaeng [Debates on Social movements in the 1980s] (Seoul: Hangilsa, 1989).

achievement of the state in good moral health. If the state fails to establish its moral legitimacy and fails to develop cultural refinement of political and moral rigor, society's cultural impulse takes upon itself the task of generating countermorality, counterpower, and counterculture. But in doing so it can become wholly political and therefore anticultural. All this may also be part of the cultural dynamic, part of the process by which a nation forges a new consciousness that will eventually encompass the necessity of community and the freedom of individuals.

Out of this consciousness may come a new politics, not without an adversarial tension with and yet not quite in utter contradiction to the aspirations for fuller humanity expressed in literature and arts. The new beginning in South Korean democracy after 1987 may be the dawn of this new politics with a capacious openness for a new cultural flowering.

6
The Corporate State in North Korea

Bruce Cumings

The East is forever being viewed through lenses forged and polished in the West, a deep, pervasive, and often unconscious "Orientalism" that brings the familiar into focus just as it obscures indigenous authenticity. It is thus no curiosity that the original political model through which Western experts interpreted the Democratic People's Republic of Korea was the East European one of "people's democracies." That is, the DPRK was little more than the imposition of a Soviet-derived system lacking legitimate revolutionary credentials. It follows therefore that, in the wake of the "revolutions of 1989," the DPRK ought to have gone the way of these same "people's democracies."[1]

Wlodzimierz Brus saw the people's democracy form as "a *model* [*sic*] of socialist structure," a transplantation and "concentrated form" of Sta-

This article draws on and revises my "Corporatism in North Korea," originally published in *Journal of Korean Studies,* no. 3 (1983), and "The Northern System," in *Origins of the Korean War,* vol. 2 (Princeton: Princeton University Press, 1990).

1. Nicholas Eberhardt, for example, read North Korea's fate through the East European lens in his "The Coming Collapse of North Korea," *Wall Street Journal* (June 26, 1990).

linism; for him the people's democracies were also "brutal instruments of foreign domination," opposed ipso facto to nationalist ideologies of legitimation.[2] This was the dominant paradigm of interpretation, the accepted wisdom, about North Korea, and very little serious work has sought to counteract it. In nearly all the Western literature North Korea has been depicted as a classic Soviet satellite and puppet in the 1940s and 1950s; only in the late 1950s did the DPRK flirt with emulating another foreign model, the Chinese, and only in the 1960s did it seek an independent path to building socialism. Few grant that North Korea even in the recent period has developed much independence, and until the late 1980s it was routinely called a Soviet satellite—yet more reason for the DPRK to follow the post-1989 demise of Soviet-aligned systems.

North Korean internal politics was almost thought to be as Soviet-influenced as any European socialist regime ever was, a pure form of "Stalinism in the East."[3] This was given an added filip with the assumption, most often tacit, that Stalinism itself was "Oriental," and that "Kimilsungism" is a wretched excess of the Stalinist-Orientalist tendency. One can hear this from Russian as well as American specialists, and from British leftists. Trotsky, Bukharin, Isaac Deutscher, and Karl Wittfogel all likened Stalin to Eastern potentates, especially Genghis Khan and Tamerlane, and thought his system a species of Oriental despotism, the worst features of the "Asiatic mode of production" coming to the fore. It is stunning to see Trotsky open his biography of Stalin with a sentence remarking that the old revolutionist, Leonid Krassin, "was the first, if I am not mistaken, to call Stalin an 'Asiatic,'" and he goes on to talk about "Asiatic" leaders as cunning and brutal, presiding over static societies with a huge peasant base.[4] Perry Anderson once wrote that in the night of our ignorance, all forms take on the same

2. Wlodzimierz Brus, "Stalinism and the 'People's Democracies,'" in *Stalinism: Essays in Historical Interpretation,* ed. Robert C. Tucker (New York: W. W. Norton, 1977), pp. 239–41, 252–53.

3. See for example Chong-sik Lee, "Stalinism in the East: Communism in North Korea," in *The Communist Revolution in Asia,* ed. Robert Scalapino (Englewood Cliffs, N.J.: Prentice-Hall, 1969).

4. Leon Trotsky, *Stalin,* 2d ed. (New York: Stein and Day, 1967), pp. 1–2, 358. See also Stephen Cohen, *Bukharin and the Bolshevik Revolution* (New York: Vintage Books, 1975), p. 291, for Bukharin's depiction of Stalin as "a Genghis Khan"; also Isaac Deutscher, *Stalin: A Political Biography* (London: Oxford University Press, 1949), p. 472: Stalin was "primitive, oriental, but unfailingly shrewd."

hue; in this case, the portrait contains the people's democracy model, Stalinism, Genghis Khan, Tamerlane, and Kim Il Sung.

This chapter suggests a very different view of the North Korean state, one that emphasizes its difference from the "Soviet model" and that may help explain the DPRK's post-1989 staying power. It seeks an answer to the nature of this state in the doctrine of corporatism.

Varieties of Corporatism

Corporatism is not an easy term to grasp. Although most American intellectuals who do not work on Latin America or Southern Europe seem bewildered when asked to define this political form, the phenomenon has a long pedigree. One might say it is the preeminent antithesis of liberal politics. It predates the emergence of liberalism; it fueled the romantics of the nineteenth and twentieth centuries who hated liberalism; and it sparks the dreams of utopians who envision a transcendence of liberalism. Liberal theory separates the political from other realms of human behavior, making politics just a part of one's existence, or a subdiscipline for study, instead of the architectonic role that politics played for the ancients, and its organic interconnection with society in corporatism.

If corporatism is known by what it rejects, it also comes in several varieties: *traditional corporatism* had three great themes—hierarchy, organic connection, and family—and three great images that corresponded to it—political fatherhood, the body politic, and the great chain. "The whole of the chain of being might be imagined as an immense organism, animated by its divine source."[5] For traditionalists, and later for Facists like Mussolini, the body politic was a living organism, literally corporeal.[6] All members of the body politic were interconnected and functional to the whole. The head (or king) was the father of the people, ruler and ruled were joined by "perfect love," and the paternal wisdom and benevolence of the leader "was to be relied upon and never doubted." The king would display loving solicitude and "fatherly care" for his subjects; in the words of the Earl of

5. Michael Walzer, *The Revolution of the Saints* (New York: Atheneum, 1970), p. 149. For a useful recent discussion see "The Material and Social Bases of Corporatism," in *State Theory: Putting Capitalist States in Their Place,* ed. Bob Jessup, pp. 110–43 (University Park: Pennsylvania State University Press, 1990).

6. Walzer, *Revolution of Saints,* p. 171; see also Franz Neumann, *Behemoth: The Structure and Practice of National Socialism* (New York: Harper & Row, 1942), p. 358.

Stratford, "princes are to be the indulgent nursing fathers to their people . . . love and protection descending and loyalty ascending."[7] The most significant corporate body was the family, and then the church, which was seen in medieval times as the visible body of Christ.[8] The leader was the object of adulation: Henry VIII of England was thought to be "the sun of man."[9] This was a politics of the medieval society of estates and communal organizations that slowly disappeared in the solvent of capitalism. The traditional corporate ideal, of course, held fastest and longest in those countries where the Catholic church remained dominant.

Conservative corporatism sought to recapture this lost age and was a prevalent ideology in the nineteenth century among romantic anticapitalists and antiliberals. It idealized hierarchy, fixed social position, commonly shared values, and closed communities. As Unger put it, "Forgetful of history, it proposed to resolve the problems of bureaucracy by reviving the very forms of social order whose dissolution created these problems in the first place."[10] Among twentieth-century dictatorships of the Right, conservative corporatism provided an ideology and a set of slogans, but not much guidance in practice. Linz's model of weak authoritarianism in late Franco Spain, Schmitter's analysis of Portugal and Brazil, and some of the interwar regimes in Eastern Europe adhered to this set of ideas, but never succeeded in establishing a real corporate hierarchy of groups and classes segmented according to work and station, and never really tried to do so.[11]

The *pathological* variant of corporatism is fascism, exemplified by Germany and Italy in the 1930s. Fascism gave corporatism the bad name that it still possesses. For example, the entry on corporatism in the 1968 edition of the *International Encyclopedia of the Social Sciences* reads simply, "see fascism." Fascists used the rhetoric of conservative corporatism toward different ends: totalitarianism, breaking up the secondary associations that real corporatism would presumably wish to preserve, an aggressive milita-

7. Walzer, *Revolution of Saints,* pp. 172, 186.

8. Ibid., pp. 171, 188.

9. Neumann, *Behemoth,* p. 86.

10. Roberto Mangiaberra Unger, *Knowledge and Politics* (New York: Free Press, 1975), pp. 188, 249–50.

11. Juan Linz, "An Authoritarian Regime: Spain," in *Cleavages, Ideologies, and Party Systems,* ed. Erik Allardt and Yrjo Littunen, pp. 291–341 (Helsinki: Academic Bookstore, 1964); Philippe C. Schmitter, "Still the Century of Corporatism?" in *The New Corporatism,* ed. Frederick B. Pyke and Thomas Stritch, pp. 85–131 (Notre Dame: University of Notre Dame Press, 1974).

rism, and a mobilized politics of the street that corporatist regimes could never muster. Facist regimes also relied on the charisma of a leader, whereas the corporate polities were led by more plodding, truly "fatherly" types. Instead of organic connection, Neumann argued that in Germany only the leader principle unified state and party, with the leader and various Nazi groups functioning to disaggregate people and leave them helpless: Nazism appealed not to organically rooted individuals but to the "least rational" stratum of the population.[12] But the corporate underpinning of great minds like Pareto, who identified society with a living organism, could not resist the attractions of this pathological variant; nor could some neosocialists who found that there is a hazy netherworld where facism and communism seem to meet.

People such as the Romanian Mikhail Manoilescu, Robert Michels, Pareto, and others, moved from a sophisticated and interesting corporate conception of socialism to more-or-less egregious sympathy with 1930s Facist regimes. But they also developed a kind of *neosocialist corporatism,* which has interesting similarities with North Korea. Their fundamental departure from Marxism was to substitute nation for class and to develop a conception of a world system of advantaged and disadvantaged (or bourgeois and proletarian) nations.

It was Karl Polanyi's great accomplishment to discern how the breakdown of the world economy in the 1930s explained both Stalin's "socialism in one country" and the behavior of the Fascist powers: "fascism, like socialism, was rooted in a market society that refused to function."[13] This breakdown was at the root of neosocialist corporate ideas. For Manoilescu, "the organic, 'productivist,' vertically structured metaphors of a harmonic political-economic order" at home and their corollary in a hierarchical world at large.[14] The international division of labor had distributed rich nations here, poor nations there; the "proletarian" nations of what we would now call the periphery should structure themselves vertically at home (to accumulate power) and horizontally abroad to redress their positions in the world economy. Here, as several writers have pointed out, was

12. Neumann, *Behemoth*, pp. 83–84, 96.

13. Karl Polanyi, *The Great Transformation* (New York: Beacon Press, 1944), p. 239.

14. Philippe Schmitter, "Reflections on Mikhail Manoilescu and the Political Consequences of Delayed Development on the Periphery of Western Europe," in *Social Change in Romania, 1860–1940,* ed. Kenneth Jowitt (Berkeley: Institute of International Studies, University of California, 1978), p. 120.

an early and sophisticated variant of dependency and world-system theory.[15]

Other neosocialists thought no practical Marxism could continue to avoid the problems that nations and nationalism posed for class analysis: class was for the nineteenth century, whereas "the concept of the nation would be the key concept of political organization in the twentieth century."[16] Such thinking led neosocialists into strong support for protectionism and the type of autocentered development associated with Stalinism in the 1930s. Neosocialist corporatism had had its most profound recent statement in the work of Roberto Mangiaberra Unger, who proposed a movement toward a corporatism embodying equality of conditions, democracy, and the overcoming of liberalism and individualism through a new conception of organic groups.[17] Unger's proposals seek once again to introduce the family as either a refuge from liberal politics or a metaphor for transcending liberalism. Unger writes that the family "comes closest to [the ideal of] community of life in our experience. . . . The modern family forever draws men back into an association that . . . offers a measure of individual recognition through love."[18] Thus we have come full circle: the logic of corporatist disgust with liberalism leads progressives to rediscover the family as a model for politics, something that the traditionalists never abandoned. In the absence of other organic groups, it is the best candidate.

It has rarely occurred to Asian thinkers to abandon the family as metaphor or reality: only Mao's China during the Great Leap Forward assaulted the family structure, and even this monumental effort was dropped rather quickly. The family has been the center piece of *Asian corporatism,* the preeminent example of which is interwar Japan. In Japan the three corporatist images of political fatherhood, a body politic, and the great chain were pronounced. The emperor was the father of all the people, the people were united by blood ties, and the blood "running through the veins of the race . . . has never changed" since time immemorial.[19] As one publicist put

15. Daniel Chirot, "Neoliberal and Social Democratic Theories of Development," in *Social Change in Romania,* pp. 31–52; also Schmitter, ibid.

16. Zeev Sternhell, "Fascist Ideology," in *Fascism: A Reader's Guide,* ed. Walter Lacquer (Berkeley: University of California Press, 1976), pp. 352–55.

17. Unger, *Knowledge and Politics,* p. 250.

18. Ibid., pp. 252, 264; see also Christopher Lasch, *Haven in a Heartless World: The Family Besieged* (New York: Basic Books, 1977).

19. Chigaku Tanaka, *What Is Nippon Kokutai?* (Tokyo: Shishio Bunko, 1936), p. 95.

it, "It is only Nippon in which national society has ensured not merely horizontal union by dint of blood and land relations but also the blood-relation-center of the society itself . . . as the authority of national society."[20] The emperor was the center of blood relations extending through the whole polity and back through time—benevolent, august, solicitous, wise, eternal, and loving.

Masao Maruyama, seeking out the unique in what he called "Japanese fascism," rested on "the family system extolled as the fundamental principle of the State structure." Its basic characteristic was that the state was always "considered as an extension of the family; more concretely, as a nation of families composed of the Imperial House as the main family and of the people as the branch family. This is not merely an analogy as in the organic theory of the State, but is considered as having a substantial meaning."[21] According to imperial officials, each Japanese family was "an independent animate body, a complete cell in itself." Radicals like Kita Ikki called Japan "an organic and indivisible great family."[22]

In the 1930s the Japanese government sought to popularize an opaque formula expressing the principle of eternal Japanese unity, *kokutai.* One can read book after book and not fathom the core meaning of this set of dicta, recited and memorized by schoolchildren. *Kokutai* means something like national essence. The character compound combines "country" *(koku)* and a term meaning "basis" (of philosophy) or "essence," that is, what makes Japan different from other countries *(tai)*. The emperor and the rulers were to govern "with the real significance of Kokutai as the center, in every national affair and in perfect order." The people were to let "every thought, idea, and action have Kokutai as its principle and clearly display the principle in national life."[23] These various emphases, always latent in Japan, were pushed forward in the 1930s as Japan joined with the Fascist powers in unity and conquest abroad and authoritarian coordination at home. This was not fascism, however, because it lacked a mass party, coherent ideology, and the raucous mass politics of the streets of Germany. The better term for this would be *conservative corporatism,* more specifically an Asian corporatism deeply influenced by the Confucian past.

20. Ibid., Appendix, p. 3.

21. Masao Maruyama, *Thought and Behavior in Modern Japanese Politics,* ed. Ivan Morris (New York: Oxford University Press, 1969), p. 36.

22. Ibid., p. 37.

23. Tanaka, *Kokutai,* pp. 102, 186.

With this review of corporatism in its many forms, we now come to the central argument: the application of the universal truth of Marxism-Leninism to the concrete realities of Korea, as the saying goes, has resulted in a peculiar and fascinating form of socialist corporatism, mingling classic corporatist verbiage and images, but growing out of Korean political history, with the progressive rhetoric and practices of Marxism-Leninism. The DPRK is a socialist state, meaning that the means of production are state or collectively owned, the goal of "building socialism" toward the distant point of communism remains the basic agenda, and politics and administration are under control of a hierarchical party structured in the typical ways that have characterized communism in this century. In other words I am not arguing that North Korea is Fascist, or "feudal-fascist," the term used for the politics of the Gang of Four in China. But it is a corporate state and a family state—perhaps the best twentieth-century example of this ancient ideal.

Origins of the Northern System

In recent years a mass of new archival materials, captured in the North during the Korean War, has been declassified and provides solid evidence for a new interpretation. These documents undermine accepted wisdom on several central issues. North Korea was not simply a Soviet satellite, but evolved from a somewhat decentralized coalition regime based on widespread "people's committees" in 1945–46, to a period of relative Soviet dominance in 1947–48, thence in 1949 (i.e., well before the Chinese intervention in the Korean War and the time from which Brus dates the Stalinization of East Europe[24]) to important ties with China, which in turn provided a realm of maneuver for the DPRK between the two Communist giants. The northern system in the late 1940s was a meld of Korean, Soviet, and Chinese experience, with much of the selection of models rooted in Korean political history. The North also diverged significantly from the Soviet Union and China, especially in its party structure and its leadership system.

In short, the "Kimilsungist" system and the self-reliant ideology *(Juche)* are artifacts of the 1940s, not the 1960s or 1970s. Whatever one may think of the system, its distinctive features have not changed for forty years.

Kim Il Sung's thought was rarely presented as a separate wellspring of

24. Brus, "Stalinism," p. 241.

ideas in the late 1940s, as it was later on when his Juche ideology was placed on a par with Maxism-Leninism. (In the 1940s Juche existed, but it was part of the general Korean desire, shared across the spectrum, for self-reliance and independence.) One 1940s text for use by lecturers in party schools, for example, followed contemporary Soviet lines, quoting from the *History of the Bolshevik Party—Short Course,* Lenin's *What Is to Be Done?,* Engel's *Peasant War in Germany,* and then dilating in typical Soviet fashion on the "revisionism" of Karl Kautsky and Edward Bernstein, Rosa Luxembourg, and others. When this same document comes to the Korean revolution, however, the dry tone disappears. The previous section is a preamble to the important thing, the purest Kim Il Sung line.

The text proceeds to dwell on the differing conditions in Korea when compared with other countries, how all methods of organization and work must be made to conform to the concrete historical situation in Korea, how the only "independent" *(chajujŏgin)* anti-Japanese movement, unaided by foreigners, was Kim's; how other Korean Communists were petty-bourgeois factionalists who had no contact with the masses, and how the North must be the base for preparing "a unified, self-reliant, independent country."

Until the liberation from Japanese colonialism, the text said, no Korean Communists were able "to organize a revolutionary, vanguard party." Instead of a unified party, there were two types of Communists: those who talked a lot about communism, but only "verbally" participated in the struggle, and the real activists, who fought hard and went among the masses. They lacked theory but they had good praxis. The first group ended up being unable to resist the Japanese, and thus after the mid-1930s quit the struggle, or did flip-flops under Japanese pressure and betrayed their comrades. The second group was best exemplified by Kim and his guerrillas. After the liberation, the first group threw obstacles in the path of the revolution with endless haggling over Korea's historical stage, the correct line for the revolution, and so forth, engaging in "bourgeois personal heroism." It went on to quote Kim as saying, "whosoever has close ties with the masses, that person will be victorious."[25]

25. Korean Workers' Party, *Tang Kŏnsŏl (kangŭi yogang);* the first ninety-four pages deal with Marxism-Leninism and the Soviet experience, and the remaining fifty or so cover Korea. This and other Korean texts cited herein come from Record Group 242, "Captured Enemy Documents," a collection at the National Records Center, Suitland, Maryland, of captured materials dating from the Korean War.

The Marxist-Leninist portion of this study moves on an abstract, disengaged track; when it turns to Korea, it forgets about the theory, even depicts Kim as lacking in theory (but so what?), and goes on to discuss actual conditions in Korea with the ring of authenticity, and with a devastating and often apt critique of the so-called domestic faction of Korean Communists and, by implication, their titular leader Pak Hŏn Yŏng.

Stalinist ideology did have one thing to teach the Koreans that fit like a glove with their own preconceptions. This was the Platonism of Stalin, the architectonic, engineering-from-on-high quality that marked his thought and his praxis. Stalin was a hegemon in the era of "late" heavy industrialization, and his discourse, like his name, clanked with an abased, mechanical imagery that valued pig iron over people, machines over bread, bridges over ideas, the leader's will over the democratic instincts of Marx. When he had Andrei Zhdanov impose his suffocating doctrine of socialist realism on the cultural realm in 1932, the metaphor of choice was that artists and writers should be "engineers of the soul," and that may serve as a general metaphor for Stalin's rule.

The Leader as Core of the State

Koreans have historically thought that a maximum leader should be an engineer of the soul, too, but through exemplary behavior instead of coercion. They think a leader should be benevolent instead of brutish. And they think good ideas come from correct thought—rectification of the mind—proceeding from the leader down through the masses, who learn the teaching by rote mastery of received wisdom. These Confucian residues melded with Soviet doctrines to make Kim a kind of benevolent Stalin, the fount of ideas, and led to the development of a profound idealism and voluntarism at opposites with the materialism of Marx. Koreans still refer to artists as engineers of the soul. They still surround Kim with a cult of personality. They still depict him as the source of all good ideas. This aspect of Stalinism stuck like glue in Korea, and if it had not existed in Moscow, it would have had to be invented in P'yŏngyang. Such "top-downism," as we might call it, is one of the key characteristics of Korean politics, reinforced in the South by Japanese rule and in the North by Stalinism.

Kim Il Sung never, from the beginning, trucked with Maoist ideas about the spontaneity and creativity of the masses, the peasantry or the proletariat as the epistemological source of good ideas, and so on. Kim's use of Maoist techniques of leadership was not a reflex of a radical epistemology, but for implementation of what the party wanted. It was always, for him, the passive tense: "the political level of the working class has been comprehensively raised"; educated people "are being turned into new intellectuals"; peasants are being "working-classized." Party cadres were not to be tested by the masses; instead Kim used the Stalinist phrase, "cadres decide everything." Kim was completely orthodox in following a Soviet conception of the role of the leader and the party center, which, as Merle Fainsod once put it, was "saturated in elitism."[26]

Although Kim became chairman of the North Korean Interim People's Committee in February 1946, his particular leadership style does not appear until mid-1947. But by then the evidence of a hagiographic and grandiose style was almost as palpable as it is today. Beginning in 1947, agents making forays into North Korea reported that pictures and posters of Kim festooned telephone poles and the like with tales of how "wise, clear-sighted, spirited, wonderful" Kim Il Sung was. At the same time, articles appeared describing him "the sun of the Nation," "a beautiful new red star in the sky," wisely guiding things with his "brilliant, scientific" methods.[27]

In an important interview with Kim's first biographer in 1946, an unnamed member of his guerrilla unit promoted a Kim Il Sung line that remains the official history today.[28] Kim set the following sort of example:

> This sort of person naturally has an extremely strong power of attraction to others. . . . And it goes without saying that a guerrilla organization with such a person at the center is incomparably strong. The sublime good fortune of our guerrilla detachment was to have at our center the Greater Sun. Our general commander, great leader, sagacious teacher, and intimate friend was none other than General Kim Il Sung. Our unit was an unshakeable one, following General Kim and

26. See for example Kim's speech on the first anniversary of the founding of the Korean Workers' Party (KWP), *Kŭlloja* (The Worker) 8 (August 1947): 27–44. See also my "Kim's Korean Communism," *Problems of Communism* (March–April 1974), for more on this aspect of "Kimilsungism" and contrasts with Maoism; and Merle Fainsod, *How Russia Is Ruled,* LC 63-1418 (Russian Research Center Studies No. 11), pp. 128–31, 183.

27. U.S. National Archives, G-2 Weekly Summary no. 99, July 27–August 3, 1947; "General Kim Il Sung Is the Leader of the Korean People," *Podo,* no. 3 (August 1947): 18–21.

28. Han Chae-dok, *Kim Il Sŏng changgun kaesŏn gi* [Record of General Kim Il Sung's triumphal return] (P'yongyang: Minju Chosŏn-sa, 1947), Han's interview with an important member of Kim's guerrilla detachment, pp. 35–65.

> having General Kim as the nucleus. The General's embrace and love are like the Sun's, and when our fighters look up to and receive the General, their trust, self-sacrifice and devotion are such that they will gladly die for him.

The detachment's "philosophy of life" was its willingness to follow Kim's orders even to the death; "its strength is the strength deriving from uniting around Kim Il Sung . . . our guerrillas' historical tradition is precisely that of uniting around Kim as our only leader."

Kim loved and cared for his followers, so this text said, and they responded with an iron discipline for which "a spirit of obedience is needed, and what is needed for that is a spirit of respect. . . . Above all, the spiritual foundation [of our discipline] was this spirit of respect. And the greatest respect was for General Kim Il Sung. Our discipline grew and became strong amid respect and obedience for him." This officer then went on to recommend the guerrilla tradition as a good principle for party and mass organizations; he might have added that it would be the principle for the organization of the entire North Korean state.

The language used by this man is fascinating. It is all moral language, bathing Kim in a hundred virtues, almost all of which are Confucian—benevolence, love, trust, obedience, respect, reciprocity between the leader and the led. It is also a language of circles: the phrase "uniting around Kim" uses a term, *chuwi,* that literally means circumference; in a neighborhood it means living around a center or *chungsim,* which literally means a "central heart." Synonyms for this, widely used in the North Korean literature, are "core" and "nucleus." The party center was also a euphemism for Kim and his closest allies, just as it became the euphemism for Kim's son in the 1970s when the succession was being arranged.[29]

29. To my knowledge only one source in all the published and unpublished literature on North Korea grasps the central importance of Kim's peculiar style of leadership: the formerly classified study done in the early 1960s by Evelyn McCune for the State Department Bureau of Intelligence and Research. She correctly terms the relationship between Kim and his close allies "a semi-chivalrous, irrevocable and unconditional bond . . . under iron discipline." It is a "deeply personal" system, "fundamentally hostile to complex bureaucracy." Kim and his allies were generalists, Jack-of-all trades who could run the government or command the army, show a peasant how to use new seeds or cuddle children in a school; Kim would dispatch them as loyal observers of officials and experts or specialists outside the inner core, i.e., in the realm of impersonal bureaucracy. McCune thought correctly that the powerful glue holding the Kim group together made it much more formidable than typical Korean political

This is also a language with religious resonance, both Shamanist and Christian. The term that the North Koreans translate as "to hold [Kim] in respect," *urŏrŏ patta,* literally means "to look up to and receive," and is used religiously for receiving Christ. It is also used in the sense of esteeming one's father. The term "Great Sun" resonates with Western usages placing a king in communion with the sun, or by extension with God, and with Japanese usages regarding the emperor. To my knowledge, the first statue of Kim erected in the North was unveiled on Christmas Day 1949, something that suggests a conscious attempt to present him as a secular Christ, or Christ-substitute.[30]

The style is always paternal, with Kim depicted as the benevolent father of the nation, and the nation compared with one large family. The strongest of emotional bonds in Korea is that of filial piety, and Kim and his allies sought to weld the nation together by drawing on vast reservoirs of duty and obligation toward one's parents, seeking to have them transferred to the state through Kim's auspices. North Korea has always been remarkable in its treatment of children: Kim personally identified himself with orphans of revolutionary fighters and, after 1953, of Korean War dead; a major school for orphans of important leaders was located at his birthplace. Children routinely called him "our father."

The process of burnishing Kim's image and uniting around him also suggests an element of chivalry, of men and women found together by oaths of fealty, duty, obligation, and possessing among them uncommon virtues of courage, daring and sacrifice. It is the language of feudal warlords, and indeed Kim in the early period always used the title *"changgun,"* translated as "general," but using the same characters as the Japanese term *shogun.*

The dynamic of this politics is centrifugal-centripetal, concentric circles radiating outward from the core, embracing first the Manchurian guerrillas and their families, then the party hierarchy, then the army, then the people; it then falls back on itself as each outer circle presumably returns trust and loyalty to the center. Somewhere in between, of course, there arose a plod-

---

factions, based on weaker patron-client relations and given to splintering in power struggle and personal competition; thus it was able to assert dominance over rival groups rather easily. She also understood the concentric circle metaphor, providing a chart of the leadership radiating outward from Kim.

30. See for example E. M. W. Tillyard, *The Elizabethan World Picture* (New York: Vintage Books, 1942). On the statue, set up in Hŭngnam, see the daily record for December 1949 in *Sun'gan t'ongshin* 3 (January 1950).

ding, dense bureaucracy that manages the day-to-day administration. But at the commanding heights this was a charismatic politics, its legitimacy resting in an overblown history and a trumpeted mythology about men with superhuman qualities.

It is so characteristic of the North Koreans, then and now, that they simultaneously paper the walls with hagiography and mythology about Kim and his guerrillas, while caring little to provide any evidence that would convince an independent observer. This bespeaks another characteristic of the Kim leadership, a profound solipsism, indeed a *national solipsism* that is also connected to the theme of concentric circles. Kim's legend and mandate would seem to stop at the national border, non-Koreans cannot be expected to appreciate its virtues. Even prewar Japan did not try to sell *kokutai* to the *gaijin* (foreigners). But the circles keep on extending, to encompass foreigners and persuade them to see the virtues so obvious to North Koreans. This is far more pronounced today, when the regime organizes and funds "Juche study groups" all over the world, treating group leaders like heads of state, but it existed in the 1940s in a solipsism that seemed to think all eyes were on Korea as the Kim leadership blazed a trail for postcolonial revolution, providing a model to emulate. It is a Korean microcosm of the old Chinese world order, radiating outward from the Middle Kingdom or central source.

Another interesting element in the 1947 interview is implicit, the suggestion that Kim Il Sung is being put forward as "Kim Il Sung," a figure larger than life, as an example for all to emulate. If all are to emulate him, he cannot put his pants on one leg at a time like anyone else—he has to be perfect. But in the conjuring of that perfection, the real man Kim Il Sung, né Kim Sŏng Ju, runs the risk of being himself a symbol of power rather than holding it, being put forward by shadowy figures as the source of everyone's legitimacy. There is a hint of an emperor system here, a figure being created who would have to be mysterious and remote.

Another person who articulated this vision of leadership was Kim Ch'ang Man, who used the familiar "Il Sung" in his writings, and who became for a time Kim Il Sung's ideological interlocutor. Kim Ch'ang Man was a Yanan Korean and, like Kim Il Sung, melded Maoist and Korean leadership methods. In a critically important article entitled "Several Questions in Methods of Leadership in Party Work,"[31] Kim argued that two methods of leadership

31. *Kŭlloja* 11 (January 1948): 12–22.

were central: the first is the mass line, and in discussing it he directly plagiarized Mao's famous 1942 speech, attributing the words to Kim; the second was fostering or rearing core leadership:

> This is the leadership method of forming in party branches and work units . . . leading nuclei [*haeksim*] based on a small number of active elements, and then rightly uniting this core and the broad masses.

The mass line linked the core and the mass, likened to "blood lines" within a family. How is core leadership formed? It "must always be formed in a real struggle":

> In an actual struggle, active elements are continuously born, while from among the original leading core a portion is cast off. . . . This is the natural growth of an organization.

Workers and peasants with low theoretical and cultural levels, he said, can be fashioned into core elements through struggle; so can all of Korea, even though it is short on a history of struggle and has many people, even cadres, who are poorly educated and culturally backward.

Koreans are nothing if not eclectic in their foreign borrowing; among other things we may see in such statements a metaphor of atomic nuclei being born and dying. But anyone familiar with Mao's writings will see in this analysis a voluntarism that assumes a people who are "poor and blank" can be honed into revolutionaries through class struggle and specific methods for attitudinal change, such as small group criticism and self-criticism. The basic materialism of Marx, which assumes that class world views are ultimately formed through epochal change, through an ethos that is inseparable from a class's historical relationship to means of production, such that one's assumptions and premises are not a matter of conscious reflection, would treat Korean efforts to remold millions of peasants overnight as the basest left-wing infantilism.

Kim and Mao made the idealist assumption that class consciousness can metamorphose through struggle and various forms of "consciousness raising." For Mao this was supposed to be something that people would be brought to through class struggle. But for Kim and for North Korea, where class struggle was telescoped (for example in the quick land reform) and where a Marxist conception of structuring from below gave way to a Hegelian conception of structuring from above, the borrowing from China melded with Kim's benevolent engineering conception. If Koreans were poor and blank, he and his "core" would write on this tabula rasa.

Koreans have assumed, implicitly and often explicitly, that the fount of wisdom, the spark of philosophy, occurs in the mind of the leader—that it resides in an exceptional person. One genius is at the core, one philosopher-king, and he tutors everyone else. But if Kim was at times an engineer from above, he also descended to the lower levels to observe his engineering through incessant "on-the-spot guidance." If he was often a remote emperor, protected by moats of security and mystery, he was also one who pressed the flesh.

It is engineering of the soul with a human touch. It is Platonism for the masses. It is Hegelian populism. It is the Confucian mass line. Indeed, hardly a cornerstone can be laid, a tunnel dug, a building topped off, without the genius-leader being present to sanctify it. The uniting of theory and practice is the catalytic action of the leader interacting with the led. His teaching was studied over and over, everywhere, in inner-sanctum–like rooms where a ghostly white bust presided, until it was established as a state of mind.

There is not just a Hegelian idealism here, but a kind of individual heroism, focused on the extraordinary "I." Korean child-rearing patterns would reinforce such a conception, where the first son is both pampered, by non-Korean standards, and given solemn responsibilities for rearing the other children. The eldest son is nurtured entirely within the nuclear family, living with the parents under the same roof after he gets married; at a certain point in his maturity he then becomes the family patriarch. When Kim's son Jong Il finally (and predictably) came forward to assume the mantle in the 1980s, the universal line was that he, personally, was a genius: traditional first-son patterns perhaps explained the careful rearing and unveiling. But such family patterns also tend to produce first sons who think they can be anything; it is often said that every first son wants to be president in Korea.

In Kim's praxis, like Confucianism, the family unit becomes a model for structuring the state, the ultimate metaphor for organizing everything under heaven, including international relations. No Communist inner core was ever more permeated with family connections than the North Korean; although the guerrilla tie is the innermost core of power, Kim's family is next. His entire lineage was, from the time of his return to Korean, projected as a model revolutionary family. His first wife (Kim Jong Il's mother) became the model woman guerrilla. Presumably alien and un-Marxist to Western Communists, this practice fits nicely with East Asian politics: Taiwan, for example, with Chiang Kai-shek preparing the way for his son Chiang Ching-Kuo, or Mao or Ferdinand Marcos of the Philippines trying to pass power to Imelda, his willful wife, or any of the big South Korean conglomerates *(chaebŏls),* two-thirds of which are held within founding families.

Such systems, traditionally in East Asia and markedly in North Korea, seem to lack a political process (at least to any public scrutiny). Always it is the absence of conflict that the regime seeks to project, all for one and one for all, a much-bruted "monolithicism." (Trotsky notes how appalled he and his Bolshevik allies were when Stalin began using this term, but the Koreans use it all the time.[32]) How could there be a political process when the leader is perfect? What is the "political process" of the deeply veiled Japanese imperial system? This is one reason, perhaps, for the absence of much public conflict since 1946, a remarkable phenomenon even when Korea is compared with other Communist states.

The Leader's Idea

By the 1960s Kim Il Sung had made everyone willing to listen aware of his Juche idea, including readers of the *New York Times,* who would frequently be treated to full-page advertisements for the concept. Kim's use of the term is thought to have begun with a December 1955 speech that, coming well before de-Stalinization and the Sino-Soviet conflict, was remarkable for its criticism of Koreans who mimicked things Soviet. The existing literature depicts Kim as a dependent Soviet today who, somehow, burst his bonds and began to criticize his former masters. But newly available materials, including originals of Kim's speeches in the 1940s that cannot have been tampered with retrospectively by regime ideologues, make clear that the elements of self-reliance and revolutionary nationalism in this concept were present from Kim's emergence as a leader in his own right in the summer of 1947.

The Koreans call it "the great Juche idea," but it is less an idea than a state of mind. The term literally means being subjective where Korean matters are concerned, putting Korea first in everything. The second charac-

32. Trotsky, *Stalin,* p. 18.

ter, *ch'e* in the Korean pronunciation, is found in the famous Chinese term of the late nineteenth-century self-strengthening movement, *ti* of *ti yong,* which stands for "Chinese learning for the foundation [*ti*] and Western learning for application"; it is also the *tai* of *kokutai,* the concept promoted in Japan in the 1930s.[33] The Koreans use Juche in much the same way, its goal being a subjective, solipsistic state of mind, the correct thought that must precede and then determine correct action. The term is really untranslatable; for a foreigner its meaning is ever-receding, into a pool of everything that makes Koreans Korean, and therefore is ultimately inaccessible to the non-Korean.

It is from this basic philosophical stance, which can be linked to a doctrine of essences, that the rest of Korean voluntarism flows—all the talk about ideas coming first, the leader coming first. In discussing "how to study appearances to reach essences," Mao once said that you start with appearances, observations, and then go on "to reveal the substance and contradictions of objective things and events." And once the essence is grasped, one can then act in the real world, linking theory or essence to concrete praxis.[34] Kim Il Sung thinks the same way, except with less emphasis on praxis. This is an Asian way to think, unsurprisingly. (If Asians place too much emphasis on states of mind, Westerners place too little.)

Although one can find uses of the term *Juche* in the 1940s in North and South, no one would notice were it not for its later prominence. But Kim's rhetoric rang with synonyous language; a variety of terms translating roughly as self-reliance and independence structured Kim's ideology in the 1940s: *chajusŏng* (self-reliance), *minjok tongnip* (national or ethnic independence), *charip kyŏngje* (independent economy). All these terms were antonyms of *sadaejuŭi* (serving and relying on foreign power), which had been the scourge of a people whose natural inclination was toward things Korean. Kim at this time was a modal if early variant of Third World revolutionary nationalism, reinforced by the Korean "Hermit Kingdom" past toward a left-isolationist tendency.

Kim has always been the major interpretor of Korean self-reliance. In

33. Peter Lowe located a British Foreign Office study of the DPRK constitution, which found predictable similarities with the 1936 Soviet constitution, but quite unexpected parallels with Japan's Meiji constitution (*The Origins of the Korean War* [New York: Longman, 1986], p. 50).

34. Mao Zedong, *Critique of Soviet Economics,* ed. and trans. Moss Roberts (New York: Monthly Review Press, 1973), p. 112.

July 1982 he gave a vintage discussion of his ideology: Korea should not become "a plaything of great powers"; "I say to our officials: if a man takes to flunkeyism [*sadaejuŭi*] he will become a fool; if a nation falls into flunkeyism, this nation will go to ruin; and if a party adopts flunkeyism, it will make a mess of the revolution." "Once there were poets who worshipped Pushkin and musicians who adored Tchaikovsky. Even in creating an opera, people patterned it on Italian ones. Flunkeyism was so rampant that some artists drew foreign landscapes instead of our beautiful mountains and rivers. . . . [But] Koreans do not like European artistic works." Koreans, he said, should always "hold fast to *chajusŏng*."[35]

Although Kim muted his nationalist self-assertion when Soviet troops were on the ground, similar ideas are not hard to find in the 1940s. In his speech on the second anniversary of the liberation in 1947, he began by thanking the Soviets profusely for their aid in defeating the Japanese. But soon he began discussing the need for an independent economy, "an economic foundation to make our Motherland a wealthy and powerful, free and independent country"; in spite of extended efforts toward this goal, he said, enemies in the South say we "intend to make [Korea] a political and economic dependency of a certain country." He went on to call for the construction of "a unified, self-reliant, independent state free of foreign interference." In another speech that same month, he went on about the glorious traditions of Korea and made a big pitch for young people to become educated so that "with our own hands" we can make everything we need ourselves—daily necessities, automobiles, trains, even aircraft, thus to realize "the complete independence of our Motherland." In a June 1946 speech, Kim referred to Koreans as "a superior people" whose contemporary backwardness was wholly attributable to Japanese oppression; unification, he said, was "a matter of restoring a free and independent state, without the interference of foreign countries, and guaranteeing the fundamental interests of our nation [*minjok*, i.e., nation or ethnic people]." Various ideologues drew attention to speeches earlier in 1947 where Kim called for "an independent national economy."[36]

35. "Conversation of the Great Leader Kim IL Sung with the South Korean Delegates to North-South the High-Level Political Talks," Korean Central News Agency (KCNA), July 4, 1982.

36. Kim's speech at the Moranbong theater, *Kŭlloja* 8 (August 1947): 2–26; Kim Il Sung, "Speech to the Youth of Korea," *Podo* 3 (August 1947): 11–17; Kim, "What Are the Demands of the Various Political Parties and Social Organizations Concerning the Establishment of a

Just before the Korean War, the Korean Workers' Party *(KWP)* Propaganda and Agitation Department put out a guide for propagandists that began by referring to Korea as having "lost its *chajusŏng*" during the Japanese period and, in the post-1945 period, as having constructed an economic and political base "that firmly guarantees our nation's interests and *chajusŏng* on the world stage." The existence of the Soviet Union and other socialist countries was the external condition that guaranteed Korea's position, and the economic basis at home would "build a rich and strong state that can guarantee our nation's *chajusŏng*." The document said explicitly that central planning "was a means of guaranteeing the *chajusŏng* of a democratic state's economy and ensuring that it does not become subordinated to a foreign economy."

In spite of praise for Soviet efforts in this document, it underlines the manner in which the Koreans took Japanese and Soviet state structures and ideas and turned them toward an autarkic conception of a self-contained national economy; it clearly referred to all foreign nations by using the term "foreign" instead of "imperialist."

Kim Il Sung was quoted many times in the document on the necessity of building "our own democratic homeland independently using our own strength and our own assets." Korea must use "our own domestic resources and our own strength," thus to avoid dependency on external sources of supply: this, too, would guarantee "the *chajusŏng* of our national economy." Perhaps most important, this document dates the adoption of these "basic principles" *(wŏlli)* from 1949, signaling the break toward an independent trajectory that, in my view, occurred after Soviet troops left Korea.[37]

The Corporate State

Kim Il Sung's ideas resonate with the Left-isolationism, predicated on a withdrawal from the world economy, that European leftists popularized in the 1930s when the world economy collapsed and some sort of withdrawal and restructuring was on the agenda of every nation (a New Order, a New

Democratic Provisional Government?" *Kŭlloja* 6 (June 1947): 2–15; Min Chu (pseud.), "Several Problems in Leadership Work in Economic Construction," *Kŏlloja* 7 (July 1947): 20.

37. KWP Agit/Prop Department, "Se hwan'gyŏng kwa se chogŏn" [The new environment and the new conditions], internal document, 1949, pp. 1–3, 6, 16–18, 32–35.

Deal, "socialism in one country"). In Kim's system in the 1940s, one discerns the rudments of a type of neosocialist corporatism, going back to the Romanian Manoilescu, who, as we have seen, substituted national struggle for class stuggle and suggested that dependent, peripheral socialist nations unite horizontally in commom cause.[38] This was precisely the Korean departure as well, incipient in the 1940s and trumpeted for all to hear by the 1960s.

Socialism over the past century either presents us with a vacuum where the political should be or has had such a varied politics—from social democracy to totalitarianism—as to be no guide at all. Marx had no political model, only a highly opaque set of prescriptions for politics under socialism (mainly the Critique of the Gotha Programme and some remarks on the dictatorship of the proletariat). It was Lenin who turned Marxism into a political theory and, some argue, transformed Marxism into a voluntaristic doctrine that left open the possibility of the extreme statism of Stalin, in which superstructural politics became the agency for engineering society. For Marxist-Leninists who opposed Stalinism—Burkharin, Trotsky, Mao, and the Gang of Four, for example—their critique always resolved to the political. Bukharin saw the Bolshevik state as a new "iron heel" oppressing the masses. Trotsky located the problem of Stalinism in the control of the commanding heights of the state by the wrong people; in the early stages of socialism there was no automatic conditioning of the superstructure by the base as had existed under capitalism, and therefore a tiny stratum could seize power and undo the revolution. At the beginning of China's Cultural Revolution this is where Mao located the problem as well, in "bad elements" and strata at the top; the Gang of Four simply completed the logic by arguing that a veritable "new class" had emerged right inside the Communist Party.[39] If politics is so fragile and critical in the early socialist stage, then of course the problem of succession becomes paramount. But the political vacuum in Marxism-Leninism also opens the way to an assertion of indigenous politics; this may even be demanded by the very paucity of political models.

38. Philippe Schmitter, "Reflections on Mikhail Manoilescu."

39. Important references here would be Samuel Huntington, *Political Order in Changing Societies* (New Haven: Yale University Press, 1968), chap. 5; Cohen *Bukharin and the Bolshevik Revolution*; Leon Trotsky, *The Revolution Betrayed* (New York: Pathfinder Press, 1937), pp. 53–54, 239, 249; on China see my "The Political Economy of Chinese Foreign Policy," *Modern China* (Oct. 1979): 411–61.

In an era of revolution that now seems almost antiquarian, Marxism-Leninism seemed to be a talisman that made all things possible, especially rapid and millennial change that wiped away the past. Recent history has demonstrated that Marxism-Leninism had a far less transformative effect than either its proponents or opponents care to admit. Marxist-Leninist ideology functioned as a new, self-conscious ethos seeking to replace an existing ethos; Lenin conceived of the replacement of old ethos with the new as the work of generations. Although the dictatorial aspect of proletarian rule should be ever-receding into the future, so he wrote, it could not be done away with until people's habits had changed, until they all got up in the morning and automatically acted like good Communists instead of good capitalists.[40]

We all know how hard it is to change old habits ("culture"); they prove far more recalcitrant than revolutionaries can know. Thus Marxism-Leninism cannot affect the deep structures of thought and behavior in any society except over a very long period: it will be grafted onto existing, long-standing roots and, while seeking to transform the roots, will itself be transformed as peoples and societies render it intelligible to their lives.

This has proved truer in Korea than in many settings for building socialism, precisely because of the very alienness of the setting to this fundamentally Western set of ideas. Korea had a minuscule proletariat, the beginnings of capitalism, and far too much internationalism (capitalist-style) by 1945. It therefore took from Marxism-Leninism what it wanted and rejected much of the rest: a state with potent organization capable of providing the political basis for independence at a future point; an economic program of rapid industrialization and a philosophy of subjecting nature to human will; Lenin's notion of national liberation; Stalin's autarky of "socialism in one country" (to become in Korea "socialism in half a country," and now, as Kenneth Jowitt once remarked, "socialism in one family"). Autarky fit Korea's Hermit Kingdom past and answered the need for closure from the world economy after decades of opening under Japanese auspices.

What does the DPRK's corporatist socialism look like? We can sketch out the model and then fill in the details:

The Leader. Functions as a charismatic source of legitimacy and ideology;

40. V. I. Lenin, *State and Revolution,* in *the Lenin Anthology,* ed. Robert Tucker (New York: W. W. Norton, 1975), pp. 379–84.

also as a father figure, head of the Korean family; also as the "head and heart" of the body politic.

The Family. Core unit of society; leader's family is the model, and the historical extension symbolizing the great chain; metaphor for the nation; interpenetrates the state.

The Party. The core the body politic; itself a living organism, it also provides the sinews linking the nation together; it represents the "blood ties" linking ruler and ruled. Metaphorical images are blood relations and concentric circles of organization. Often termed the "mother party."

The Collective. Social organization mediating between party and family; model is family; pools state and family property.

The Idea. Juche (chuch'e), the symbol of the nation and the leader; source is leader's mind; the metaphor for the people acting as one mind.

The Revolution. The leader's biography, stretching back half a century through him and a century through his family; model for how to apply Juche.

The Guide. The leader's progeny; symbolizes the future; establishes the principle of family-based succession.

The World. Structured by a national solipsism in which the Sun (the leader) is the center; the sun spreads its rays (Juche) outward; the world tends toward the Sun.

This model suggests all the phenomena we have associated with corporatism in its nonpathological forms: organic solidity; the family as metaphor and model; the great chain connecting past, present, and future; the fatherly role of the leader (whether a traditional king or a charismatic revolutionary); the subsuming of the individual by family, collective, or state (all three in the DPRK); the hostility to liberalism in politics and modernity in culture (bourgeois decadence being reviled both by conservative and socialist corporatists); and the principle of hierarchy (modified more or less by general equality and democracy, depending on the type of corporatism).

In North Korea, the determinant causes for the peculiarities of the model are Korea's Hermit Kingdom and Confucianist past, its history of colonial opening and penetration by the market, followed by closure and development on an autarkic model, and peculiarities of the domestic political economy and demographic base at the time of regime formation.

The first point is to have one leader, onto which everyone is expected to project the fondest ideals of the nation, and around which everyone is expected to unite. The phrase, "uniting around Kim Il Sung" ("Kim Il sŏng chuwi e tan'gyŏl") expresses the notion that the leader is the center and the source of all good ideas, and an organizational principle of concentric circles spreading out from the leader. Second, the leader surrounds himself with a core, usually rendered as nucleus *(haeksim)*, but sometimes by a rare term that carries the connotation of marrow *(kol'gan)*. Third, the critical core group is the leader's family: it is virtuous (i.e., revolutionary), it is exemplary (all the relatives were virtuous), and it is a chain linking past with present (e.g., the great-grandfather led the first blows struck at U.S. imperialism, in 1866). Fourth, the core holds all effective political power. (From the 1930s until the 1980s, that core has consisted of Kim, his family and relatives, and those Manchurian guerrillas who either fought with him or quickly united with him after the liberation.) Fifth, the leader spreads love and benevolence (the classic Confucian virtues), and the followers respond with loyalty and devotion, and with fulsome accolades designed to enhance the leader's stature.

Since Kim passed his sixty-year cycle (1972), a point beyond which Korean elders are venerated generally, he has been venerated particularly—veneration that, by non-Korean standards at least, knows no bounds. At Kim's sixty-fifth birthday it was stated that "our whole society has become a big revolutionary family, all members of which are firmly united in one ideology and one purpose." Kim was also described as the "tender-hearted father" of the million or so Koreans living in Japan.[41] In November 1978, for the first time to my knowledge, Kim was termed "the supreme brain of the nation," a formation that later changed to "heart" (*maŭm*, a Korean term that can mean heart, mind, or both).[42] Long termed "the fatherly leader" *(ŏbŏi suryŏng)*, Kim now became simply "our father," and the country the "fatherland" or "motherland."

In October 1980, North Korea arranged to have Kim's son Jong Il intro-

41. KCNA, April 17, 1977.
42. KCNA, November 23, 1978.

duced as his effective successor at the Sixth Congress of the Korean Workers' Party. At that time organic metaphors proliferated one after the other. Kim Il Sung's report to the congress referred to "the organizational will" of the party and the party's "pulsation," always felt by the masses; the party was called "one's own mother"; "infinite loyalty" to the party and the establishment of an "iron discipline" were expected of everyone, "under which the whole party acts as one body under the leadership of the party central committee. It is a fixed practice in our party that all its organizations move like an organism according to the principle of democratic centralism."[43]

In the aftermath of the congress the party newspaper published several editorials and articles full of organic metaphors. "Father of the People" in February 1981 said the following:

> Kim Il Sung is . . . the great father of our people . . . possessed of greatest love for the people. Long is the history of the word "father" used as a word representing love and reverence . . . expressing the unbreakable blood ties between the people and the leader. Father. This familiar word represents our people's single heart of boundless respect and loyalty. . . . The love shown by the Great Leader for our people is love of kinship. . . . Our respected and beloved Leader is the tenderhearted father of all the people.
>
> Love of paternity . . . is the noblest ideological sentiment possessed only by our people, which cannot be explained by any theory or principle or fathomed by anything.[44]

Another article argued that "the blood ties between our party and the people [mean that] . . . the party and the people always breathe one breath and act as one. . . . The creed of the people [is] that they cannot live or enjoy happiness apart from the party . . . today our party and people have become an integrity of ideology and purpose which no force can break. The Workers' Party of Korea . . . is the Mother Party bringing boundless honor and happiness to the people . . ."[45] In March Kim Il Sung got a new name: "Great Heart" *(widaehan maŭm):*

43. KCNA, October 14, 1980.
44. *Nodong sinmun,* February 13, 1981; KCNA, February 16, 1981.
45. *Nodong sinmun,* February 4, 1981; KCNA, February 7, 1981.

> Only a man of great heart . . . possessed of rare grit and magnanimity and noble human love can create a great history. . . . His conception of speed and time cannot be measured or assessed by established common sense and mathematical calculation. . . . The grit to break through, even if the Heavens fall, and cleave the way through the sea and curtail the century [is his]. . . . His heart is a traction power attracting the hearts of all people and a centripetal force uniting them as one. . . . His love for people—this is, indeed, a kindred king of human love. . . . No age, no one has ever seen such a great man with a warm love. . . . Kim Il Sung is the great sun and great man . . . this great heart. . . . Thanks to this, great heart national independence is firmly guaranteed. . . . As there is this great heart, the heart of our party is great. As the heart of our party is great, the victory of the cause of Juche is firmly guaranteed . . . and the entire people [are] rallied in one mind and thought.[46]

Here the organic metaphors are joined with religious references; the language is reminiscent of the Nippon *kokutai* material referred to earlier and, of course, the kings and princes of medieval Europe.

At about the same time, *Nodong sinmun* (Workers' daily) published a full-page editorial, "Spirit of Korea," which linked "the glorious party center" (Kim Jong Il) with "the eternal spring of Mankind" and a new, "youthful spirit," "alien to decrepitude," now marching through Korean land. "A solid foundation" (the succession) had been laid, so that "our people will sing of the prosperous Fatherland down through generations . . . in one mind and one purpose."[47]

North Korean socialist corporatism possesses a pronounced voluntarism before which Maoist will and vision pale by comparison. We have already detected the frequent use of the term "will": iron will, leader's will, steel-like will, and so forth are frequently seen. The Korean propagandists frequently state that "everything is decided by idea."[48] Such emphases have been around from the beginning, the result both of the cult of the leader and his Juche thought, and the inevitable prominence of the superstructure in a socialism that must, in part, create its own base (thus the engineering

46. KCNA, March 12, 1981.
47. *Nodong sinmun,* March 25, 1981; KCNA, March 26, 1981.
48. See, for example, KCNA, June 20, 1981.

metaphors of Stalin). Voluntarism, of course, was yet another characteristic of corporatism, especially the pathological Hitler version.

"The Idea," Juche, seems at first glance to be readily understandable. It is defined as self-reliance and independence in politics, economics, defense, and ideology. On closer inspection, however, the term's meaning is less accessible. For example, "self-reliance" is often translated as *charyŏk kaengsaeng,* the same four-character expression used by the Maoists; "independence" can be *charip, chajusŏng,* or *tongnip.* Juche seems to stand above and to encompass these other meanings. Yet Juche is used in ways that the other terms are not.

The North Koreans say things like "everyone must have Juche firm in mind and spirit"; only when Juche is firmly implanted can we be happy"; "Juche must not only be firmly established in mind but perfectly realized in practice"; and so on. The closer one gets to its meaning, the more the meaning recedes. it is the opaque core of Korean national solipsism. Few would have much guidance for how to get up every morning and "perfectly realize" Juche. In fact it seems to be used much like *kokutai* in interwar Japan, or *volkische* in Germany, or Mao Zedong Thought in China: a term defining an emotion that puts the nation first, or the leader's wishes first, in everything. As we have said, Juche shares the same character as *kokutai* (*kukch'e* in Korean); *chu* means something like main or master, so that the liberal translation of Juche would be "main" or "master" principle.

Corporatism seems to be a flexible framework within which Left and Right can meet, something many have noted about interwar Europe. Korea is no different. Juche resonates with *kokutai* and other such phrases precisely because of its diffuse and all-purpose meaning; an emotion masquerading as an idea, it appeals to nationalists of all persuasions. Thus it is that Kim Il Sung's ideology calls up comparisons with perhaps the most extreme right-wing figure in postwar South Korea, Yi Pŏm Sŏk, the founder and leader of the early postwar Korean National Youth (KNY).

In the 1930s, Yi had studied European corporatist and Fascist youth groups, and worked with the Kuomintang Blue Shirts and Special Services in China.[49] On his return to Korea in 1946 he organized some 70,000 youths into a classic rightist vehicle of the streets; by 1948 the KNY had

49. See Gregory Henderson, *Korea: The Politics of the Vortex* (Cambridge: Harvard University Press, 1968), p. 141; also Cumings, *Origins of the Korean War,* vol. 1 (Princeton: Princeton University Press, 1981), chap. 5.

over a million members and made Yi second only to Syngman Rhee in power. His pet slogan, "minjok chisang, kukka chisang" (nation first, state first), expressed his German learning;[50] he was among the first Korean political figures explicitly to exalt not just the nation, but the state. He opposed Korean reliance on foreigners (*sadae chuŭi* or "flunkeyism," as the North Koreans translate it), advocated independence, lambasted those politicians who were "un-Korean," and urged Koreans to adopt a standpoint of juche, which in his usage meant complete subjectivity where everything Korean was concerned. He preferred economic autarky to any external international involvements that might subordinate Korean interests. He urged a pan-national Korean solidarity based on racial purity: "the Nation is the race and the race is the nation." Talk of "racial essence" and "blood-lines" *(hyŏlt'ong)* runs throughout his work: this for him was the key characteristic defining Korea, and the essential element in its corporate and organic unity. As for the mind and spirit, he thought only the strongest national consciousness *(minjok ŭisik)* could save Korea from predatory great powers. He lived in the era of "the masses," he said, and therefore leaders must "understand and love" the masses, always be among them and never separate from them. One race, one blood, one nation, one state, and inseparable unity between leaders and led would create "a great family" that would endure.[51]

The resonance with Kim Il Sung's idea is clear. Yi was, however, a romantic and conservative corporatist. He exalted the state, thought leaders should be patriots above politics, railed against the concept of class struggle, and in his bias against capitalism and material pursuits sought not to overcome it in socialism but to return to an earlier era of community. But his experience and his success in the South suggests that if there is one kernel idea linking postwar Korean leaders it is corporate national unity at home and autarky vis-à-vis the rest of the world, a combination that is overdetermined by Korea's past history of internal factionalism and disastrous external penetration in the imperial era of the nineteenth century, and its political and economic autarky (thus the "Hermit Kingdom") in the three hundred years after the Hideyoshi invasions in the 1590s.

A socialist (or a conservative) corporatism also appeals to a people with a very strong extended family system, a high consciousness of lineage ("the

50. Yi Pŏm-sŏk, *Minjok kwa ch'ŏngnyŏn* [Nation and youth] (Seoul, 1948), p. 27.
51. Ibid, pp. 9–13, 29–30.

great chain"), major cottage industries putting out genealogies, and the Confucian background that justifies and reinforces it all. The hierarchical language, with verbal endings and even grammatical markers differing according to the station of the person speaking and being spoken to, is deeply embedded in Korean family practices—so much so that, surprisingly, the North Koreans have not done much to eliminate it. The DPRK constitution defines the family as the core unit of society. Furthermore, marriages are apparently still arranged in the North, family themes are exalted in the arts, and the regime has never sought to break up the family unit. For these and other reasons, North Korea often impresses foreign visitors precisely in its cultural conservatism: a Japanese visitor old enough to remember prewar Japan remarked on the similarities he found and noted the "antiquarian atmosphere" in North Korea.

The Mass Party

The Korean Workers' Party (KWP) from the beginning in 1946 was designated a "mass party of a new type," not a class party with its typical small, vanguard unit. Korea has always had the highest percentage of the population enrolled in the party of any Marxist-Leninist regime, fluctuating between 12 and 14 percent. Kim argued that almost anyone should be able to join the party, so long as he or she was a patriot who put the nation and the revolution first. For young people not eligible to join the party, and the adult population not in the party, there were extensive mass organizations of youths, workers, women, and peasants that made it virtually obligatory for everyone to join something.[52] The unique symbol of the KWP places writing brush across the hammer and sickle, acknowledging the inclusive policy toward intellectuals and experts: Kim has rarely if ever denigrated them, as did Mao, and explicitly authorized their widespread introduction into positions of authority.

The Koreans also established a vague category, *samuwŏn,* meaning clerks, petty-bourgeois traders, bureaucrats, professors, and so on. My own research into the late 1940s suggests that this category served two purposes: for the regime, it retained educated people and experts who might otherwise have fled South; for many Koreans it provided a category within which to hide "bad" class background. In membership lists for mass organi-

52. Cumings, *Origins,* vol. 2, chap. 11.

zations, giving class background of members and their families, the *samuwŏn* are very prominent.[53] *Samuwŏn* also show up prominently in aggregate statistics on KWP membership. In 1946 the percentage was 48 percent; by 1956 *samuwŏn* had dropped to 13 percent and peasants had increased to 61 percent, mostly the result of the war (many *samuwŏn* moved South or were killed, or were working the fields in the mid-1950s amid all the destruction). Thus the Korean revolution, far from polarizing the population exclusively into good and bad classes, pursued an inclusive, all-encompassing mass politics.

This organizational history also expresses the corporate character of the DPRK. Its doctrine says that the core leadership must be constantly steeled and hardened, while moving outward in concentric circles to encompass other elements in the population. This is the primary method of Korean organization, cited over and over in Kim's works. More fundamentally, this history suggests that, in good corporate fashion, the Koreans have envisioned their society as a mass, the gathered-together "people," rather than a class-based and class-divided society. The union of the three classes—peasant, worker, *samuwŏn*—excluded few but the landlords of the old period who, after all, were much stronger in southern than in northern Korea. In striking contrast to China before Mao died in 1976, the Koreans have not since the 1950s mounted campaigns against "the old bad classes," nor have they suggested that the socialist period may spawn new classes, the clarion call of the Cultural Revolution.

Police and Intelligence

Nothing in the preceding discussion should be construed as meaning that North Korea uses "familial benevolence" in dealing with its perceived enemies. If we accept Michael Mann's distinction between "despotic" and "infrastructural" power, with modern authoritarian states deploying both effectively, North Korea might be taken as the classic meld.[54] Just as with the South, the security apparatus was very large in the North; the difference is that North Korea systematized this function very early, whereas South

53. See original materials on the Tongmyŏn youth corps and party organizations, 1946, in SA 2005/4/35-39, RG (Record Group) 242, "Captured Enemy Documents."

54. A useful summary of his distinction can be found in Mann, "The Autonomous Power of the State: Its Origins, Mechanisms and Results," in *States in History,* ed. John A. Hall, pp. 109–36 (Cambridge, Mass.: Basil Blackwell, 1987).

Korea did not before the early 1960s. An "extremely secret" document on the people's committee administrative structure shows that the intelligence *(chŏngbo)* section of each provincial committee always had more members than any other section, about twenty per province, with the provincial committee staff totaling 353 to 362, depending on the region. In cities, 55 members of the Ministry of the Interior [*naemuwŏn*] were attached to each committee, and the size of these committees ranged from 141 members in Nanam to 185 in Sinŭiju, excluding the capital, which had 341 members. P'Yŏngyang appeared to have 218 *naemuwŏn* in addition to the ordinary committee staff members. At the county level, of a total of 10,499 staff, more than one-third (3,732) were *naemuwŏn*. These personnel, of course, included ordinary neighborhood police, and even the intelligence function encompassed routine things like control of narcotics and poisons, that is, it was not just oriented to political cases. Furthermore the total numbers of police appear much smaller than in the South.[55]

A secret report in 1947 by Pak Il U of the Department of Peace Preservation *(poan'guk)* made clear that political cases were a matter of direct concern. He admonished province chiefs, "in spite of your awareness of political criminals, [your] struggle against profiteers and evil capitalists is weak." The chiefs should be sure "to examine the class background and the thoughts" of all neighborhood leaders (*panjang*s) in their jurisdiction, and bring problem cases to the attention of the people's committee. Apparently discipline was lax among provincial police, for he said they were not paying enough attention to laws and directives from the center and did not keep proper records. The class enemy was, obviously, given next to no rights under this system.

In the same document, however, Pak urged the chiefs to develop "the character of all-around revolutionaries"—people who abjure improper or immoral behavior, dispense justice in a strict but impartial manner, and relate means to the ends revolutionaries should seek. They were to "serve the people," he said, using the same characters that Mao did, earn their trust and the trust of the whole country. Weekly meetings should be held to explain policies, the political situation, and to conduct "thought training" *(sasang hullyŏn):* "protect our intimate ties with the people, the political

55. RG242, SA2009, item 9/113, North Korean people's committee, *To, si, kun, inmin wiwŏn-hoe chigu chŏngwŏn mit samu punjang* [district administrative staff and duties in province, city, and county people's committees], "extremely secret," no place, no date.

parties and social organizations, especially lower-level people's committees." Pak even appreciated the weaknesses policemen are sometimes prone to, and urged them to repent:

> Everyone has an appetite for food and loves the opposite sex. But this is something that the patriot conquers. Debauchery, indolence . . . are just for the benefit of one's self and are in opposition to patriotic thought.[56]

These and other materials also make it apparent that the term translated as "liberalism," *chayujuŭi,* means to Koreans a kind of license in which the individual departs from the group, benefits his interests at the expense of others, and lacks a proper conception of morality. Pak frequently referred to getting rid of *chasa* and *chari,* which would translate literally as self-interest or self-profit, and of course the character *cha* is common to all these terms, symbolizing something produced out of the individual self rather than out of the group, and therefore selfish or immoral or hard to control, or all of the above. By contrast, the "all-around revolutionary" [*man'nŭng hyŏngmyŏngga*] possesses manifold moral virtue, like the Confucian ideal of the *Junzi,* or true gentleman.

However "virtuous" these new policemen were, their functions included a total system of thought control and surveillance that would horrify a believer in basic political freedoms. The regime organized secret networks on a grand scale to report political statements, including rumors and hearsay, both as a means of checking on citizen loyalty and of providing the leadership with a rudimentary guidance to public opinion. One internal directive from the occupation of the South in August 1950, which can be assumed to be representative of North Korean practice, if in wartime conditions, says the following:

> The most important mechanism for impressing the masses with the correctness and superiority of people's sovereignty is the question of grasping what their opinions are, and how they can be changed. Therefore, it is of the utmost importance to strengthen the organized collection network . . . and through it broadly to collect and report mass

56. RG242, SA2005, item 6/11, *Saŏp kwan'gye sŏryu* [work documents], "secret."

> opinions, so as to sweep away anti-democratic phenomena and incorrect thoughts among the village people.

The document called for the organization of inspection networks that would ascertain the names, addresses, class backgrounds, party affiliations, preliberation activities, and good and bad attitudes of everyone—to be reported as they are, without editorials.

Studies done using prisoner of war interviews during the war bore out this general picture of repression combined with law and order in the North—a highly penetrative structure that required correct behavior of everyone, as the regime defined it. At the same time, most citizens seemed to believe that this apparatus was a distinct improvement over that of the Japanese period. One POW said the police were "severe," but "no third degree measures were ever used"; the result was that people came to look upon the police as "guardians of peace."[57]

A final aspect of this corporate socialism links the domestic system with the international sphere. North Korea was perhaps the supreme example in the postcolonial developing world of conscious withdrawal from the capitalist world system (South Korea is perhaps the leading example of the opposite model, too, a fact worth pondering). Franz Neumann once remarked that "autarky is the philosophy of a fortress about to be beleaguered," but in North Korea the fortress has always been beleaguered.[58] Few countries have a more unfortunate geopolitical position, jammed cheek-by-jowl against two feuding socialist giants with an always tense confrontation with the United States and South Korea along the demilitarized zone. The combination of external political pressure and internal ethnic homogeneity is almost enough to predict a tight little polity. But the Koreans have, since the late 1940s, quite consciously sought an autarkic and self-reliant development policy. Late industrial development has always suggested neomercantile strategies abroad and unity and strong states at home, and in the 1930s the late developers (Japan, Germany, Italy) turned corporate or Fascist as well. What about "late late" development? A fortiori, the later the industrialization the stronger the necessity for coordination and unity at home? The experience of both Koreas would suggest a positive

57. MacArthur Archives, Record Group 6, box 81, POW interrogation reports, esp. Interrogation Report no. 612, August 19, 1950; there are many others that could be cited.
58. Neumann, *Behemoth,* p. 329.

answer, not simply because of DPRK corporate socialism, but because the intense pressures of late late development in South Korea have helped to generate an unprecedentedly strong state as well. In any case the strong domestic unity, the political economy of development, and no doubt the wretched excesses of North Korea, are in part the precipitate of world system pressure in the periphery.

This chapter closes with one last observation. In *Knowledge and Politics* Roberto Unger distinguishes between an inner and an outer circle in contemporary politics. The inner circle represents power and domination, exercised everywhere by the few. The outer circle includes all the rest, and their search for community, decency, and participation through the architecture of politics. Nowhere has the problem of the inner circle been resolved, he argues, and therefore in the outer circle "the search for community is condemned to be idolatrous, or utopian, or both." In Unger's sense, the inner circle—Kim's nucleus—is clearly the problem in North Korea; in the absence of a nonfamily and impersonal principle for constituting the core, the outer circle is condemned to idolatry. It may be that the apparent stability of this state masks instability at its center, in the failure to constitute a politics that can extend beyond the circle of family and personal relations. Or it may be that the North Koreans, with their singular meld of premodern and socialist politics, will be able to weather the problem of succession that bedeviled the other Communist systems. In any case, with Kim Il Sung's passing drawing ever closer, the problem of the core moves front and center. The inner circle will be tested in a way that it has not been since the Korean War. When that time comes, the outer circle will hang in the balance. A politics that, whatever else one may say about it, has brought remarkable stability to Korea for nearly half a century, will be put to the test.

7
Strong State and Contentious Society

Hagen Koo

What clearly emerges from the analyses presented in this book is that Korea's path to modernity and industrialization has not been a smooth evolutionary process but rather a discontinuous, uneven, and conflict-ridden one determined not by some immutable logic of modernism but by historical contingencies and a dialectical process of social change. At the core of this historical process is the relationship between the state and society, which itself has undergone dramatic changes on a nonlinear path of evolution. Although the state has played a critical role in setting the dominant direction and framework of social transformation in Korea, concrete processes of social and political change have not been determined simply by the state's directives but have been intimately shaped by the specific ways in which individuals, groups, or social classes have reacted to state actions and to their experiences of social change. The discussions presented in this collection demonstrate that neither a state-centered nor a society-centered perspective is appropriate for comprehending the unique features of social change in contemporary Korea. For the latter, we must go beyond the unnecessary dichotomy of these two approaches and direct attention to complex and dynamic relationships between the state and society and dialectic processes through which their relationships change.

What is particularly interesting about state-society relations in contemporary Korea is that despite the state's unusual strength and pervasive presence, civil society in the South has never been completely stifled but has always demonstrated a subversive, combative character. Thus the asymmetrical relationship between the state and society, which has mostly been the norm, has required extra vigilance and shows of coercive power on the part of the state in order to maintain it, and many times in modern Korean history, this vertical relationship has been overturned by sudden eruptions of social forces. Though short in history and relatively underdeveloped in institutional features, civil society in South Korea has always contained both elements of strong resistance to state power and violent eruptions.

An important phenomenon that must be explained is not simply the origins of the strong state but the origins of the simultaneous presence of a strong state and a strong, contentious society in South Korea and the reasons for the volatile relationship between the two. This is not a simple question to answer. A satisfactory answer would require a wholesale reconceptualization of state power and civil society in the Korean context, which is beyond the scope of this essay. What I attempt here is merely to outline such an answer by reanalyzing Korea's major historical changes since the colonial period, focusing on state-society relations. The analyses presented in this volume provide essential materials for this interpretive analysis.

Probably the most prevalent view of the origin of Korea's strong state is to define it as a product of Japanese colonialism. Observers of contemporary Korean history are in wide agreement that the modern state in Korea has a gestation period under Japanese colonial rule (1910–45). They also note that the Confucian monarchy of the Yi Dynasty (1392–1910) hardly represented a strong state, since it had neither the organizational capacity to penetrate into society nor effective autonomy from the dominant classes. While state power was highly centralized and autocratic during the Yi Dynasty, its autonomy was severely restrained by the powerful *yangban* class (aristocracy). Palais has made this argument most forcefuly: "Despite the existence of the apparatus of absolute despotism, the centralized structure of government masked the limitations on royal authority by the *yangban* aristocracy. The most important reason for these limitations was that the sources of power, wealth, and prestige were not controlled exclusively by the crown; they were also based on inheritance of status and landownership."[1] While land officially belongs to the state, Palais explains, it came to be controlled through the hereditary rights of *yangban* families in the latter period of the Yi Dynasty. Using their monopoly access to civil service exams, the *yangban* class turned the government bureaucracy into a bastion of their own class interest. A long period of political stability was maintained based on checks and balances between the monarchy and the aristocracy, but this balance of power prevented the Yi state from exercising sufficient power and from being able to mobilize social forces to respond positively to the onslaught of imperial forces.[2]

Japanese rule brought drastic changes to both state organization and class structure in colonial Korea. The feeble and discredited Korean monarchic system was dismantled, and in its place was implanted a modern bureaucratic colonial government with an improved ability to penetrate society and control the population. "The colonial state was a far cry from the decrepit Yi," Cumings writes, since "it soon came to possess a comprehensive, autonomous, and penetrating quality that no previous Korean state could possibly have mustered."[3] The colonial rulers modernized the government bureaucracy, built a vast network of police and security forces, introduced modern land surveillance and taxation, laid down railroads, and developed transportation and communication systems. If state power, as Skocpol argues, is ultimately based on the ability to extract resources and control the people's behavior, the Japanese colonists clearly did their job very well in Korea.[4] The nature of state power also changed: if the traditional Korean state rulers enjoyed only "despotic power," in Mann's terms, the colonial state came to possess much "infrastructural power," or more correctly a combination of both.[5]

1. James Palais, *Politics and Policy in Traditional Korea, 1864–1876* (Cambridge: Harvard University Press, 1976), p. 10.

2. The most concise and informative source book on modern Korean history is Carter Eckert, Ki-baik Lee, Young Ick Lew, Michael Robinson, and Edward Wagner, *Korea Old and New: A History* (Cambridge: Korea Institute, Harvard University, 1990).

3. Bruce Cumings, *The Origins of the Korean War,* vol. 1: *Liberation and the Emergence of Separate Regimes, 1945–1947* (Princeton: Princeton University Press, 1981), p. 10.

4. Theda Skocpol, *States and Social Revolutions: A Comparative Analysis of France, Russia and China* (New York: Cambridge University Press, 1979).

5. Michael Mann defines despotic power in terms of "the range of actions which the elite is empowered to undertake without routine, institutionalized negotiation with civil society groups." Infrastructural power is "the capacity of the state actually to penetrate civil society, and to implement logistically political decisions throughout the realm." See Mann, "The

The colonial government ended the *yangban* status system, which had in any case lost much of its integrity in the late nineteenth century. However, colonial rulers kept the landlord structure more or less intact, to bolster their control and exploitation of the indigenous population. Although this change may be interpreted simply as a transition from one form of stratification to another (i.e., from an estate to a class system), with no significant change in the distribution of power, it actually entailed a fundamental change in the relationships between state power and social classes. Stripped of their traditional status, and now totally dependent on the colonial government for their landholdings, the landlord class ceased to be the state's strongest competitor for power. Not only did the landlords lose power vis-à-vis the state, but they also lost social power and moral authority over the subordinate classes; indeed, they became "Japanese collaborators," and the object of an intense national hatred that continues even to the present.

The balance of power between the state and society shifted irrevocably in favor of the former. Now a highly developed central bureaucratic state stood above society, which no longer possessed powerful social classes or social organizations. This was clearly an "overdeveloped state," using Alavi's terms—overdeveloped relative to the nature of class structure and in proportion to the level of social differentiation in civil society.[6] As in other postcolonial societies, this overdeveloped state apparatus became an important legacy in postcolonial Korea; its bureaucratic organizations, its instruments of coercion, and its political practices provided an essential institutional foundation for postcolonial state formation in Korea.

In this regard, it is impossible to understand the processes of modern state formation in Korea, both North and South, apart from the Japanese colonial legacy. It is inaccurate, however, to attribute the strength of both Korean states entirely to the colonial power. To do so ignores the importance of both postcolonial contexts and the influence of Korea's long history, and infers too simplistic an understanding of the meaning of the colonial experience for Koreans and Korean society.

First, it is necessary to have an accurate understanding of the precolonial

Autonomous Power of the State: Its Origins, Mechanisms and Results," *Archives Européennes de Sociologie* 25 (1984).

6. Hamza Alavi, "The State in Postcolonial Societies: Pakistan and Bangladesh," *New Left Review* 74 (1972): 59–81.

historical legacy. Although during the late Yi Dynasty, the crown's power was relatively weak, throughout Korea's long history, the state has been the most dominant and powerful institution. The state existed not simply as the most powerful among other competing social organizations, but it was a supreme entity that stood above society and gave meaning and direction to both individuals and social groups under its sovereign power; state power represented moral authority with a "heavenly mandate" to create and maintain a morally integrated community. All other forms of social power and privilege were ultimately to be derived from state power. Though the Yi state was deeply penetrated and controlled by the powerful *yangban* class, the *yangban* did not have an autonomous source of power, unlike feudal lords or the bourgeoisie in Europe. Legally, all land belonged to the state and the *yangban* had to reclaim their status continuously through the state-controlled civil service exam. Thus the relationships between the state and the dominant class in the Yi Dynasty were essentially symbiotic rather than competitive. The *yangban* class had no interest in weakening state power; rather, it sought to use state power only for its own interests. In fact, the application of a dualistic model of state versus class power seems inappropriate to traditional Korea, where the legal system and the structure of the economy allowed no institutional base of autonomous power of any class, and where society was subsumed under the state.

So even though the Yi state was relatively incapable of controlling the behavior of the dominant class, it nevertheless left behind the legacy of a powerful centralized state authority. In this regard, Nettl's insightful early writing on the state as a "conceptual variable" is particularly useful.[7] Conceptualizing the state as "essentially a sociocultural phenomenon," he argues that the degree of "stateness" or "statelessness" depends on historical, intellectual, and cultural factors. "Is there a historical tradition in any particular society for the existence, primacy, autonomy, and sovereignty of a state?" "Do the political ideas and theories of the society past or present incorporate a notion of state, and what role do they assign to it?" "To what extent have individuals generalized the concept and cognition of state in their perceptions and actions, and to what extent are such cognitions salient?" These are the crucial questions we must ask, Nettl argues, in order to determine the degree of stateness of a particular state. Clearly, in terms

7. J. P. Nettl, "The State as a Conceptual Variable," *World Politics* 20 (1968): 559–92.

of all these dimensions, the Yi state enjoyed a high degree of stateness. The state as a hegemonic institution in Korean society was not a creation of the colonial government. Although the colonists may be credited for modernizing Korean state organizations, they were clearly the creator neither of a new state nor of the cultural notion of the state.

The highly centralized state power that existed in traditional Korea engendered a distinct pattern of politics, which Henderson describes as "politics of the vortex": "the imposition of a continuous high degree of centralism on a homogeneous society has resulted in a vortex, a powerful, upward-sucking force active throughout the culture. This force is such as to detach particles from any integrative groups that the society might tend to build—social classes, political parties, and other intermediary groups—thus eroding group consolidation and forming a general atomized upward mobility."[8] Although his depiction of Yi society as a "mass society" is a puzzling application of this sociological concept, Henderson is right in stressing the centripetal dynamics of Korean politics and a center-oriented political culture associated with this pattern of power.[9] This political culture has strong ramifications for the ways in which state power is exercised in contemporary Korea. And this cultural element is one major reason, as Cumings suggests, for the similarities between North and South Korea in terms of their state organizations and leadership patterns, despite their diametically opposed paths of political and economic development.

Returning to the Japanese colonial legacy, one must look beyond what kinds of organizational and infrastructural changes the Japanese introduced to comprehend the nature of colonial experiences undergone by the Korean people and the ways in which these experiences transformed the nature of Korean society. Colonial rule changed the structure of the Korean state and caused a profound transformation of Korean society and its relationship with state power, leaving another important legacy that is not well acknowledged in most scholarly discussions on South Korean development. The most crucial aspect of this social change was the separation of the state from society. The extremely coercive and exploitative nature of Japanese rule in Korea and the intense anti-Japanese struggles among Koreans cre-

8. Gregory Henderson, *Korea: The Politics of the Vortex* (Cambridge: Harvard University Press, 1968), p. 193.

9. Norman Jacobs regards this as a Korean form of patrimonialism. See his *The Korean Road to Modernization and Development* (Urbana: University of Illinois Press, 1985).

ated a widening gap between the state and society. In proportion to the development of the colonial state's coercive apparatus, civil society became increasingly politicized and mobilized for anticolonial struggles. A tremendous amount of social change occurred during the colonial period, including the displacement of many peasants from their land, the rapid rise of wage workers, forced military service on Japanese war fronts, and large-scale emigration to Manchuria, Japan, and Russia. Thereafter Korean society could not remain a peaceful, quiescent peasant society. While civil society became differentiated and increasingly politicized, colonial power maintained itself through coercive power, with only tenuous links to society, mainly through a small number of Korean collaborators.

In the face of the continuously recalcitrant colonial society, the colonial government relied heavily on the notorious police and surveilance systems it developed in Korea. The "sophisticated cultural policy" it adopted after the massive 1919 independence struggle did little to reduce the indignation of the Korean people over Japanese rule. State power was thus completely detached from the social base; strong as it was, it drew from the power of the metropole, not from the society where it was located. Antistatism became a deeply ingrained Korean intellectual orientation during this period, and this antistatist tradition has continued.

Thus the Japanese colonial legacy must be understood in its dual character. On the one hand, it bequeathed to modern Korea a set of institutions essential for the formation of a strong modern state and changed the balance of power between the state and society. On the other hand, it gave rise to a highly agitated, mobile society with suppressed desires for undoing past injustices and deep antagonism against alien-controlled state power. In short, the colonial experience simultaneously brought about a strong state apparatus and a contentious civil society.

The nascent civil society that began to develop during the colonial period was not primarily the outcome of capitalist development and social differentiation. The level of capitalist industrialization was still at a very low level, and the repressive control of the colonial government was simply too thorough and penetrating to allow much space for autonomous associational life. What existed in colonial Korea was largely subterranean networks of resistance movements, peasant and labor organizations, and intellectual circles, as well as a few officially sanctioned voluntary associations.

Strictly speaking, therefore, we cannot say that a "civil society" really existed during the colonial period. It must be remembered that in a Hegelian definition, civil society is identical to a bourgeois society, that is, civil society is an integral feature of capitalist economy and bourgeois institutions. The concept of civil society is basically a Western, more accurately West European, notion, shaped by the twin influences of capitalism and the French revolution.[10] An essential idea at the base of this concept is the Western liberal principle of "free, self-determining, autonomous individuality with equal right to social justice and to attainment of satisfaction."[11] The idea of the separation of society and the state, and the importance given to the sphere of social life as distinct from the state, derives essentially from this nineteenth-century Western liberal political thought.

Such an idea is alien to Confucian political thought, in which state and society constitute a moral and ethical unity, inseparable from each other. If society is subsumed under the state, state power is also subordinate to a higher morality that ought to govern both of them (see chapter 5 by Uchang Kim in this book). However, Japanese colonial rule brought an important change. As argued above, colonial experience led to an alienation of society from the state, of the people from state power, and of national culture from alien culture. Nationalism thus became the fulcrum of a new political consciousness. To a large extent, Korean nationalism is the product of Japanese colonialism. Although it began to arise in the second half of the nineteenth century in reaction to the penetration of imperial forces, it was during the colonial period that nationalism became the most potent ideology, with a clearly articulated ideology with an obvious reference point, and with concrete experiences and emotions attached to it. And it was the intellectuals who became the principal bearers of nationalism. In short, the nascent civil society was a product not so much of capitalism or Western political liberal ideas as of the nationalistic reactions to alien power. The significance of civil society during this period is not to be found in the growth of autonomous associational life, but in the separation of society

10. See John Keane, "Despotism and Democracy: The Origins and Development of the Distinction between Civil Society and the State, 1750–1850," and Jeno Szucs, "Three Historical Regions of Europe," in *Civil Society and the State: New European Perspectives,* ed. Keane (London: Verso, 1988); Ellen Meiksins Wood, "The Uses and Abuses of 'Civil Society,'" *Socialist Register 1990,* ed. Ralph Miliband, Leo Panitch, and John Saville (London: Merlin Press, 1990).

11. Jean L. Cohen, *Class and Civil Society: The Limits of Marxian Critical Theory* (Amherst: University of Massachusetts Press, 1982), p. 30.

and state power and the ways in which this political alienation formed the political consciousness of Korean intellectuals.

Postliberation political development in Korea was intimately affected by these complex colonial legacy—by the organizations, ideologies, transformed class relations, strong sense of injustice, and experience of collective struggles, all accumulated during thirty-six years of harsh colonial rule. The major actors and themes of the drama to be played were more or less determined by this colonial experience. Yet the play itself was not written by the actors but by outsiders, causing Koreans great anguish. In interpreting postcolonial Korean political history, and the evolution of state-society relations, it is crucial to understand the significant influence that geopolitical forces and, in particular, the Korean War have exerted on political development in Korean peninsula.

With the sudden ending of Japanese colonialism in 1945, the subterranean networks of Korean civil society erupted onto the surface. As described in Chapter 1 by Jang Jip Choi, a dizzying array of political organizations, peasant and labor organizations and youth, student, women's, religious, and cultural groups were formed in a short time to make their voices heard in determining the destiny of the new nation state. As Choi points out, no serious schism existed at the beginning in the ideological orientations of these political organizations, since they were all wrapped up within the same ideology of nationalism and claimed their raison d'être with this ideology; indeed, nationalism was an essential tissue with which Koreans, Left and Right, North and South, all sought to construct an independent state. But what subsequently developed was the mutilation of these nationalist aspirations. The destiny of postwar Korea had been, in fact, determined even before Japan surrendered to the allied forces. The nation was arbitrarily divided by the interests of two superpowers, the United States and the Soviet Union, thus setting the stage for divided and antagonistic state formation.

What followed in the South, as well described by Choi, was a forceful demobilization of civil society and propping up of the conservative, reactionary regime of Syngman Rhee by the U.S. occupation forces. With this development, both the colonial apparatus of coercion and the people who allied themselves with colonial masters and gained status under colonial rule were revived, in direct contradiction to the masses' pent-up grievances and desire for radical change. Consequently, the state and society became alienated from one another again, and as before, the ruling power's lack of legitimacy was the most sensitive element in state-society relations and a focal point of political consciousness among Korean intellectuals.

In the North, the legitimacy question was largely absent because a harmony of interest existed there among the Kim Il Sung regime, internal social forces, and the Soviet Union. Immediately after coming to power, the Communist Party swiftly eliminated landlords, old colonial bureaucrats, and other Japanese collaborators, and carried out a thorough land reform in 1946. By 1948 a strong communist state was fully in place with a solid social base, strong ideological hegemony by the state, and well-developed state organizations copied from the Soviet Union. But what gave the North Korean state such remarkable stability and strength, as Cumings argues in chapter 6, was not just communist ideology and organizations but also the ways in which North Korean rulers used nationalism to construct their own distinctive corporatist system, in which the state and society were woven together under the nationalistic ideology of *Juche.*

The democratic republic in the South, however, was weak. Neither the colonial bureaucracy and the police forces nor the U.S. military occupation forces provided the South Korean state with sufficient authority to exercise effective control over society. In addition, the Rhee regime was internally undermined by incessant factional infighting, Rhee's autocratic leadership style, mismanagement of the economy, and the penetration of the bureaucracy by dominant economic interests. Had there been no strong U.S. military and economic support, most observers agree, Rhee would surely have fallen. Yet, notwithstanding all his political and economic problems, Rhee's regime did not collapse but enjoyed autocratic power for twelve years. Why? U.S. support and the powerful coercive organs at the service of political power were, of course, major factors. More important, however, was the impact of the Korean War.

No single event in modern Korean history has influenced state formation in Korea more than the Korean War. State organizations, state ideologies, and the dominant patterns of state-society relations were all shaped by the impact of the war. The war was particularly important in consolidating an anti-communist state in the South, and it achieved several things for the Rhee regime: it eliminated leftist elements and sources of peasant rebellions; it bolstered Rhee's political authority and provided political tools to control opposition groups; it led to a firmer U.S. commitment to the security of South Korea as a bulwark against communism; and it established anti-communism as the state ideology. "The Korean War," Choi argues, "transformed the South Korean state from an extremely unstable and fragile anti-communist state into a powerful bureaucratic state." Civil society, on the other hand, was fatally demobilized, and a strong state–weak society relationship was reestablished on new ground.

The significance of geopolitics and war for state formation is well recognized in recent theoretical understandings of the state. Tilly, for example, considers war a driving force of state formation and sees war-making and state-making as inseparable phenomena.[12] He argues that different paths to state formation in Europe cannot be satifactorily explained without considering geopolitical factors. Mann, in a similar vein, argues that the ruling-class strategy of state building in Europe has been historically determined not so much by internal class struggles as by the consequence of war.[13] This line of formulation was suggested earlier in Otto Hintze's writings, which pointed out the limitations of both liberal and Marxist understandings of the state and directed attention to military rivalry as a crucial mechanism of state formation in Europe.[14]

By and large, scholars of European state formation tend to focus attention on the effect of war making on the development of military organizations and other coercive resources of the state. In Korea, too, the most immediate and tangible effect of the war can be seen in the enlargement of the military forces and a hypermilitarization of society. But perhaps more powerful and pernicious was the ideological effect of the war experience, that is, its role in establishing anti-communism as a hegemonic ideology in South Korea, and anticapitalism and anti-Americanism as its counterpart in North Korea. It should be noted that both capitalism and communism were alien ideologies, thus abstract and remote from people's daily experiences (although Korean political leaders clung to one or the other from the days of their anticolonial resistance movements). But the war brought this ideological conflict to the level of daily experiences, to the level of individual psyches and social relationships. The facts that the war had never officially ended and that both states have been subjected to constant mutual military threats made the impact of this war particularly penetrating and enduring.

12. Charles Tilly, *Coercion, Capital, and European States, A.D. 990–1990* (Oxford: Basil Blackwell, 1990).

13. Michael Mann, "Ruling Class Strategies and Citizenship," *Sociology* 21 (1987): 339–54.

14. Otto Hintze, *The Historical Essays of Otto Hintze,* ed. Felix Gilbert (New York: Oxford University Press, 1975).

However, the newly established state-society relationship contained seeds of conflict and opposition that could not be removed by either the greatly enhanced coercive organs of the state or powerful anti-communist ideology. While suppressed by the intense Cold War atmosphere, civil society and especially the intellectuals have not really forgiven the "original sin" of the Rhee regime: its reactionary character, its revival of the colonial structure, and its overreliance on the United States for power maintenance. In addition to this, U.S. intervention introduced a new element of contradiction, centered on the ideal of democracy. The contradiction consisted in the fact that the United States installed a formally democratic government structure in the South with a public commitment to parliamentary democracy as a universal political goal, but in reality it had to support a regime that blatantly violated such an ideal in its daily practices. A cleavage, in Choi's words, thus developed along the axis of democracy and authoritarianism, with the United States playing the contradictory role of supporting both of them simultaneously. This contradiction eventually led to the April 19 Student Uprising in 1960 and to the violent overthrow of the First Republic.

Civil Society was once again resurrected, and so were the old issues of nationalism, unification, and social justice. Yet South Korea's first democratic government (1960–61) headed by Chang Myon was incapable of meeting these demands, partly because its social base was still predominantly in the propertied classes, partly because of its weak political leadership and lack of internal elite unity, and partly because of excessive demands on the new government from the hypermobilized civil society.

The military regime that came to power in 1961 opened a new chapter in South Korea's political and economic history. The first two or three years of the Park Chung Hee regime were a period of drastic restructuring of state organizations and state-society relations. Again, using the powerful instruments of coercion and ideological weapons of anti-communism and nationalism, the holders of state power quickly succeeded in demobilizing civil society and in reestablishing the strong state–weak society relationship.

Park, however, did more than restructure state-society relations; he initiated, with the help of the United States, several important institutional innovations to create a "developmental state"—a state possessing a sufficient amount of autonomy from societal interests and the organizational resources to regulate and guide the economy with a consistent mix of development policies. As Haggard and Moon explain in Chapter 3, the strength and effectiveness of a developmental state are based not simply on the state's coercive power but on the insulation of the economic bureaucracy and the well-coordinated institutional mechanisms of policymaking and implementation. It is Park's unique contribution that he transformed a relatively weak, ineffective state into a strong, developmental one.

Again, however, the Park regime was afflicted by fatal weaknesses: its illegitimate birth stemming from the usurpation of power from a democratic government by force, its harsh repression of civil rights, and the close ties it developed with Japan in order to pursue export-oriented industrialization. Thus from the beginning the Park regime had to face strong opposition from society, especially from students, who had acquired enhanced political efficacy from toppling the authoritarian regime only a year earlier. Park Chung Hee's strong developmental orientation had a lot to do with this political environment. As Haggard and Moon suggest, Park's prime motivation in pursuing rapid economic growth was to buy popular support. For Park and his followers, economic growth was not a goal, but rather a means of establishing the regime's political legitimacy.

Rapid economic development after the early 1960s did expand the social base for the Park regime. But this economic success generated a new source of social cleavage: the issue of distribution and economic justice. This new problem occurred as a consequence of the Park government's development policies, which stressed accelerated growth at the expense of equitable distribution. Thus, despite a spectacular rise in the nation's wealth, the number of exploited people increased proportionately, and the issue of economic justice became a political and intellectual issue beyond the daily problems of the poor.

Nowhere was economic inequality more acute than in the industrial arena. Millions of new industrial workers, fresh from the countryside, adapted relatively smoothly to factories and became productive workers making few demands on their employers. But the effect of intense labor exploitation and despotic labor relations eventually forced them into an aggressive posture beginning in the early 1970s. One of the most distinctive features of the South Korean labor movement, as I explain in Chapter 4, is that it developed close linkages with political conflicts outside industry, supported organizationally and ideologically by the larger *minjung* (the people's or the masses') movement, while supplying a major social base and an arena for democratization struggles among students. These factors explain why South Korea developed a much stronger working-class movement than did other East Asian NICs.

As Nettl suggests, one good indication of a high level of stateness (or state strength) in a given country is that social conflicts and social movements are largely directed against the state. A strong state, however, shapes the organizational form, language, membership, and agenda of social movements.[15] The merging of the working-class movement and the *minjung* movement indicates the strength of the South Korean state and the power of nationalism. A product of Japanese colonial rule, nationalism has played a dual, somewhat contradictory role in South Korea. On the one hand, it served as the state's ideology to mobilize people for economic development as well as to suppress the sectional interests of society; on the other hand, it was used by civil society as a means of multiclass social mobilization against the authoritarian state. *Minjung* combined nationalist sentiment and populist ideology, and provided economic, political, and cultural movements in the 1980s with a powerful antihegemonic ideology (see Chapter 4).

Thus an irony of South Korea's economic development is that the very success of the economy brought into being a social force that turned against its own creator with increasing resentment. As the South Korean economy continued to develop at a rapid pace, and as the chorus of outsiders' admiration of South Korean economic success became louder, internal opposition to the Park regime grew broader and deeper, eventually leading to Park's assassination by his own intelligence chief in 1979. Thereupon followed a new cycle of resurrection of civil society, the "Seoul spring" of 1980, and its brutal suppression by the military. Again, we saw a direct confrontation of the two forces: the state, equipped with immense resources of coercion and ideological repression on the one side, and a highly contentious and resilient society, on the other side. One important difference between 1980 and previous periods of political transition was that South Korea's economy and society had become far more complex and differentiated than before. By 1980, South Korean society had become a class society, with a highly visible capitalist class, a large working class, and sizable urban middle classes, while the agrarian sector had diminished to a third of the

15. Theda Skocpol, "Bringing the State Back In: Strategies of Analysis in Current Research," in *Bringing the State Back In,* ed. Peter Evans, Dietrich Rueschemeyer, and Theda Skocpol (New York: Cambridge University Press, 1985).

population. Thus the dominant direction of change in civil society and in state-society relations was determined, to a great extent, by the dynamics emanating from relations between those classes.

In this regard, one of the most interesting features of South Korea's class society is the absence of bourgeois hegemony. This is the theme Eckert explores in depth in Chapter 3. His analysis points out several causes of this phenomenon: the nationalistic context in which capitalism was first introduced to Korea at the turn of the century, heavy moral demands placed on the capitalists' role for the good of the nation, the collaboration of the early Korean capitalists with the Japanese, the greedy manner in which big business amassed wealth at the expense of small entrepreneurs, and the capitalists' extremely poor record in material concessions to the working class. But more important than any other factor is the intimate collusion that existed between the *chaebŏl*s (conglomerates) and the authoritarian state. It is widely recognized that some thirty *chaebŏl* groups were able to accumulate so much wealth, in such a short time, and starting from almost nothing, mainly thanks to excessive state protection and privileges granted them, and that these groups, in turn, supported the authoritarian regimes both rhetorically and financially. This meant that insofar as the military regimes lacked political legitimacy, big business leaders were similarly devoid of social and moral authority. In a generally hostile intellectual and cultural environment, the Korean capitalist class has assumed, at least until very recently, an ideologically passive and defensive posture, embracing the old, uncomfortable ideology of nationalism or a new statist ideology of developmentalism rather than asserting its own capitalist ideology.

The capitalist state of South Korea, for its part, has not helped the capitalist class to establish hegemony over society. While amicably performing the capital accumulation function, the South Korean state has been either unable or unwilling to act as a legitimating mechanism of bourgeois hegemony. As mentioned above, the Park and Chun regimes pursued economic growth mainly for the sake of their own regime's legitimacy, that is, to buy political legitimacy with economic performance. Consequently, the negative social attitudes toward the *chaebŏl* class forced the state to keep an arm's-length posture, and sometimes to be openly hostile, toward big business for its own political reasons. Interestingly enough, every new regime since the First Republic used an anticapitalist campaign, in particular against those who had engaged in "illicit accumulation," as a strategy for earning popular support. Therefore, the accumulation and legitimation functions of the state, the two vital functions of a capitalist state, have frequently clashed in the South Korean state's actions, making it difficult for the Korean capitalist class to achieve ideological hegemony over civil society.

Here, we can see an interesting anomaly in the rise of South Korea's civil society. As in the West, the growth of civil society in South Korea in recent decades has been directly related to capitalist industrialization and to the social differentiation and plurality of interests generated by industrial transformation. But unlike Western societies, South Korea's civil society arose not under the leadership of the bourgeoisie, but in opposition to it. The absence of bouregois hegemony was both a cause and a consequence of a highly politicized civil society. The failure of the bourgeoisie to establish its hegemony allowed the antihegemonic forces to penetrate and moiblize civil society more easily; on the other hand, however, it is the virility of the political and cultural movements in civil society that has kept the capitalist class on the defense. In such a sociopolitical environment, ideological and cultural hegemony was, by and large, in the hands of the intellectuals.

To a large extent, this was because of the privileged status accorded to intellectuals in the Confucian political system. In Confucian thought, as Uchang Kim explains, culture is given a privileged status over the state and society, since rulers are supposed to rule by example, not by force. Much of the political dynamics in Korean history, as in China and Japan, has involved struggles over culture among state rulers, bureaucrats, intellectuals, and segments of the dominant class. The colonial and postcolonial political experiences have intensified these struggles over culture, producing a high level of politicization of culture, as most vividly demonstrated in the themes of Korean modern literature presented by Kim. The continuous process of politicization and depoliticization of Korean literature, Kim argues, is a consequence of ongoing struggles over culture in the ideological terrain of civil society, in which the state and the dominant class faced a highly politicized community of intellectuals and students. In such a contentious environment, contemporary Korean literature was not allowed to pursue pure aesthetic concerns but became engulfed by political and ideological currents.

During the 1980s, South Korea's economy and civil society grew significantly larger and more complex, while the state's grip on both gradually slipped. By the mid-1980s, the South Korean economy had become too complex and internationalized for the state to manage effectively, and pressure for economic liberalization from domestic and international capital had grown too powerful for the government to resist. With economic liberalization, the economic power of big business vis-à-vis the state has grown noticeably, along with a pluralization of interests manifested in many different arenas of economic and social life. The differentiation of social classes developed further, engendering relatively distinct class identities and class-based interest groups as well as a powerful working-class movement. So social development in South Korea since the 1980s can be explained, in part, by the liberal pluralist theory of social change—only in part, because political transition in South Korea even during this period did not occur in a gradual, continuous fashion as a consequence of this social differentiation, but discontinuously through violent confrontations between civil society and the state.

The civil uprising in the summer of 1987 was a culmination of the tensions that has been building up between the authoritarian state, which was adamant in upholding the status quo, and civil society, which had grown larger and stronger, with heightened interest in broader political participation. What made this critical transition possible was the joining of the segments of the middle class with those groups that had long fought for democracy so tenaciously, students, political dissidents, labor activists, and progressive intellectuals. By the mid-1980s, the latter groups enjoyed a great deal of social and moral authority, and the antihegemonic *minjung* ideology had penetrated the culture and discourse of the middle classes.

The extent to which the post-1987 political change under the Roh Tae Woo regime represents a democratization process is debatable. But there has been an indisputable trend toward political and ideological stabilization, since the post-1987 transition to democracy, however halting and limited, substantially reduced the salience of previous sources of social conflict and politicization. The questions about political legitimacy and the nationality aspect of political power are no longer burning issues and are no longer powerful enough to politicize broad segments of society. Even on other sources of social cleavage, that is, economic distribution and national reunification, the Roh government was able to act preemptively, reducing conflict and politicization to a considerable degree. Yet political and economic liberalization have resulted in a substantial reduction of the state's autonomy and allocative power, while strengthening the position of big business. And the liberal political environment has stimulated the mushrooming of voluntary associations and all varieties of social and cultural movements, as if the civil society has finally come into its own. The dominant character of this civil society increasingly reflects the temperament and the ideological inclinations of the middle classes, which have become considerably more conservative since 1987. In this new drift of social change, the winner is most likely to be the capitalist class, not particularly in terms of economic power but of political and social power. Thus it is quite possible that the maturation of civil society in a highly developed capitalist economy will, after all, invite the ascendance of a hegemonic bourgeoisie.

To summarize, what has been described above is a continuous process of conflicts between a strong state and contentious society. Only through exploring their mutual opposition and accommodation can we understand the essential character of the Korean state and society. The origins of Korea's strong state are historical and geopolitical: a long tradition of a centralized state structure, the colonial legacy of a strong state apparatus, the impact of the Korean War and national division, and the intense Cold War environment in which the Korean peninsula found itself. But the same historical experiences brought into being a relatively strong and highly politicized society. Japanese colonial rule proved, in many ways, to have the most critical influence on Korean society. It was during this period that the state and society began to bifurcate, fostering an antistate orientation as an important trait of Korean intellectual political culture. And it was the bitter experience of Japanese rule that gave rise to strong nationalism among the Korean people.

The contentious and unruly character of South Korea's civil society stemmed basically from the fact that subsequent political development in Korea continuously denied the Korean people opportunities to restructure state power according to their nationalist ideals and democratic political values. Their frustration began with the end of colonial rule, which brought not a genuine liberation but another form of foreign domination, unwanted national division, and the revival of colonial apparatuses of control. The Korean War and strong U.S. support prolonged the life of the politically illegitimate Rhee regime. The student uprising in 1960 toppled this regime and introduced another opportunity for a radical change, but again the people's hopes were dashed only a year later by a military coup. A third opportunity came in 1979 but it too was stolen, by a military coup in 1980.

Civil society in South Korea developed in this political context, not simply as an institutional manifestation of a bourgeois society but as a nationalistic political reaction to the nature of state power. Thus to the extent that one can talk about the strength of South Korean civil society, it is a strength residing not in the multiplicity of independent civic organizations or in the existence of powerful social classes but in a stubborn and resistant political culture and a latent mobilizational capacity of civil society, both the products of tumultuous political history of contemporary Korea. This political history prevented both the state and the capitalist class from establishing stable hegemony over civil society. The contentious nature of South Korean civil society was both a cause and a consequence of unhegemonic state power. Only by focusing on the contingent and dialectic nature of state-society relationships can we grasp the truly fundamental character of Korea's transition to modernity in the twentieth century.

Index

AID. *See* U.S. Agency for International Development
"Alien Land, The" (Hwang Sŏgyŏng), 184–85
Amsden, Alice, 57–58
Anderson, Perry, 198–99
Anti-communist ideology, 18–24, 136, 147
April 19 Student Uprising, 3, 25–26, 29–30, 42, 242
Authoritarian state development, 24–28. *See also* Bourgeoisie; Capitalism; Chaebŏl; State-society relations

Ball Shot Up by the Dwarf, The (Cho Sehi), 183–84
Bank of Korea, 107–8
Bare Tree, The (Pak Wansŏ), 178
Bisson, T. A., 101
Blue House, 75–76
Bourgeoisie, 22–24, 26, 29, 31, 35, 95–130, 244–47. *See also* Chaebŏl; State-society relations
  and authoritarian politics, 127–28
  and Confucianism, 117–20
  development of, 97–101
  and economic inequity, 120–25
  and leadership, 115–20
  and society, 110–11
  and state, 101–10, 125–27
  and working class, 111–15
Brown, Gilbert, 72–73
Brus, Wlodzimierz, 197–98

Capitalism, 19–20, 244–47. *See also* Bourgeoisie; Chaebŏl; Postwar economy
  and the arts, 176–80
  and Confucianism, 117–20
  history of, 97–101
  and Korean War, 22–23
  Western, 129

Index

Catholic and Protestant Farmers Federations, 34
Catholic Farmers' Association, 87
Catholic Young Workers Association, 74
Chaebŏl. *See also* Bourgeoisie; Postwar economy
  and authoritarian politics, 127–28, 245
  and economic inequity, 120–25
  influence of, 104–10
  and moral leadership, 110–11, 115–20
  and state controls, 101–4
  and state privilege, 79–80, 125–27
  and working class, 111–15
Chang, Dal-joong, 53
Chang Glisan (Hwang Sŏgyŏng), 185–89
Chang Key Young, 70
Chang Myon, 3, 64–65, 242
Children of Cain, The (Hwang Sunwŏn), 170–71
China, 198, 202, 204
Cho Bong Am, 42
Cho Chŏngrae
  Taebak Mountains, The, 185–86, 191–93
Chŏlla province, 35n
Cho Sehi
  Ball Shot Up by the Dwarf, The, 183–84
Cho Soon, 91
Chun Doo Hwan, 31, 81, 89–90, 142
  and labor movement, 146, 148–51
  regime of, 3–4, 35–40, 102–3, 105, 115
Chung Ju Yung, 47, 92, 102, 105–6, 108, 110–11, 124–27
Chun Tae Il, 33–34, 74, 138–39, 148
Church movement, 34, 140–41, 150
Civil society concept, 6–7, 13–14, 237–38, 248–49
Class consciousness, 151–55, 183–85. *See also* Bourgeoisie; Chaebŏl; *Minjung;* Socioeconomic status; Working class
Cold War, 42, 129
Committee for the Preparation of Korean Independence (CPKI), 15–16
Communism. *See also* North Korea
  and the arts, 190–92
  and labor movement, 134–36
Confucianism, 238, 246
  and capitalism, 117–20
  and culture, 163–65, 167–68
  and labor movement, 136–37
Corporatism. *See* North Korea
CPKI. *See* Committee for the Preparation of Korean Independence
Culture
  and agrarian literature, 169–74
  and historical novels, 185–92
  and industrialization, 176–80
  and Japanese colonialism, 166–69, 190–92
  and Korean War, 174–76
  and labor movement, 136–37
  and populist literature, 180–85
  and state-society relations, 163–66, 192–95
  and working class, 151–55
Cumings, Bruce, 53, 233, 236, 240

Daewoo Group, 104–6, 156
Dawn of Labor (Pak No Hae), 154–55
Democratic Justice Party, 86, 90, 108–9
Democratic Liberal Party (DLP), 45, 91, 109–10
Democratic People's Republic of Korea (DPRK), 197–99, 204, 225–26. *See also* North Korea
  corporatist socialism model, 218–20
Democratic Republican Party, 28, 66, 76
Democratization, 18–21, 39–40
DLP. *See* Democratic Liberal Party
DPRK. *See* Democratic People's Republic of Korea

Index

Economic liberalization
  and chaebŏl, 106–10
  and postwar economy, 80–89
Economic Planning Board, 64–65, 67, 70
8-3 Decree of 1972, 104, 107–8
Eisenhower, Dwight, 61
Entrepreneurs, 98–100
Evans, Peter, 55

Fainsod, Merle, 207
Fascism, 200–204
Federation of Christian Farmers, 87
Federation of Korean Industries (FKI), 66, 87, 107–9, 158
Federation of Korean Trade Unions (FKTU), 18–19, 79, 135, 157–58
Fifth Republic, 37, 81
First Republic, 13–14, 20–21
Five-Year Plan, 69
FKI. *See* Federation of Korean Industries
FKTU. *See* Federation of Korean Trade Unions
"Flower of Fire, The" (Sŏnu Hwi), 172–73
Foreign aid, 22–23. *See also* Postwar economy; U.S. Agency for International Development; U.S. military government

GDP. *See* Gross domestic product
General Motors, 106
General trading company (GTC), 79
Gould, Jay, 121
Graft of Humanity, The (Hwang Sunwŏn), 174
Grain Management Fund, 82, 87
Gross domestic product (GDP), 61–62, 73, 81, 92
GTC. *See* General trading company

Han, Sang-Jin, 145
Han, Wan-Sang, 145
Hanmindang (Korean Democratic Party), 17, 20–21, 60
Henderson, Gregory, 236
Heroic Age, The (Yi Munyŏl), 191
Hintze, Otto, 241
Hobsbawm, Eric J., 110
Hwang Sŏgyŏng
  Alien Land, The, 184–85
  Chang Glisan, 185–89
  "Illegal Slaughtering," 186–87
Hwang Sunwŏn
  Children of Cain, The, 170–71
  Graft of Humanity, The, 174
  "Tightrope-Walker, The," 174
  Trees on the Stiff Hill, 174
Hyundai Group, 47, 92, 99, 101, 102, 104–6, 156

Ilhae Foundation, 102–3
"Illegal Slaughtering" (Hwang Sŏgyŏng), 186–87
International Monetary Fund, 75

Japan, 101, 202–3, 205, 216
Japanese colonialism. *See also* Postwar economy; State-society relations; Working class
  and the arts, 166–69, 190–92
  and bourgeoisie, 97–98
  and labor movement, 133–34
  and postliberation, 3, 14–18
Johnson, Chalmers
  MITI and the Japanese Miracle, 57, 101–2
Jowitt, Kenneth, 218
Juche ideology, 213–16, 223

KAPF. *See* Korean Proletarian Artists' Federation
KCIA. *See* Korean Central Intelligence Agency
KDP. *See* Korean Democratic Party
Kennedy, John F., 69
Kim, Seok Ki, 107
Kim Ch'ang Man, 210–11

Kim Chuyŏng
Middlemen, The, 185–86, 188–89
Kim Dae Jung, 34–35, 45, 74, 109
Kim Il Sung, 204–13
and Juche ideology, 213–16
and socialist corporatism, 216–25
Kim Jong Pil, 68, 91
Kim Ku, 16n, 18n
Kim Tongri, 167
Records of Yellow Earth, The, 169
Kim Tongsŏk, 167
Kim Wonil, 191–94
Kim Woo Chung, 105–6
Kim Yongwan, 118
Kim Young Sam, 34–35, 45, 91
Knowledge and Politics (Roberto Unger), 230
KNY. *See* Korean National Youth
Koo Cha Kyung, 109
Korea Employers' Federation, 112
Korean Central Intelligence Agency (KCIA), 65, 69, 141
Korean Communist Party, 135
Korean Democratic Party (KDP), 17, 20–21, 60
Korean National Youth (KNY), 223–24
Korean People's Republic (KPR), 15–17
Korean Proletarian Artists' Federation (KAPF), 168–69
Korean Provisional government, 18n
Korean War
and the arts, 174–76
and bourgeoisie, 99–100
and the economy, 60–62
and land reform, 19n
and state-society relations, 21–24, 240–42
Korean Workers' Party (KWP), 216, 225–26
KPR. *See* Korean People's Republic
Kukje Group, 88, 103–5, 108
Kŭm River, The (Sin Donghyŏp), 182–83
Kwanchon Essays (Yi Mungu), 178
Kwangju, 4, 35–36, 74, 142, 148
KWP. *See* Korean Workers' Party

Labor Dispute Law, 82
Labor movement, 18–19, 29–31, 38–39, 46n, 243–44. *See also Minjung;* Postwar economy; Student movement; Unions; Working class
and Chun regime, 146, 148–51
and Church, 140–41, 150
and communism, 134–36
and culture, 136–37
and Japanese colonialism, 133–34
and regionalism, 44–46
and Yushin (revitalization) system, 139
Land (Pak Kyŏngri), 185–86, 189–90
Landlordism, 98–100, 113–14, 234
Land reform, 20–21, 60
"Lands and Rivers of Azalea" (Sin Donghyŏp), 182
Latin America, 142–43, 199
Left, 15n, 18, 110. *See also* North Korea; Postwar economy
and the arts, 167, 169–70, 190–92
and labor movement, 134–35
Lévi-Strauss, Claude, 192
Liberal Party, 33, 60–61, 63–64, 102
Linz, Juan, 200
Literature. *See* Culture
Loans, 63, 72, 104
foreign, 77–78
Locke, John, 117
Lucky-Goldstar, 99, 104, 109

Mann, Michael, 226, 233, 241
Manoilescu, Mikhail, 201, 217
Mao Zedong, 214
Martial law, 29–31, 70, 76
Maruyama, Masao, 203
Marx, Karl, 129, 136
Marxism, 5, 166–67, 183. *See also* North Korea

Middle class
  and Chun regime, 35–40, 87
  and industrialization, 28–35
  and working class, 44
Middlemen, The (Kim Chuyŏng), 185–86, 188–89
Military. *See* Postwar economy; Soviet Union; U.S. military government
Military coup (May 1961), 26, 65, 135–36
Mill, John Stuart, 164
Ministry of Commerce and Industry, 71
Ministry of Commerce and Trade, 84
Ministry of Finance, 62–64, 107
Ministry of Reconstruction (MOR), 63–64
Minjung, 17–18, 46, 243–44. *See also* Working class
  formation of, 131–33
  and land reform, 19n
  movement, 142–48
MITI and the Japanese Miracle (Chalmers Johnson), 56
Monetary Board, 107
Monopoly Regulation and Fair Trade Law, 84, 87
Moon Hi Gap, 91
MOR. *See* Ministry of Reconstruction

NAM. *See* National Association of Managers
National Assembly, 60, 74, 76, 89–90, 92, 109–10
National Association of Managers (NAM), 158
National Council of Korean Trade Unions (NCKTU), 18–19, 134, 157–60
National Council of Workers' Cultural Movement Organizations, 160
National Federation of Business Organizations, 112
Nationalism, 18, 23, 238–39
  and the arts, 167
  and capitalism, 117–21
National Security Law, 20, 42
NCKTU. *See* National Council of Korean Trade Unions
Nettl, J. P., 235, 244
Neumann, Franz, 229
New Democratic Party, 34–35, 74, 141
New Democratic Republican Party, 91
New Village Program, 79, 103
Nixon, Richard, 75
No-hak yŏndae (worker-student alliance), 37, 150
Nordpolitik, 41–43
North Korea
  corporatism ideologies of, 199–204
  and intelligence, 226–29
  in international sphere, 229–30
  and Juche ideology, 204–5, 213–16, 223
  and Korean Workers' Party, 225–26
  and land reform, 20n
  leadership, 206–13, 240
  and reunification, 41–42
  and socialist corporatism, 216–25
  and South economy, 33
  as Soviet satellite, 197–99
  system origins of, 204–6
North Korean Interim People's Committee, 207

Office of National Tax Administration (ONTA), 103
ONTA. *See* Office of National Tax Administration
Our Village (Yi Mungu), 178–80
Overdeveloped state. *See* State-society relations

Paek Nakch'ong, 181–82
Pak Hŏn Yŏng, 206
Pak Hyŏnch'ae, 111, 145
Pak Il U, 227–28
Pak Kyŏngri, 185–86, 189–90

Pak No Hae
Dawn of Labor, 154–55
Pak Wansŏ
Bare Tree, The, 178
"Ramparts of Mother, The," 177
Unsteady Afternoon, The, 177–78
Palais, James, 232–33
Park Chung Hee regime, 3, 35, 100, 102, 242–43. *See also* Postwar economy
and labor movement, 139, 146
and socioeconomic status, 26–32
Party for Peace and Democracy (PPD), 45, 109
"People of the Village of Cranes, The" (Yi Bŏmsŏn), 171–73
People's committees, 15, 204
People's Theology, 34
Polanyi, Karl, 201
Postliberation
and bourgeoisie, 98–99
and land reform, 19–21
and state-society relations, 3, 14–18, 239–40
Postwar economy, 51–93. *See also* Chaebŏl; State-society relations
and economic liberalization (1980–1987), 80–89
and export growth (1964–1970), 70–73
and external constraints, 53, 55, 58–60
and import-substitution (1954–1960), 60–64
and industrial deepening (1971–1979), 73–80
and military interregnum (May 1961–December 1964), 65–70
and Second Republic (April 1960–May 1961), 64–65
and state-society relations, 55–57
and "strong state" paradigm, 57–58
PPD. *See* Party for Peace and Democracy
Presidential Task Force on Korea, 68
Protestant Ethic and the Spirit of Capitalism, The (Max Weber), 126

Racial purity, 224
"Ramparts of Mother, The" (Pak Wansŏ), 177
Records of Yellow Earth, The (Kim Tongri), 169
Regionalism, 44–46
Representative Democratic Council, 16n
Republic of Korea Army (ROK), 22
Reunification, 26, 40–43
Reunification Democratic Party, 91
Rhee, Syngman, 3, 16n, 17, 33, 55, 58–59, 100. *See also* Postwar economy
regime of, 20–21, 23, 25–26, 33, 126–27, 135, 239–40
Right, 15n, 18
and the arts, 167, 169–70, 190–92
and corporatism, 223
and labor movement, 134–35
Roh Tae Woo, 37–38, 90–91, 112
and Nordpolitik, 41–43
regime of, 158, 247
and socioeconomic status, 46–48
ROK. *See* Republic of Korea Army

Samsung, 99, 101, 104, 156
Samuels, Richard, 101
Schiller, Friedrich, 180
Schmitter, Philippe C., 200
Schumpeter, Joseph, 128
Second Republic (April 1960–May 1961), 64–65
Sin Donghyŏp
Kŭm River, The, 182–83
"Lands and Rivers of Azalea," 182
Sixth Republic, 90–91
Skocpol, Theda, 233
Slavery, 113–14
Smith, Adam, 117
Sŏ Chŏngin
"Valley, The," 181

Index

Socialism. *See* North Korea
Socioeconomic status. *See also* Bourgeoisie; Chaebŏl; *Minjung;* Working class
  and Chun regime, 35–40
  and class consciousness, 151–55, 183–85
  landlords, 98–100
  and Park Chung Hee regime, 26–32
  and reunification, 42–43
  and Roh regime, 46–48
  yangban, 95–96, 232–35
Sŏnu Hwi
  "Flower of Fire, The," 172–73
Southern Army, The (Yi T'ae), 192
Soviet Union, 43, 99, 129. *See also* North Korea
  and military intervention, 15–17
Special Law Concerning National Security, 79
Stalinism. *See* North Korea
State-business relations. *See* Bourgeoisie; Chaebŏl; Postwar economy
State-society relations. *See also* Bourgeoisie; Chaebŏl; Culture; *Minjung;* Postwar economy; Working class
  and capitalism, 244–47
  Chun regime, 35–40
  and culture, 163–66, 192–95
  and democratization, 18–21
  and economic justice, 32–35, 243–44
  and effect of political opening, 43–48
  and industrialization, 28–32
  Japanese colonialism, 232–34, 236–39, 248
  Korean War, 21–24, 240–42
  Park Chung Hee regime, 242–43
  postliberation, 3, 14–18, 239–40
  post-1987 period, 247–49
  postwar, 24–28
  precolonial period, 232–33, 234–36
  reunification, 40–43
"Stray Bullet, The" (Yi Bŏmsŏn), 174–76
Student movement, 33–34, 37. *See also* Labor movement; Unions
  and April 19 Student Uprising, 3, 25–26, 29–30, 42, 242
  and no-hak yŏndae, 37, 150

Taebaek Mountains, The (Cho Chŏngrae), 185–86, 191–93
Taxation, 71–73, 77, 103–4, 123–24
  Bureau, 71
  as forced donations, 109
Third World, 34, 141
Thirty-eighth parallel, 15
Three-Year Plan, 64
"Tightrope-Walker, The" (Hwang Sunwŏn), 174
Tilly, Charles, 241
Tonghak Uprisings, 2–3, 17n, 182–83
Trade Union Law, 82
Trees on the Stiff Hill (Hwang Sunwŏn), 174
Trotsky, Leon, 198, 213, 217
Twilight (Kim Wonil), 191–94

Unger, Roberto Mangiaberra, 200, 202
  Knowledge and Politics, 230
Unification National Party (UNP), 47, 92
Unions, 18–19, 29–31, 34. *See also* Labor movement; *Minjung;* National Council of Korean Trade Unions; Student movement; Working class
  and no-hak yŏndae, 37, 150
  and postwar economy, 56, 79, 90
United Nations Command, 62
UNP. *See* Unification National Party
Unsteady Afternoon, The (Pak Wansŏ), 177–78
Urban Industrial Mission, 34, 74, 115, 140–41
U.S. Agency for International Development (AID), 69–71

U.S. military government, 99, 239–40, 242. *See also* Rhee, Syngman: regime of
  and anti-communism, 18–24
  and labor movement, 134–35
  and U.S. occupation, 15–18
U.S.–Soviet Joint Commission, 16n

"Valley, The" (Sŏ Choñgin), 181
Vietnam War, 100–101
Vogel, Ezra, 53

Weber, Max
  Protestant Ethic and the Spirit of Capitalism, The, 126
Women's workforce, 37, 140, 156
Working class
  and bourgeoisie, 111–15
  and Chun regime, 38–40
  and class consciousness, 151–55, 183–85
  European, 160–61
  formation of, 131–33
  and middle class, 44
  and *minjung,* 142–48
  1920s–1950s, 133–37
  1960s–1970s, 137–42
  1980–1987, 148–51
  post-1987, 155–60
  and socioeconomic status, 29–30
World War I, 98–99

Yangban, 95–96, 232–35
Yang Chung Mo, 108
YH Company, 141
Yi Bŏmsŏn
  "People of the Village of Cranes, The," 171–73
  "Stray Bullet, The," 174–76
Yi Dynasty, 232–36
Yi Mungu
  Kwanchon Essays, 178
  Our Village, 178–80
Yi Munyŏl
  Heroic Age, The, 191
Yi Pŏm Sok, 223–24
Yi T'ae
  Southern Army, The, 192
Yi Tong Ch'an, 112
Yŏm Muung, 181–82
Yoon, Jeong-Ro, 110
Young Catholic Workers, 115
Yu Kilchun, 117, 119, 122
Yushin (revitalization) system/constitution, 26–27. *See also* Postwar economy
  and labor movement, 139
  and middle-class development, 32–33

Zhdanov, Andrei, 206

Library of Congress Cataloging-in-Publication Data

State and society in contemorary Korea / edited by Hagen Koo.
p. cm.
"The papers in this volume grew out of workshop sponsored by the Joint Committee on Korean Studies of the Social Science Research Council and the American Council of Learned Societies"—P. preceding CIP t.p.
Includes bibliographical references and index.
ISBN 0-8014-2867-X (cloth : alk. paper). —ISBN 0-8014-8106-6 (paper : alk. paper)
1. Korea (South)—Politics and government—1948–1960—Congresses.
2. Korea (South)—Politics and government—1960–1988—Congresses.
3. Korea (South)—Politics and government—1988– —Congresses.
4. Korea (South)—Economic conditions—1948–1960—Congresses.
5. Korea (South)—Economic conditions—1960– —Congresses. I. Koo, Hagen, 1941– . II. Joint Committee on Korean Studies.
JQ1729.A15S73 1993
306.2'095195—dc20
93-25325